Late Glacial Long Blade Sites in the Kennet Valley

Excavations and Fieldwork at Avington VI, Wawcott XII and Crown Acres

Roy Froom

Edited by Jill Cook

The British Museum Research Publication Number 153

Publishers
The British Museum
Great Russell Street
London WC1B 3DG

Production Editor
Kiley Edgley

Series Editor
Dr Josephine Turquet

Distributors
The British Museum Press
46 Bloomsbury Street
London WC1B 3QQ

Late Glacial Long Blade Sites in the Kennet Valley
Roy Froom
Edited by Jill Cook
Front cover: The Kennet Valley, 'The Wilderness' between Hungerford and Newbury; Long Blade artefacts at Avington VI

ISBN 086159 153 4 (9 78 0861 59 153 4)
ISSN 0142 4815

Note: the British Museum Occasional Papers series is now entitled British Museum Research Publications. The OP series runs from 1 to 150, and the RP series, keeping the same ISSN and ISBN preliminary numbers, begins at number 151.

For a complete catalogue of the full range of OPs and RPs see the series website: www/the britishmuseum.ac.uk/researchpublications
or write to:
Oxbow Books, Park End Place
Oxford OX1 1HN, UK
Tel: (+44) (0) 1865 241249
e mail oxbow@oxbowbooks.com
website www.oxbowbooks.com
or
The David Brown Book Co
PO Box 511, Oakville
CT 06779, USA
Tel: (+1) 860 945 9329; Toll free 1 800 791 9354
e mail david.brown.bk.co@snet.net

Printed and bound in the UK by 4-print

Contents

List of Figures

All of the figures in this book have been drawn by the author and are his copyright.

List of Tables

List of Plates

Foreword

This book gives an account of the Late Glacial Late Upper Palaeolithic Long Blade sites discovered and excavated in the Kennet Valley by Roy Froom. It is a strong reminder that an independent archaeologist with an intimate knowledge of his or her local landscape can make a major contribution to a professionalized and academic subject in which funding, institutional responsibilities, research reviews and just too much information can impose limitations that are hard to overcome.

Working independently, Froom has been able to spend some 40 years studying what he knows and loves best: the Kennet Valley and its Palaeolithic and Mesolithic archaeology. Patiently exploring his patch he has been able to recognise, excavate and record the sites of Avington VI, Wawcott XII and Crown Acres, as well as the isolated finds described in this volume. These sites are crucial to our understanding of the archaeological implications of the transition from the Late Glacial to the early Holocene. They constitute a major part of the known evidence for this period in England and are crucial to our understanding of comparable assemblages in Belgium, France and Germany. Even before they have been fully published these sites, particularly Avington VI, are frequently referred to in learned works on the Late Glacial. Without Roy Froom's diligence and persistence they would probably not even have been discovered.

In this volume he provides a full report of his work and offers what he would call his parochial conclusions to help push back the boundaries which inhibit progress in understanding the early Holocene in Britain. Like him, I hope that both this book and the collections from the sites which are to be curated in the British Museum will be well used.

Jill Cook
Department of Prehistory and Europe
The British Museum

Preface

Even as young child growing up in the countryside around Newbury I was aware of the prehistoric past. This interest was given awareness and direction when, as a pupil attending St Bartholomew's Grammar School, I was taught by Douglas Connah who was an active member of the Berkshire Archaeological Society. Connah's enlightened teaching of history included archaeology and led to the foundation of the school Archaeological Society of which I was founder member. In those days it was possible for Connah to include excavations amongst the society's activities and these he directed with great enthusiasm. After graduation and a period of teaching elsewhere, I returned to St Bartholomew's, now Newbury Grammar School, to teach Chemistry. When Connah retired in the mid-1960s I assumed direction of the Archaeological Society.

Whereas Connah's interests had focussed on Romano-British remains, under my direction the Society concentrated on the investigation of the local Mesolithic. I had been introduced to the Mesolithic through what amounted to rescue excavations during the construction of the Kintbury Sewerage Works in 1950. Since that time I have devoted an enormous amount of time and effort in pursuit of the Mesolithic of the Kennet Valley which also led to the discovery of Late Glacial Long Blade sites. In this volume I have started the task of setting down the results of these labours supported with great enthusiasm by the senior students of the Grammar School who assisted with field walking and excavating, as well as in the laboratory, processing and analysing the finds.

The excavation of Avington VI described here was to be the last episode in the history of the St Bartholomew's Archaeological Society. Upheavals in secondary education in the 1980s led to its demise but its achievements are remembered through these pages and in the collections of the British Museum.

Acknowledgements

The work at Avington VI could not have been carried out without the permission granted by the late Lord Howard de Walden and the assistance of his agent for the Hungerford Park Estate, Mr. W.J.C. Scrope. The excavations at this site would not have been possible without the help during the various seasons of members of St. Bartholomew's Grammar School Archaeological Society, which at this time also drew members from The County High School for Girls; over the years the following played a particularly prominent part often working under adverse conditions: Philip Burge, Bruce Jackson, Vivienne Lawson, Michael McWalter, Roger Shelton, John Weaver, Paul Welch, John Welham. Simon Froom, Paul Froom, Alison Harrod, John Norris, Michael Part, Mark Side, Diana Skipper, Euan Smith, Ian Cunliffe, David Goodship and Gerald McConnon. I am also grateful to my wife Dorothy who painstakingly cleaned every exposed flint in the Long Blade Horizon without disturbing it before photography. In both 1978 and 1979 Ian Fenwick and David Holyoak of the Geography Department, The University of Reading, made valuable contributions and their help is gratefully acknowledged.

In the case of Wawcott XII the writer is indebted to the late Mr. C.R. Sutton, then resident Director of the Marsh Benham Estate, part of Sir Richard Sutton's Settled Estates, and to the then Resident Agent, the late Mr. F. Howes for allowing access. The tenant farmer, the late Mr. W.W. Allen, was always helpful and a source of useful information.

My description of the Crown Acres site was much assisted by discussions with Mr. Peter Tosdevine, the original discoverer of the site, and by help received from the Planning Department of West Berkshire District Council.

During the writing of this volume, the staff of Newbury Museum, particularly Mr. Paul Cannon, have been most helpful and have rendered great assistance.

I also owe a great debt of gratitude to John Wymer for help and encouragement going back over 40 years; it was he who unwittingly set me on the quest for Long Blades which has resulted in this volume. More recently, Jill Cook of the British Museum has been an essential source of information and encouragement. All the Figures were drawn by the author, who is grateful to Stephen Crummy for preparing them for publication.

Finally, and most importantly, I am indebted to my wife and sons who all too often found that they shared a home with an archaeologist rather than their husband or father.

Chapter 1

Long Blade Sites in the Kennet Valley

Location

The Kennet is one of the more significant rivers of southern England; it rises in the Avebury area of Wiltshire and flows in a generally easterly direction before joining the River Thames at Reading, Berkshire (**Fig. 1.1**). It is some 70km in length and has a number of tributaries: the most notable are the Dun entering at Hungerford, the Lambourn which joins between Newbury and Thatcham and the Enborne which enters at Aldermaston. The system has a significant catchment area which is geologically diverse. In the west it is predominantly Cretaceous whereas to the east Tertiary deposits become increasingly important. Both of these sequences were superficially modified during the Quaternary. This varied geology attracted ancient peoples because it supported different types of habitats containing a wide range of plants and animals. Furthermore, the Kennet connects to the River Thames, forming an obvious route to and from the east which in the early post-glacial would probably have linked directly to the Continent. Via its minor tributaries, the Upper Kennet provided access to the southern rivers such as the Itchen, Test and Hampshire Avon and thence to the south coast, while to the west the Upper Kennet leads to the Vale of Pewsey and the west of England.

As prehistoric peoples moved along this corridor they left their marks. For many years the oldest known and most investigated sites were those of the Mesolithic (Peake, 1931; Froom, 1963, 1965, 1970, 1972a, 1972b, 1976; Froom *et al.*, 1994; Rankine, 1956; Wymer, 1962 *inter alia*) and it was not until the 1970s that some older occupation characterised by 'Long Blades' became the focus of attention.

Long Blades: a definition

In this volume the term Long Blade will be used to denote any assemblage in which the blades are significantly longer than those found at Mesolithic sites and not in any more narrowly defined sense. Local Early Mesolithic sites rarely, if ever, produce blades exceeding 100mm in length and the local Late Mesolithic sites contain even shorter blades. Assemblages characterized by Long Blades are now generally recognized as being Late Last Glacial/ Late Upper Palaeolithic in age, *c.* 10,300 years old, and are found not only in southern Britain but also France, Belgium, the Netherlands and Germany.

The discovery and distribution of sites

The first Long Blade site to be recognized in the Kennet Valley in modern times was that at Crown Acres, Thatcham, Berkshire, which was found early in the 1960s (**Fig. 1.2**). It was approximately 1km east of the complex of Early Mesolithic sites originally identified and excavated by Peake and Crawford in the 1920s, and subsequently extensively reinvestigated by John Wymer in the 1950s (Wymer, 1962). All traces of Crown Acres have been obliterated by gravel extraction but some of the material found there is curated at Newbury Museum. In conversation with Ray Sheridan, an independent archaeologist who worked at the site, the writer was informed that the site was found by field-walking but subsequent exploratory excavation revealed that all stratification had been destroyed by ploughing. Originally, the worked flints had been deposited on or just above the gravel of the low terrace and were covered by a comparatively thin layer of later sediment. However, the site may once have been more deeply buried as allowance must be made for the probable removal of peat and allied deposits during historical times (Peake, 1935). A detailed account of the Crown Acres site can be found in chapter 7 of this volume.

In 1964 two Long Blade sites were discovered by the writer: Avington VI and Wawcott XII (**Fig. 1.2**). One of these, Wawcott XII was found by field walking. The field had rarely been ploughed but despite this, exploratory excavations showed that any stratification had been destroyed as at Crown Acres. However, a considerable assemblage has been accumulated from the site, mostly by surface collecting (Froom, 1972b). In contrast to Crown Acres, Wawcott XII is situated on what would appear to be flood plain gravel although whether or not it was strictly flood plain in the Late Glacial–Early Post Glacial is open to question. Exact comparison of the two sites is rendered difficult by the fact that between the two sites the River Lambourn joins the main valley at Newbury, altering the character of the valley. At Wawcott XII the worked flints were localised: the great majority came from an area at the most some 10m in diameter and were associated in the main with a patch of fine grained marl which was on, or in the surface of, the gravel. It is worth noting that there was no nearby concentration or even a background scatter of diagnostically Mesolithic material and, although a trapezeform microlith and a few blades may be the latter, the assemblage can be regarded as a discrete occurrence of Long Blade artefacts. There were faunal remains but due to the disturbed nature of the stratigraphy, they could not be securely associated with the assemblage. This site is described in more detail in chapter 6.

The site of Avington which is the main subject of this volume was also discovered in 1964 although its full significance did not become apparent until initial excavations had taken place there in 1972. These excavations and the description and refitting of the assemblage are the subject of the main part of this volume.

Isolated finds

Other occurrences of what appears to be Long Blade material in this part of the Kennet Valley are more enigmatic. In 1965 investigations at Wawcott XV produced an Early Mesolithic assemblage in which the flint was not patinated with the exception of a large well-made blade struck from a core with a retouched platform. This blade was deeply patinated and would not be out of place in any Long Blade assemblage (Froom, 1972a:

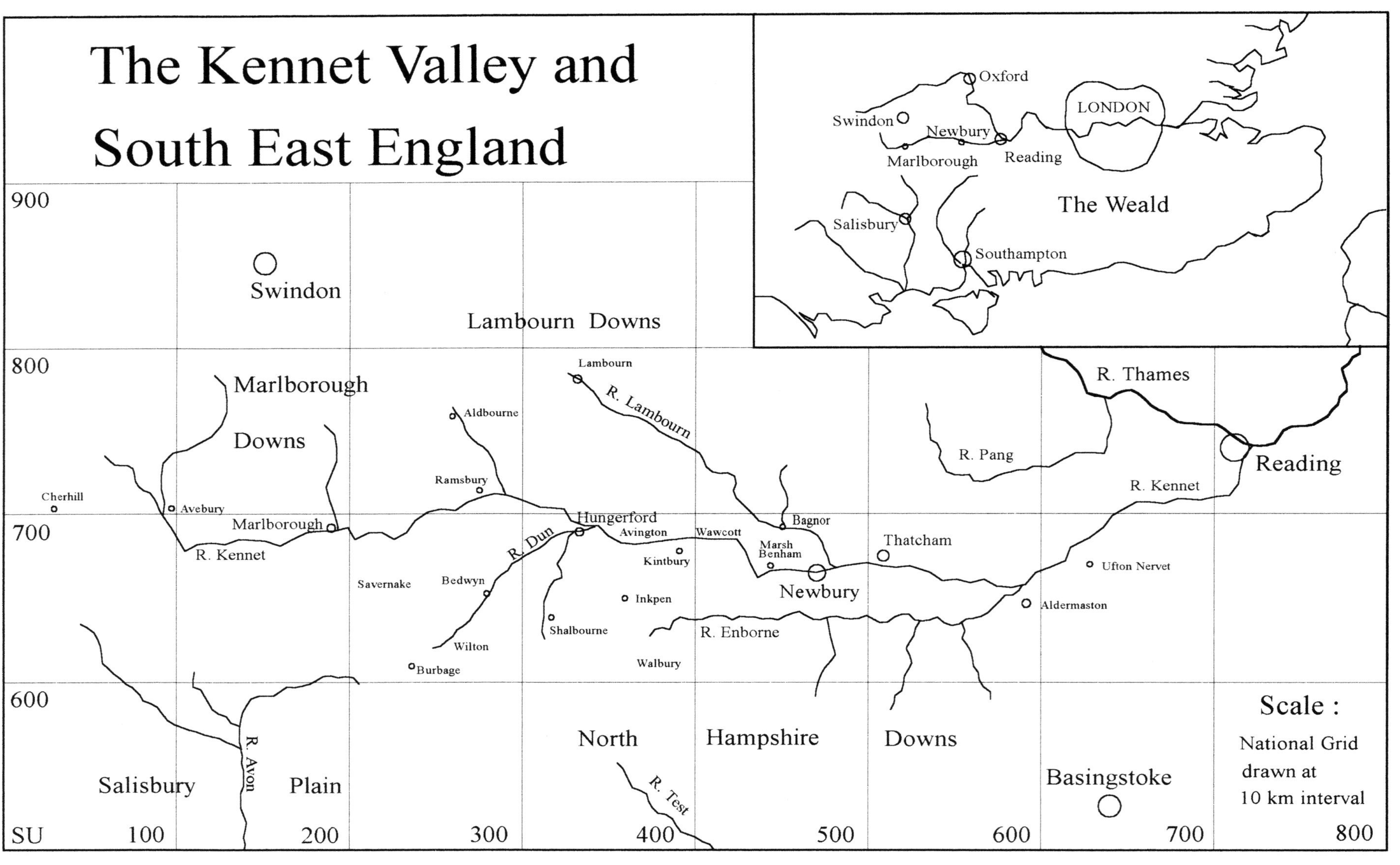

Fig. 1.1 The Kennet Valley and south-east England

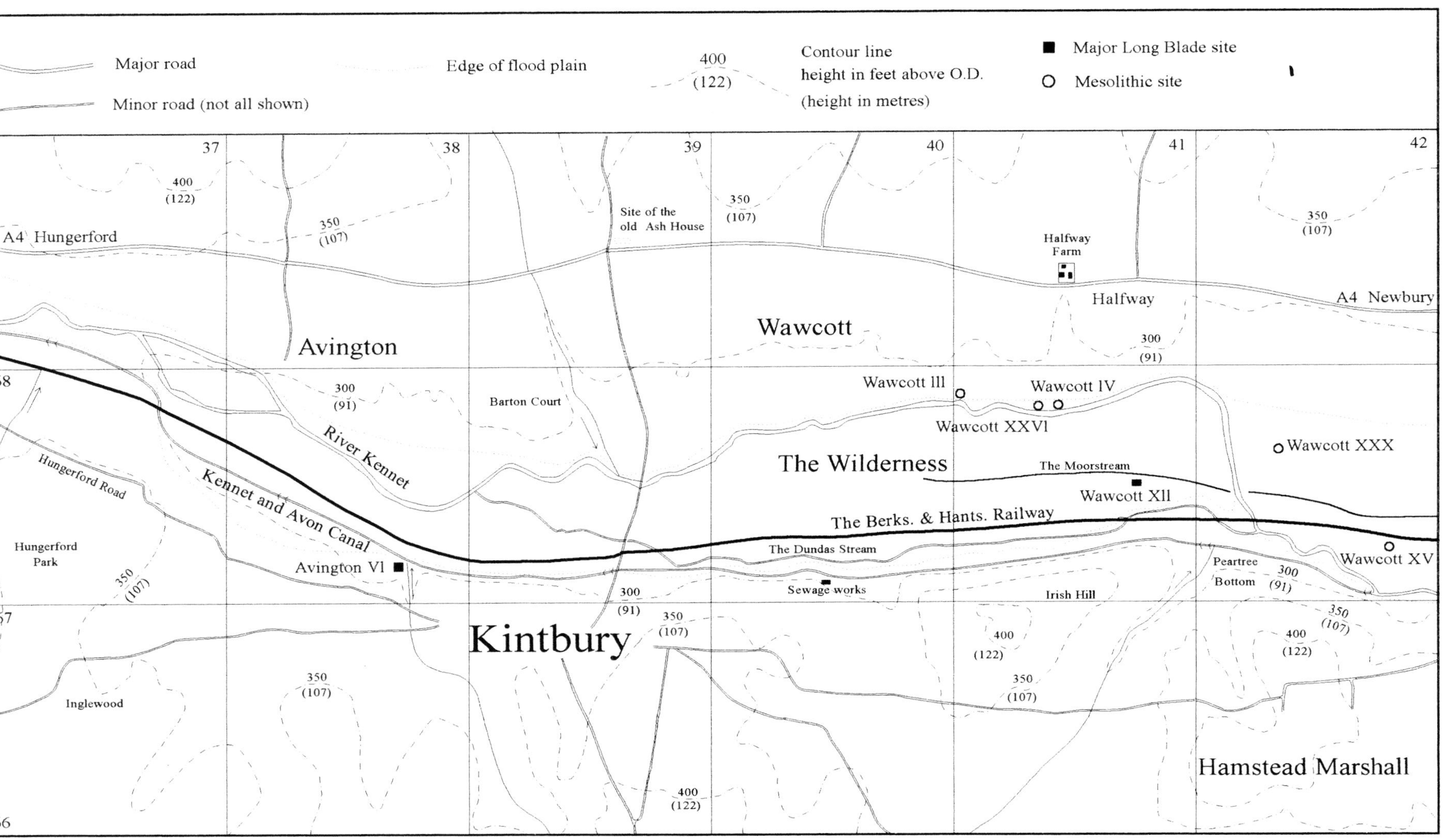

Figure 1.2 Long Blade sites in the Kennet Valley

18, fig. 4.8). Not far away, in the area of Wawcott XXX (Froom *et al.*, 1994), especially to the east, the odd abnormally large flake or core has been recovered when surface collecting but despite diligent searching no concentration has yet been found. However, such a concentration could be more deeply buried here. Similarly, at the major Mesolithic site of Wawcott III (Froom, 1976 and in preparation), where the overall stratification closely parallels that at Avington VI, two heavily patinated Long Blade fragments were recovered from the upper part of the clay underneath the loam containing the Mesolithic artefacts. At least one of these blades came from a core with a retouched platform (Froom, 1976: 99, fig. 50.36, 37). The indications are that the sequence of silty loam on clay extends for 0.5km or more west of Wawcott III. Unfortunately, Long Blade sites would not be revealed by normal agricultural operations across this area as they would be too deeply buried. However, a single, isolated core found in this area does exhibit typical Long Blade characteristics although, equally, it would not be out of place in the context of the local Mesolithic.

Immediately to the east of Wawcott III there are two enigmatic sites, Wawcott IV and XXVI, both on the northern edge of the flood plain. The bulk of the material from these sites is Early Mesolithic, some of the artefacts are patinated but some are not patinated. Among the patinated pieces there are items, all patinated, that would not be out of place in a Long Blade context. What is almost certainly the proximal fragment of a large well-made long blade was found recently during field walking about 1km west of Avington VI. Although broken by agricultural machinery and heavily abraded, the retouched butt is discernible.

In 1987–89 an archaeological assessment was made, in advance of development work, at Undy's Farm on the northern outskirts of Hungerford, close to where the valley of the River Dun joins the Kennet Valley (NGR: SU 335692). This has subsequently become known as the Charnham Lane Development. Field survey recovered finds which were wide ranging in age and included worked flints of both Mesolithic and Neolithic character, as well as a few more interesting Long Blade artefacts, including three large two-platform cores, a crested blade and a scraper made on a crested blade (**Figs 8.2; 8.3; 8.4**). The fresh condition of these pieces led to the excavation of some exploratory trenches by Steve Ford of Thames Valley Archaeological Services but, unfortunately, no concentration was located and the pieces appeared to be isolated finds (Ford, 2002). However, it is possible that a concentration may still be present further upslope outside the area investigated as part of the planning process. The writer visited the site several times while the investigations were in progress and recorded that some of the sections were similar to those at Avington VI. Sections observed during the construction of the garden centre near Hungerford (NGR: SU 346688) also showed a comparable stratigraphy. These sites are discussed further in chapter 8.

The most enigmatic reference to Long Blades known to the writer is that by Putman (1931) who refers to implements of Le Moustier type with Aurignac influence and assigns them to the Upper Palaeolithic. Writing in 1931, Putnam would have been familiar with the elegant long narrow blades characteristic of the early Aurignacian. His description of his Kennet Valley finds as of Le Moustier type suggests that he thought that they were not quite right for Aurignacian but, as Late Glacial Long Blades were not recognized at that time, he had no other category for his finds. Putnam found this material at Horsepool Field, Speen, Newbury. There are artefacts in Newbury Museum labelled as coming from Horsepool Field but it is by no means certain that they are the finds referred to in the above reference, various finds having been made in this area over a period of years.

Distribution pattern

In approximately 20km of the Kennet Valley there are or were three well defined Long Blade sites with additional usually isolated finds hinting at the existence of others. At present, the possible existence of Long Blade sites out of the main valley, perhaps associated with the small lateral streams joining from the south, must remain a matter of pure conjecture although the writer was once shown an unusually large blade from the watercress beds at Shalbourne, 5km to the south of Hungerford. The connection of the Kennet to the Thames with two large Long Blade sites in its tributary the Colne and thence from the Thames to the Somme and Seine where such sites are also coming to light is notable.

The location of Avington VI in a tributary valley off the Kennet flood plain is similar to those of the Long Blades sites at Three Ways Wharfs, Uxbridge, Middlesex (Lewis, 1991) and Church Lammas, Staines, Surrey (Anon. 1995) both in the Colne Valley tributary to the Thames. Their situation may even be tentatively suggested as a reflection of the Late Glacial age of these sites; tributary valleys would offer a more hospitable and sheltered situation than the broad flood plains, wet and difficult with braided channels and lacking much vegetation. By contrast Wawcott XII and Crown Acres are situated on the Kennet flood plain and there are aspects of their assemblages that suggest that they might be a little more recent.

Chapter 2

The Site of Avington VI

Discovery and excavations

During 1964 the construction of an electricity substation began immediately to the west of Kintbury on land then part of the Hungerford Park Estate (**Fig. 2.1**). The writer was able to monitor the building work, recovering a significant number of worked flints, the majority of which were not patinated and correlated well with the local Late Mesolithic. However, a minority did not and, in particular, there were two fine examples of Long Blades, quite unlike anything in the local Mesolithic, whether Early or Late. As the building work progressed a series of observations were made with respect to the stratigraphy at the site but no further Long Blades or allied artefacts were recovered and the exact origin of the initial Long Blade material remained in some doubt.

In 1972 an extensive trial excavation was undertaken by the writer together with members of the St. Bartholomew's Grammar School Archaeological Society, mostly Sixth Form students, and senior pupils from the Girls Grammar School. The substation is situated in the north-east corner of the field and a gravel track forms its eastern boundary and that of the field. To the north the substation and the field are bounded by the Kennet and Avon Canal. A grid was set out covering the area to the south and west of the substation using an aliquot of 10m; a 1m² trial in each of the 10m squares was then excavated. This yielded an insight into the general stratigraphy of the area covered by the grid and revealed the considerable extent of the Late Mesolithic artefacts across the site. The field had been walked over the years but little had been recovered from the surface since, as the trial trenches showed, the bulk of the Mesolithic material was at least 75cm below the surface.

During this first season of excavation Long Blade artefacts were only located in one narrowly defined area close to the boundary fence of the substation. This small area was systematically excavated in 1978, 1979 and 1981, again involving members of the schools already identified. The further excavation was justified and necessary because the writer had been warned that further development of the substation was being considered which would have led to the destruction of the site. It is probable that the whole of the south-east quadrant of the site has been excavated but excavation was deliberately stopped short on the western side of the site in order to leave a witness section for future work in the event of significant

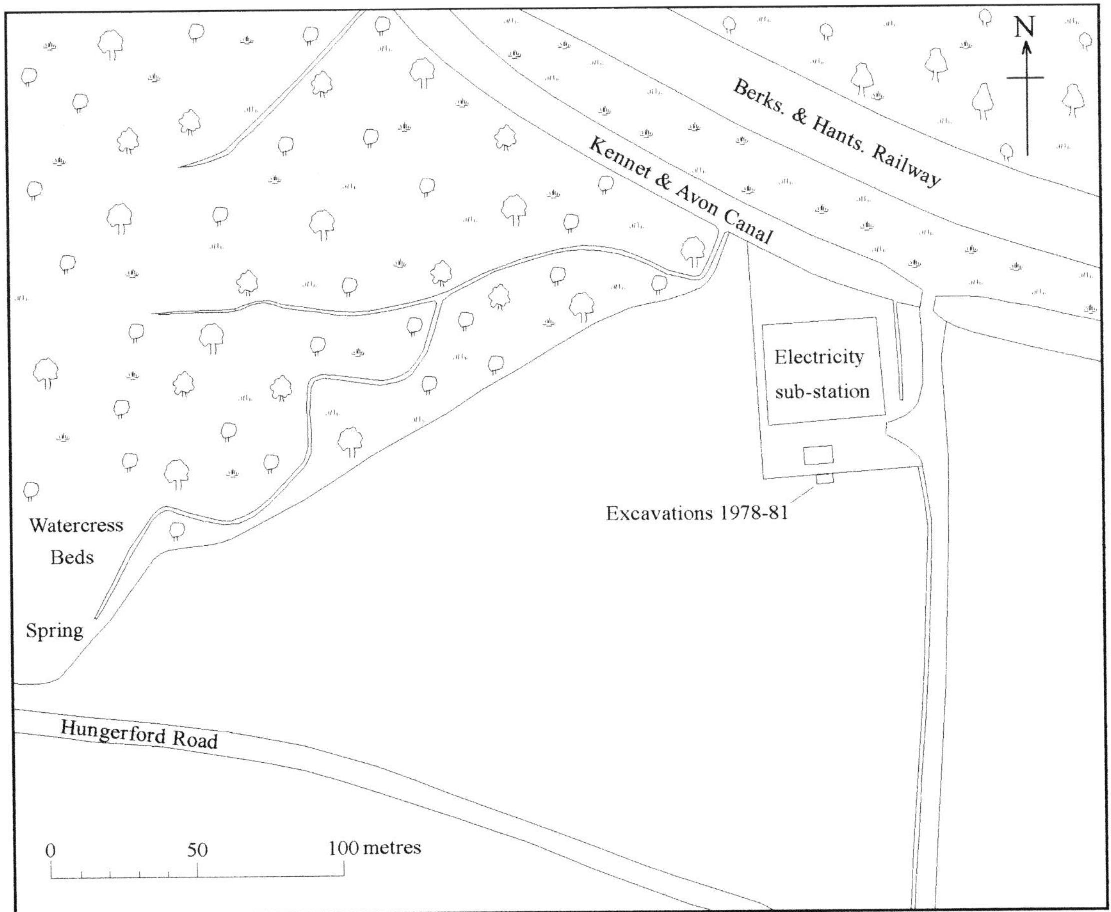

Figure 2.1. Avington VI: location

developments in archaeological science. There may also be material immediately to the north, within the substation, which it is hoped will remain undisturbed for the foreseeable future. It now seems likely that the Long Blade artefacts collected in 1964 came from the foundation trenches of the brick building at the substation.

During the excavations of 1978 and 1979, samples for environmental analyses were taken by members of the Geography Department at Reading University, notably David Holyoak, at that time a postgraduate student. Reference will be made to some of this work later in this report. Geomorphological and palaeobotanical investigations at Woolhampton, Berkshire (Collins *et al.*, 1996) and Brimpton, Berkshire (Worsley and Collins, 1995) provide further evidence of the fluvial regime and local vegetation in the Kennet Valley during the Late Glacial.

In October 1995 the area originally excavated in 1978–79 was reopened largely by means of a mechanical excavator, to expose some of the original sections (Barton *et al.*, 1998). The purpose of this exercise was to recover further samples to allow a more detailed assessment of the stratigraphy and palaeoecology of the site and also to collect samples for dating in view of the advances in this respect which had accrued over the intervening period. The mechanical excavator was also used to cut a number of trenches in the immediate area of the site, covering much the same ground as the 1972 exercise carried out by the writer. These new cuttings confirmed the stratigraphic and archaeological observations made in 1972 and enabled new sampling for palaeoenvironmental and dating purposes. The 1995 work was organised by Sabrina Dumont, a postgraduate student at the Donald Baden–Powell Quaternary Research Centre, University of Oxford, under the supervision of Dr. R.N.E.Barton, Oxford Brookes University. The three optical luminescence age estimates discussed below are the only results so far published (ibid).

Location

The site is situated on the south side of the Kennet Valley (NGR: SU 377671) at 89.4m OD, just off the edge of the modern flood plain at a point where a small lateral side stream joins the main river (**Figs 1.2, 2.1**). The valley of this stream can be traced southwards for several kilometres; in the experience of the writer, it only carries a significant amount of water in periods of prolonged wet weather. The stream originates from several small springs overlooked by the high chalk ridge (290m, OD) which forms the watershed between the Kennet-Thames system and the Hampshire rivers to the south. There are several such bournes between Newbury and Hungerford, having their sources in the area of Tertiary strata which exist between the Kennet Valley proper and the chalk ridge 5km to the south. It is likely that the site was near to the stream, whereas the Kennet may have been close or, equally, it may have been 100m or more away. Immediately to the south-east of the site the ground slopes markedly and, after ploughing, chalk is visible; a little further away chalk may also be seen in the cutting of the Hungerford to Kintbury road. To the west the ground slopes more gently but, some 250m from the site, the chalk is close to the surface, at the foot of a small chalk cliff, there is a strong spring which was used in historical times to feed watercress beds. In the absence of tree cover, the site is comparatively exposed, deriving just a little shelter from south-east winds from the somewhat higher ground, on which the village of Kintbury is built.

The local stratigraphy

In outline, the stratification at Avington VI follows a pattern which the writer has observed at several locations in the Kennet Valley, from Marsh Benham in the east to Hungerford in the west (**Fig. 2.2**). The lower slopes of the valley, especially on the north side, are commonly covered by gravel. This gravel appears to extend, without any discontinuity, underneath the current flood plain. Typically, the gravel is some 3m in thickness. It was presumably deposited and no doubt reworked during the Last Glacial. At the junction of the modern flood plain with the valley side a stony-clay varying to a clayey-gravel is commonly encountered on top of the gravel. The upper surface of this subsequent deposit is irregular and, in sections exposed in pipe-laying trenches and large-scale construction work, often appears undulating. The thickness of the clayey-gravel is variable but it can amount to as much as 2m or more. This is interpreted as a solifluction deposit. A layer of clay is normally found on top of the stony-clay/clayey-gravel. The upper surface of this clay is much more regular and its thickness varies but where the underlying layer is less developed it may be as much as 2m. The Long Blade assemblage at Avington VI was found in the surface of this clay.

Commonly, these two units of stony-clay/clayey-gravel and clay respectively are overlain by a third unit consisting of silty loam. Usually but not always this extends to the present surface. An exception to this was encountered approximately 3km to the east at the site Wawcott XXIII (Froom, in preparation), where further deposits covered the loam. These included a peaty soil above which there were two layers of marl separated by a narrow band of peaty material strongly suggestive of flood plain deposits swamping the site. Reconstruction of the ancient environment of this part of the Kennet Valley is somewhat problematic because of the extensive peat digging which took place in historical times (Peake, 1935). Worked flints which may be assigned to the Late Mesolithic are a common occurrence in the silty loam.

Stratigraphy at Avington VI

In the area of Avington VI, the silty loam is comparatively constant in thickness at approximately 1m. At the site four units were recognized: plough soil, loam, clay and gravel (**Fig. 2.2**). Within the loam and clay distinct sub-units were observed. These deposits are described from the top down as excavated.

Plough soil

The field has been subjected to ploughing for some considerable time. The modern plough soil is a dark brown loam 20–25cm in thickness. Its colour probably derives in part from its marked humus content. This soil contains some clasts but in no great numbers and flint artefacts are rare: those that are present are abraded and often appear polished indicating that they are derived. Numerous pieces of charcoal have been noted and these most likely came from fires associated with hedge cutting and tree felling in historical times. Similarly, the small granules of chalk noted in the soil are probably evidence of 'liming' the fields to neutralize soil acidity. This has been a common agricultural practice since the 18th century and, as most of the chalk observed here has almost dissolved away, it is unlikely to have occurred at Avington for some time.

Loam

Beneath the plough soil a loam was observed all over the sites. Three sub-units were recognised in it from top to bottom as follows:

Upper loam

The transition from the plough soil to the loam was barely perceptible as the top of the latter showed few distinctions. Clasts were comparatively rare and there were few artefacts; those flint implements that were present showed every indication of being derived. The frequency and size of the chalk granules continued to decrease towards the bottom of this deposit as a result of percolating water causing solution. In colour the loam was generally paler than the plough soil but, as seen in both horizontal and vertical section, there was some variation. This can be ascribed to movement of iron compounds and associated redox phenomena in the section, as well as lower humus content. At the junction of this sub-unit and the one below, inspection of the section commonly revealed an incipient layer of clasts about 40cm below the surface. The formation of such a layer of stones beneath a comparatively clast free layer is considered to be the result of a prolonged period of earthworm activity.

Middle loam

From 40–75cm below the surface the loam takes on a different character. The clast content was much higher, both sub-angular and rounded flint pebbles and cobbles were present, the latter presumably from the local Tertiary deposits. The pebbles were commonly 10–30mm in size but there were occasional cobbles up to 100mm; the sub-angular flints shared a similar size range. This middle loam contained more flint artefacts including examples, especially those from towards the base of the sub-unit, which are comparatively sharp. There were also quantities of hydrated iron oxides, presumably precipitated when surface water containing iron compounds in solution percolated down and reacted with the alkaline ground water. Currently, the ground water table in this field is known to vary widely through the year. Towards the base of this sub-unit a few sherds of rather nondescript pottery were recovered, they are probably Romano-British. Similar pottery has been seen in rabbit scrapes approximately 100m to the west and one of the machine cut trenches of 1995 yielded a fragment of Samian ware.

Lower loam

This lowest sub-unit of the silty loam can be differentiated both by its reduced clast content and its higher clay content. It is in the upper part of this sub-unit, between 75–85cm below the surface, that the bulk of the Late Mesolithic industry was stratified. The flint artefacts are invariably sharp and generally not patinated. A considerable quantity of unworked but burnt calcined flint occurred with them. The lower 15cm of this sub-unit varied from one part of the site to another, over much of the site its archaeological content is low to minimal, containing only small numbers of Mesolithic artefacts which have been displaced downwards but rarely encroach upon the underlying layer. However, there were areas where there had been some disturbance, caused either by activities on the part of the

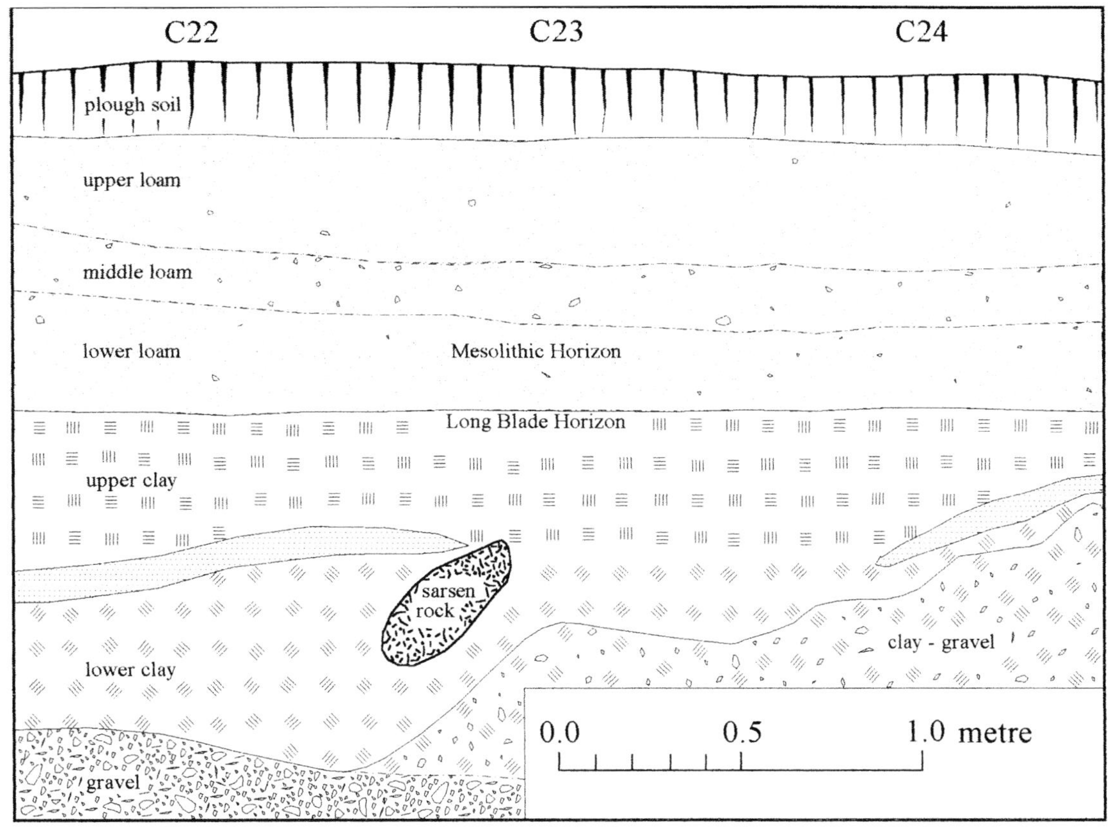

Figure 2.2 Avington VI: section across the north face of transects C22-24 at Avington VI as observed in 1979. The discontinuous black band referred to as the Intermediate Clay subunit is stippled. The 'sarsen' or fine grained sandstone boulder is of local origin

Mesolithic occupants of the site or by burrowing animals. The junction of the silty loam with the underlying clay could usually be recognized to within a few centimetres and was normally 1m below the surface.

Clay

The clay unit was investigated in 1972 and again in 1978–79. The Long Blade artefacts were found in the top of this layer which had a maximum thickness of approximately 1.3m and consisted of three sub-units wherever it was observed. These were as follows:

UPPER CLAY
Ochreous in colour.

INTERMEDIATE CLAY
Formed a thinner dark grey-black layer, usually about 10cm thick and with a high organic content. This was distinctive where it occurred but was not completely continuous over the whole site.

LOWER CLAY
Occurred beneath the intermediate sub-unit and was variable in appearance. The upper zone consisted of patches of ochreous clay set in a more general pale grey clay whilst below was a zone of dark grey clay; the various colours no doubt owing their origin to iron compounds in different oxidation states.

Gravel

This deposit was not exposed or investigated to any depth. It consisted of a mixture of unsorted flint and broken chalk gravel-size clasts with a matrix of fine sand and silt. It also included occasional sarsen boulders. Although little of this deposit was exposed, the absence of any fine sedimentary structures, the character of the sediments and its uneven upper surface suggest that it had been subjected to solifluction.

Interpretation

The stratification is straightforward. The clay deposit, in the surface of which the Long Blade artefacts were found, is probably a colluvium formed as a result of slope processes although the incline down to site is slight. It is uncertain when these sediments were deposited but given the nature of the clay it is probable that much of its thickness accumulated during the Late Glacial when a cold climate is known to have caused marked development of colluvium across southern England. This interpretation is supported by the results of pollen analyses on samples obtained by David Holyoak from trenches dug in 1978 and 1979. These suggest that although pollen and plant macrofossils were scarce, the three sub-units of clay described above could be assigned to Pollen Zones I, II and III with reasonable certainty (Holyoak, 1980). Samples from the clays contained little pollen but yielded an open country spectra with a low proportion of arboreal pollen suggesting there was open grassland and no woodland in the vicinity. The paucity of arboreal pollen and the presence of *Juniperus*, *Empetrum* ('Crowberry', a dwarf carpeting shrub), *Lycopodium* ('Club moss' a moss-like perennial) and *Artemisia* suggest a Late Devensian, Zone III profile, older than that obtained from Thatcham Reedbeds and Avenell's Cottage, Thatcham, where *Juniperus* was not found (ibid). Pollen of open country herbs and marsh plants such as *Filipendula* was also present. At Woolhampton (Collins *et al.*, 1996) pollen from the lower part of the Wasing Sand Bed (WSBa) showed a similarly treeless environment with *Juniperus* at the valley margins and *Filipendula* rich meadows. Radiocarbon age estimates on plant macro fossils from this deposit suggest an Allerød/Windermere age for this spectrum (ibid, 368). On this basis, the Long Blade horizon at Avington VI could be assigned to the end of Zone III or possibly to the beginning of Zone IV. One age estimate obtained by Barton *et al.* (1998, 24) is consistent with the proposed late glacial age of the lower deposit although Holyoak's (1980) correlation to the Allerød oscillation could not be confirmed.

Whether deposition ceased at this point or slowed down is not clear. It was certainly a low energy process as even the tiniest spalls of flint, less than 1mm, were left *in situ* within the Long Blade horizon. Furthermore excavation did not reveal any discontinuity between the Long Blade horizon and what may be termed the Late Mesolithic zone in the stratification. However, the vertical separation between these two is only some 15–20cm; such evidence as exists at present would imply that during Pollen Zones I, II and III, totalling approximately 3,000 years, 1m or more of deposit accumulated whereas from the Long Blade period to the Late Mesolithic, probably at least 4,000 years, much less material, a maximum of 25cm, was deposited. Given the difference in the climates and consequential changes, this is by no means remarkable. Stabilization of the surrounding soils by vegetation would presumably slow down slope processes. What happened after the Late Mesolithic is not of crucial importance to the study of the Long Blade episode since by this time a reasonable depth of deposit was covering the Long Blade artefacts and they were essentially safe from further disturbance. After the Late Mesolithic period, possibly less than 6,000 years to the present day, approximately 75cm of deposit accumulated; unlike the earlier sediment which was generally clast free, at least the initial 35cm contained a significant quantity of clasts, suggesting rather different conditions from those previously operating. Pottery sherds found at a depth of 65–75cm are probably significant in this respect. There are many traces of Romano-British occupation in the Newbury-Kintbury-Hungerford area and Kintbury was certainly occupied in Saxon times. The inference is that for much, if not most, of the last two millennia there has been agricultural activity over and around the site.

There is one final question to be addressed when discussing the Avington site history: could there have been an Early Mesolithic occupation there? The Kennet Valley, especially in the Newbury area, is rich in Early Mesolithic sites. An Early Mesolithic occupation at this site would clearly have to exist at or above the level of the Long Blade horizon but below that of the Late Mesolithic. Certainly no discrete horizon of worked flints between the two major occupations was observed during excavation. Again, the probability is that the artefacts from an Early Mesolithic occupation would have become strongly patinated, making them easily distinguishable from Late Mesolithic artefacts but similar, if not identical, to those from the Long Blade assemblage. However, for any confusion to arise, the Early Mesolithic occupation would have to have fallen within the boundaries of the Long Blade site. In the writer's experience, Early Mesolithic sites commonly consist of several concentrations set in a background scatter. None of the various trenches cut in 1972 or 1995 yielded any evidence for an Early Mesolithic occupation. Finally, all the truly Early Mesolithic sites as yet discovered in the Kintbury (Wawcott) Marsh Benham area have been located on or immediately above the surface of the flood plain gravels which are quite different from the situation being considered here. At Wawcott III (Froom, 1976) where the stratification closely parallels that at Avington VI, the lowest horizons did produce an assemblage dominated by simple obliquely blunted points, but the worked flints at this site, almost without exception, were not patinated. It is pertinent to observe that although some of the Early Mesolithic sites on the flood plain have yielded patinated worked flints, many, possibly a majority, of the Early Mesolithic sites have produced assemblages that are not patinated, for example, Greenham Dairy Farm, Marsh Benham and Wawcott XV and only a small proportion of the flint artefacts from the Thatcham sites are patinated. In the writer's view there are only two industries present at Avington VI: the Long Blade and the Late Mesolithic.

The Long Blade horizon

After the discovery of at least one concentration of Long Blade material in 1972, the excavations of 1978–79 and 1981 set out to characterize the nature of this aspect of the site within the limitations imposed, most notably by the presence of the electricity substation preventing work on the north side of the site (**Fig. 2.1, 2.3**). The general technique in the main excavations was to remove the upper 75cm of the loam and then to divide the trench into 1m² transects. The sediment was then removed by hand using trowels. The main part of the Late Mesolithic phase was removed in one or more vertical units, transect by transect, and the Long Blade horizon was approached and revealed in the same manner. At this point, much time and effort were expended in cleaning the Long Blade horizon; as far as possible each artefact larger than about 15mm was exposed and washed clean without disturbance so that an extensive photographic record could be made (**Pls 1–4**). Once this was done, the flints were removed and the underlying clay checked to a depth of approximately 15–20cm. Immediately beneath the major concentrations and occasionally elsewhere, patches of closely packed spalls, 5–20mm in size, were commonly observed together with even smaller waste. During this phase of the excavation there was no evidence of discrete horizons below the previously exposed Long Blade horizon. After the exposure, cleaning and photography the larger artefacts were lifted and a considerable quantity of the clay beneath them was sampled for wet sieving. This resulted in the recovery of further artefacts down to 1mm in size. The number of artefacts recovered from below the initially exposed horizon varied considerably; in the northern half of the 1978 trench where only a relatively small number of artefacts were initially exposed, few were found any deeper whereas in the southern half the number of artefacts recovered from below the prepared surface was often comparable to those in the surface. As might be expected, large numbers were recovered from below the major concentrations.

Density and distribution of the artefacts

The Long Blade horizon as initially revealed by the 1978 excavation was essentially a background scatter of Long Blade artefacts which were easily recognizable by virtue of their distinctive appearance, particularly their size and patination. The density of these artefacts as exposed was commonly of the order of 5–50 per 1m². In such areas the pieces were lying more or less horizontally (**Pls 1–4**). In two areas however, the density was much greater, in total as many as 1,000 sizable pieces per 1m² were recorded. In these concentrations, the artefacts could be found piled up and, on occasion, they had little or no clay matrix between them: flint rested on flint. The summits of these concentrations projected above the general level of the Long Blade horizon. As defined by the exposed artefacts, the Long Blade horizon presented a comparatively flat and uniform surface over the site as a whole. Where there was no later disturbance and only a modest number of worked flints, the impression was gained when excavating that the Long Blade artefacts were in the top rather than on the top of the clay, that is to say the Long Blade occupation dated to the closing phase of the clay deposition. As already noted, some artefacts were found below the initially exposed surface, occasionally as much as 15cm below, in many cases these were at a variety of angles and were consistent with having been trodden down.

The main objective of the 1979 excavation was the recovery of the remaining part of the second major concentration first recognized in 1978. It became apparent that beyond the concentration to the east there were no further Long Blade artefacts. A significant part of the trench proved to be sterile in this respect. The Long Blade horizon could thus be said to have a sharply delineated boundary beyond which there was no background scatter.

In 1981 an attempt was made to define the southern edge of the Long Blade horizon. This proved inconclusive because of a major Mesolithic disturbance but a narrow strip, approximately 0.5m wide and 4m in length, did reveal a comparatively low density of Long Blade artefacts (**Pl. 4**). As previously noted, no attempt has been made to define the western limit of the artefact spread.

When clearing down towards the Long Blade horizon in 1978, two groups of Long Blade artefacts were located higher in the profile than expected, in transects B18 and D21 respectively. The group in B18 was subsequently associated with the edge of a pit, apparently dug by the Mesolithic people. The artefacts appeared to rest on or in a block of clay spoil originating from the pit. Excavation of the pit was comparatively straightforward, it had penetrated some 25cm into the clay below the Long Blade horizon and had subsequently silted up with the more sandy loam of the Mesolithic later period; the pit fill contained numerous calcined flints as well as artefacts which are not patinated and typical of the Late Mesolithic industry already recovered from the loam. The pit was regular, steep-sided and a natural explanation for its origin is difficult to advance: it certainly did not resemble the holes created by uprooted trees. Initially, the anomalous artefacts in transect D21 appeared to be an upward extension of a major concentration that subsequently appeared in that transect and its neighbour, C21, which obviously extended beyond the eastern limit of that trench. This concentration was the main objective of the 1979 excavation. Subsequently, the 1981 excavation revealed other items of Long Blade material that had apparently been displaced upwards in transects E18/19/20/21 by a massive pit dug in Mesolithic times. This pit was at least 4m or more in length; it was not

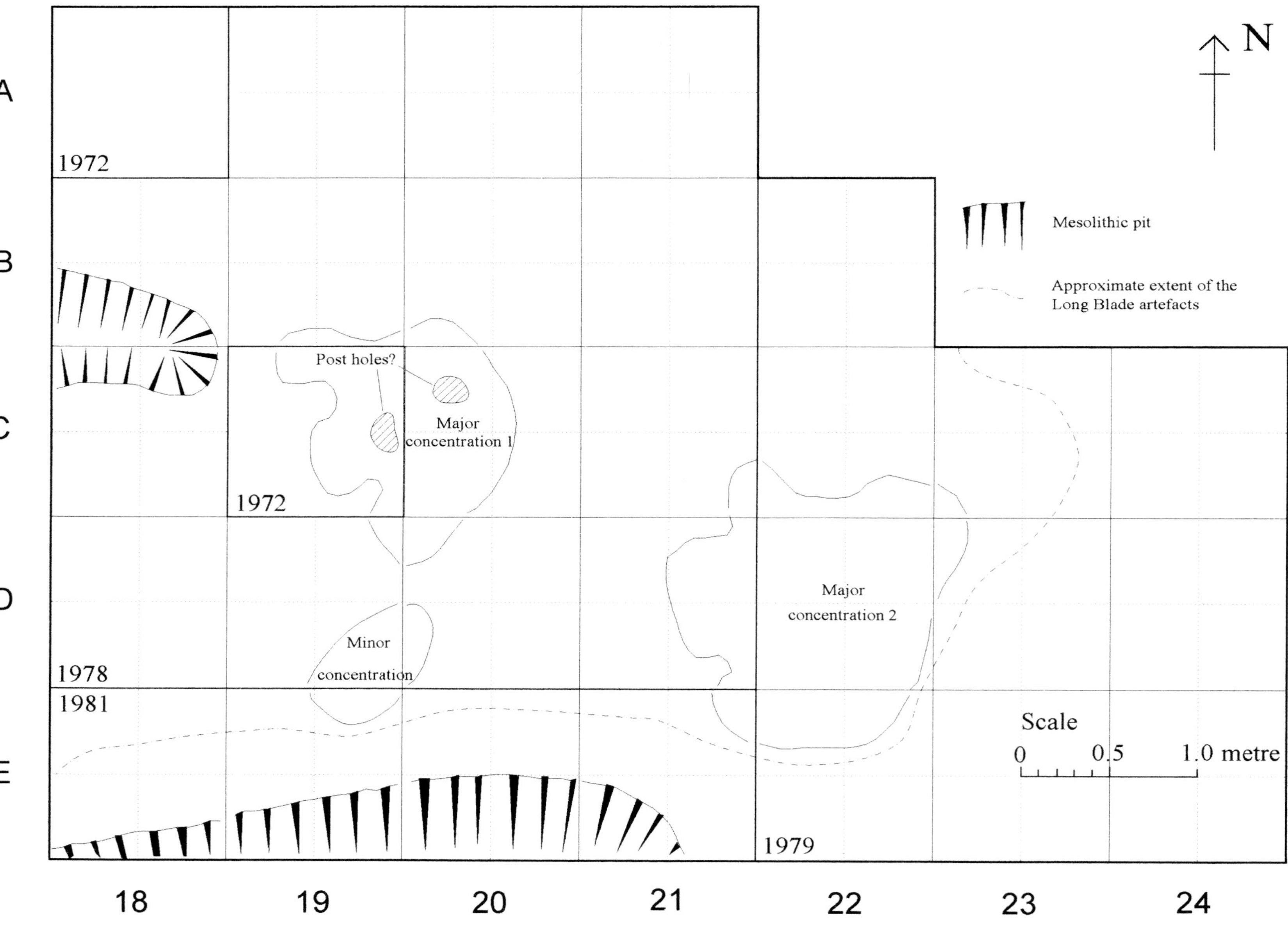

Figure 2.3 Avington VI: plan of the Long Blade surface as observed from 1972 to 1981

extensively investigated. The displaced items in D21 may also owe their origin to the digging of this pit. In both cases, some of the upwardly displaced artefacts have been refitted to other artefacts from nearby undisturbed contexts showing that they had not been moved far.

The excavations of 1978 also revealed signs of an incipient disturbance in the area of transect A20–21 which resulted in calcined flints and Mesolithic artefacts continuing down to much deeper levels than normal. However, there was no great development of the Long Blade horizon in this immediate area. Similar observations were made in 1979 in the area of transect E22 but here, after the removal of the prepared Long Blade artefacts, further excavation disclosed what was probably the outline of an animal burrow, possibly part of a badger set.

In summary, disturbance of the Long Blade site had been caused by two major pits attributable to the Late Mesolithic period and there were other areas of more minor disturbance, possibly Mesolithic in origin or more probably due to animal activity. Some degree of animal disturbance is only to be expected over a period of several millennia.

Putting together the results from all the excavations, the first impression is one of an area covered by a background scatter of Long Blade artefacts containing two major concentrations, one of which has an adjoining less intense concentration. There appears to be a demonstrable limit to the artefacts in the east which is surprisingly sharp. To the south the edge is obscured by the major Mesolithic disturbance in this area but the indications are that it was not notably different from the eastern edge. The western and northern limits lie in the unexcavated areas but here again Mesolithic disturbance cannot be ruled out. That the one observable limit is so sharp is intriguing: was there some barrier during the occupation that prevented further spread of the artefacts? Excavation produced no evidence for a barrier in the form of post-holes or even large stones but not all structures leave such enduring evidence. However, features recorded in 1972 and 1978 warrant description in this regard. All the excavations used the same grid, consequently the trial of 1972 corresponds exactly with transect C19 of 1978. When the Long Blade flints were being removed from C19 in 1972, it became apparent that below the uppermost layers the artefacts at one point tended to dip down and, in part, formed the fill of a small hole. Excavation revealed this regular hole to be D-shaped in plan, 15 x 20cm across and with a depth of 15cm (**Pls 1–2**). This feature was covered by a concrete slab in anticipation of future work. In 1978, when preparing the major concentration in C20, part of which (C19) had been removed in 1972, an examination of the cleaned flint concentration clearly showed another more circular feature (**Pls 2–4**). When the upper flints were removed and further investigations were made, a second hole was revealed; again the fill included a large number of worked flints that appeared to have slumped down into the hole because something had been removed or decayed away. This second hole was 20cm in diameter and penetrated the clay some 10cm below the general level of the flint concentration (**Fig. 2.3**). The function of these holes is open to speculation. It may or may not be significant that they were surrounded by a mass of flaking debris. According to the evidence available, in Long Blade times timber would have been at least scarce but there are ethnographic parallels for timber poles, supports for skin/hide shelters, being transported quite long distances. Given the nature of these holes, as revealed by excavation, it seems more probable that they are post holes contemporary with the occupation of the site by Long Blade makers than that they were natural in origin.

Another aspect to which attention may be drawn is the precise arrangement of the worked flints as revealed by the final stages of cleaning and preparation. The writer would question whether or not they would have appeared as they did had they fallen on ground covered with vegetation. As noted previously, there were many instances where patches of small spalls formed thin layers in which the spalls were often contiguous and were invariably lying flat. Again, in the major concentrations, larger artefacts were found lying one on another. To the writer's mind the most probable interpretation is the deposition of the worked flints on essentially bare ground. There is some slight evidence to corroborate this in the botanical data which include a single dandelion (*Taxacum*) seed filament or achene from the Long Blade horizon; dandelions commonly grow on open disturbed ground.

There is no reason why the sharply delimited eastern edge to the artefacts, the possible post-holes in C19, 20 and the postulated deposition of the artefacts on bare ground, should be in any way connected but taken together, they suggest the existence of some form of shelter. Given the probable exposed nature of the site and the climate of the time, the existence of such a shelter would not be surprising. Furthermore, it should also be noted that whereas the Late Mesolithic layer produced burnt artefacts and numerous calcined flints, the Long Blade horizon produced neither and there was no substantial evidence for fire in the Long Blade period.

Chapter 3

The Long Blade Assemblage from Avington VI

Preliminary considerations

On completion of the excavations, the numerous bags of worked flints labelled with transect data were washed and sorted into three groups according to their depth: the main Mesolithic levels; the intermediate levels and the Long Blade horizon and below. Some mixing was evident in the intermediate group but separating items from the Long Blade assemblage from the Mesolithic material rarely posed any problem. There were relatively few items of Long Blade material in the main Mesolithic zone of the loam. Similarly, the Long Blade horizon was generally free of intrusive material, except in the areas of the two well defined pits and the other less extreme disturbances already described; little difficulty was met with when setting aside the Mesolithic artefacts that did exist. Thus at the end of the initial sorting it was felt with some considerable confidence that the two industries had been separated. Only the Long Blade assemblage is considered here. The Mesolithic material will be described in a further publication (Froom in preparation).

Raw material

All of the artefacts in the Long Blade assemblage are made of flint and are patinated. Refitting shows that conjoining pieces can differ markedly in appearance and that such variation cannot be used as a means of distinguishing different types of the flint. However, differences in cortex thickness and texture suggest that flint from different sources were used. The majority of the cores which retain cortex have a thin (less than 1mm) smooth cortex, which contrasts with a thicker (3–4mm), sometimes deeply pitted cortex on a small number. The rarity of truly ancient fracture surfaces is also noticeable suggesting that the knappers preferred to select fresh, unmodified nodules of flint that were completely enveloped in cortex and less likely to be flawed. These probably came from local deposits of clay-with-flints, from exposures in weathered chalk or, out of the Tertiary strata. However, some nodules may have come from the flood plain gravels where they could have been derived from over a much wider area.

Vertical distribution

Once separated, each artefact of any consequence in the Long Blade assemblage was assigned an index number to identify it uniquely; generally this applied to any piece larger than about 15–20mm, although smaller diagnostic pieces such as microlith fragments were also treated in this way. All the relevant data were entered into a central catalogue, thus any flint carrying an index number can be traced to its parent transect and its particular depth, in many cases its original find spot may be identified to within a few centimetres. **Table 3.1** summarises the distribution of the Long Blade material by depth excluding small waste such as spalls of less than 4mm. It shows that the Long Blade material is concentrated within and below the Long Blade horizon but there has been some upward displacement of artefacts. This is confirmed by the many instances of artefacts from the intermediate and Mesolithic zones which refit to artefacts located in the main Long Blade horizon. It should also be noted that in most instances the displacement was not great; the larger proportion of the Long Blade items in the intermediate group were recovered during the final clearing and cleaning of the Long Blade surface and were not more than approximately 5cm above it. However, as far as possible the following report on the Long Blade assemblage is based on those artefacts recovered from the exposed Long Blade surface and below.

Horizontal distribution

Frequent reference will be made to the two major concentrations within the Long Blade horizon. Initially, refitting failed to reveal any connections between these two major concentrations suggesting that they could be defined as truly separate areas. Within these interest focussed on some cores with extended series of conjoining flakes and blades which had been recovered from discrete scatters within each area. However, as refitting continued, several cores had flakes and blades refitted from both concentrations; these will be discussed in more detail later in this report. These aspects of isolation and

Table 3.1: Frequency of Long Blade artefacts by depth

Artefact types	Long Blade horizon and below	Intermediate	Mesolithic
Finished forms (retouched tools & microliths)	56	12	3
Specialized waste (cores, crested blades & rejuvenation flakes)	224	28	14
Large waste	4,530	88	249
Totals	4,810	928	266

connection within the horizontal distribution, as well as their significance in terms of spatial organisation will be discussed further in relation to the various artefact types.

Assemblage composition

A total of about 6,000 artefacts may be assigned to the Long Blade occupation at Avington VI. **Table 3.2** summarises the frequency of tools such as microliths, scrapers and burins, as well as bruised edge blades or *lame machûrées* and utilised pieces, diagnostic waste including cores, core rejuvenation flakes, crested blades, unmodified, flakes and small debitage. The bruised edge blades, like the microliths, are typical of Long Blade assemblages both in Britain and northern Europe.

Table 3.2: Long Blade assemblage composition

Microliths and associated forms	34
Endscrapers	9
Burins	2
Utilized pieces including awls and a microdenticulate	11
Cores	60
Hammerstones	4
Crested blades including 11 bruised edge pieces	59
Core rejuvenation flakes	101
Blades including 43 bruised edge pieces	2,531
Flakes including 10 bruised edge pieces	1,700
Miscellaneous	299
Subtotal	4,810
Small waste	9,750
Total	**14,560**

Table 3.3: Microliths and associated forms

Form	Number
Identifiable microliths	
Type A1a	7
Type A1c	4
Type B	9
Tanged	2
Microlith fragments	**6**
Debitage	
Microburins	3
Proximal remnants	1
Distal remnants	2
Total	**34**

Microliths and associated forms

The term microlith is used to denote a small blade which has been shaped by retouch, normally resulting in the removal of the bulb of percussion, and which can be identified in the typology devised by Clark (1933; Clark & Rankine,1939). In the Avington VI assemblage, complete microliths are between approximately 30 and 60mm in length. **Table 3.3** summarises the types present. There are 22 pieces which are sufficiently complete to identify and all but two of these are obliquely blunted points and backed blades: Clark's Type A and B respectively. Both of these types, particularly the obliquely blunted point, occur in the Mesolithic of the Kennet Valley and with other Long Blade sites such as Sproughton, Suffolk and Uxbridge, Middlesex (Barton, 1992: 241).

Most of the obliquely blunted points are retouched on the left-hand side as normally viewed (**Fig. 3.1: 1– 7**). The retouch is abrupt, marginal and limited to part of the edge just below the tip. The retouched section is usually straight although one of the right-handed forms (**Fig. 3.1: 9**) is markedly concave. On the two other right-handed examples (**Fig. 3.1: 10– 11**) the blunting extends further along the edge and these microliths are at least superficially transitional with Type B microliths otherwise known as backed blades. In two examples, an A1a and an A1c (**Fig. 3.1: 6, 9**), the retouch has been applied both from the edge and in the opposite direction from a dorsal arête. The obliquely blunted points range from 32.5mm–46.2mm in length and in width from 5.9mm–13.1mm although most are10–12mm. Thickness varies from 1.9–3.3mm with three pieces thinner than 2.5mm. Four examples appear to have lost the distal tip of the blade in antiquity and only in five cases does the retouch form a sharp neat point with the opposing blade-edge. Two examples (**Fig. 3.1: 3, 7**) terminate in an oblique fracture which probably results from the way in which the microlith was produced using the notch technique: if the twisting fracture used to detach the required segment is successful then a microburin would result, but if the fracture fails the microlith blank may detach abruptly in an irregular manner from the unwanted proximal end fragment (**Fig. 3.1: 13, 19**). Two other pieces exhibit a remnant of the blade butt and again may represent microliths abandoned unfinished (**Fig. 3.1: 2**). As the classification implies, in none of the examples is there any sign of convergent retouch on the opposite edge of the tip as is characteristic of types A1b and A1d. All of the 10 microliths described above are firmly associated with the Long Blade horizon; three of them were recovered from its base during the final phase of clearing.

Of the nine microliths assigned to Type B, two are quite distinctive and stand somewhat apart from the other seven, although only one is complete and this was found as two comparatively closely spaced fragments having been broken in antiquity. This rebuilt microlith has been identified as a Blanchères or Malaurie Point and the writer is indebted to Sabrina Dumont for this identification (**Fig. 3.1: 12**). Such points may have a convex or, as in this case, a straight backed edge and a retouched basal truncation which is often but not always perpendicular to the main axis of the piece. A feature of the Type B microliths is that they all appear to have been broken in antiquity, in some cases into three or even more pieces (**Fig. 3.1: 12–20**). Although in most cases the fracture has the character of a transverse snap, in two cases it appears to have resulted from longitudinally applied impact (**Fig. 3.1: 13, 19**). The fact that only one microlith has been completely rebuilt suggests that fracture may have occurred away from their find spots, perhaps away from the site, with only some sections of the broken microlith being retained by the original handle or shaft to be released on replacement. As far as can be inferred, taking into account the incomplete nature of these microliths, retouch was applied to the whole length of one side. The retouched edge is straight rather than curved and in the two more extreme examples, the Blanchères Point and fragment, some retouch has been applied from a dorsal arête as well as from the edge. Where it is possible to see such detail, retouch has been applied to the left-hand side of the blade as usually viewed; there is no positively identified example where it was otherwise. The

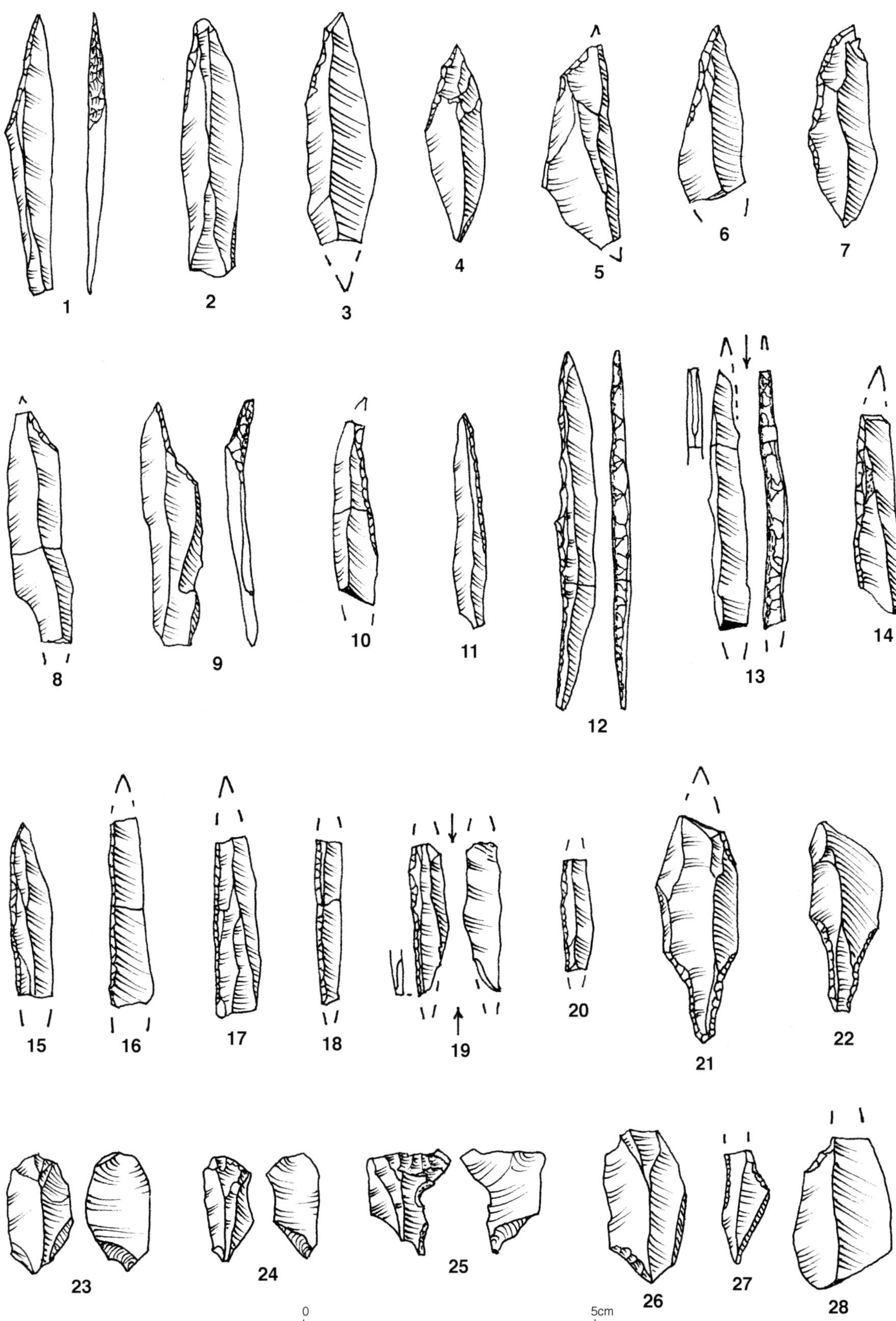

Figure 3.1. Avington VI: points, microliths, and microlith debitage

length of these microliths is difficult to ascertain for certain due to breakage. The only definitely complete example is 59.5mm, several others could well have approached or even exceeded 50mm, but others were more likely to have been in the range 30–40mm. Widths are more certain and range from 4.2mm–7.7mm, with six being 6.0–7.5mm; thickness varies from 1.7mm–3.6mm. This group of nine microliths is again firmly associated with the Long Blade horizon; four were recovered from near its base.

There are two other artefacts which may be classified as microliths; they were found less than 1m apart. One is made from a small well-formed blade; a distinct tang has been created at the proximal end by typical microlith blunting, and, although much of the distal end is missing, it almost certainly had a sharp retouched point as traces of retouch survive on the right edge (**Fig. 3.1: 21**). These characteristics are typical of an Ahrensburgian Point as defined by Clark, (1938: fig. 1.5 and 6) and the piece is identified as such. The second artefact (**Fig. 3.1: 22**) is similar in outline having a tang formed by typical microlith retouch at the proximal end of a less elegant blade. However, it lacks the distal retouch of the first piece. A parallel for this microlith is recorded by Clark from the Ahrensburgian sites (1938, fig. 1.4). This second form may be an unfinished version of the first or simply an example where it was thought unnecessary to add further retouch.

There are six pieces which have been identified as fragmentary microliths. One appears to be the proximal end of a typical A1a, one piece appears to be the mid-section of an A1a microlith and there are two sections of Type B microliths. None of these four pieces extend the range of observations already recorded. Of the remaining two items, one is a small fragment with typical microlithic blunting; the other is of some interest, it appears to be the tip or possibly butt of a microlith detached by a longitudinal impact fracture. It is 13.4mm long, triangular in cross-section and has retouch on all three faces.

A further six items have been identified as being associated with the manufacture of microliths. Three proximal ends of blades exhibit clear traces of a notch formed by typical microlithic blunting together with a curving scar. Two of these microburins were associated with microliths blunted on the left edge and the other the right (**Fig. 3.1: 23–25**). One other proximal end fragment is present but instead of the characteristic curving scar of the typical microburin it exhibits a simple fracture sometimes identified as an attempt at a microburin which failed (**Fig. 3.1: 26**). This explanation is possible but it may equally represent a premature and unwanted fracture prior to the application of the microburin technique or, alternatively, it might be the intentional result of a simple technique. As noted above, some of the Type A microliths (**Fig. 3.1: 13, 19**) exhibit the type of fracture scar indicative of this accidental or deliberate method of detaching the unwanted proximal end (p. 14). Two blade tips are present which exhibit traces of a notch worked by typical microlithic retouch together with a transverse fracture; these are consistent with the manufacture of Type B microliths (**Fig. 3.1: 27, 28**). Attempts to reunite broken or fragmentary microliths with the various forms just described did not meet any success.

Distribution diagrams plotted for the microliths and allied forms show some clustering (**Fig. 3.2**). No clear distinction emerges in the distribution of Types A and B; both types occur in much the same areas, within the boundaries of the major concentrations of worked flints but also elsewhere. It is

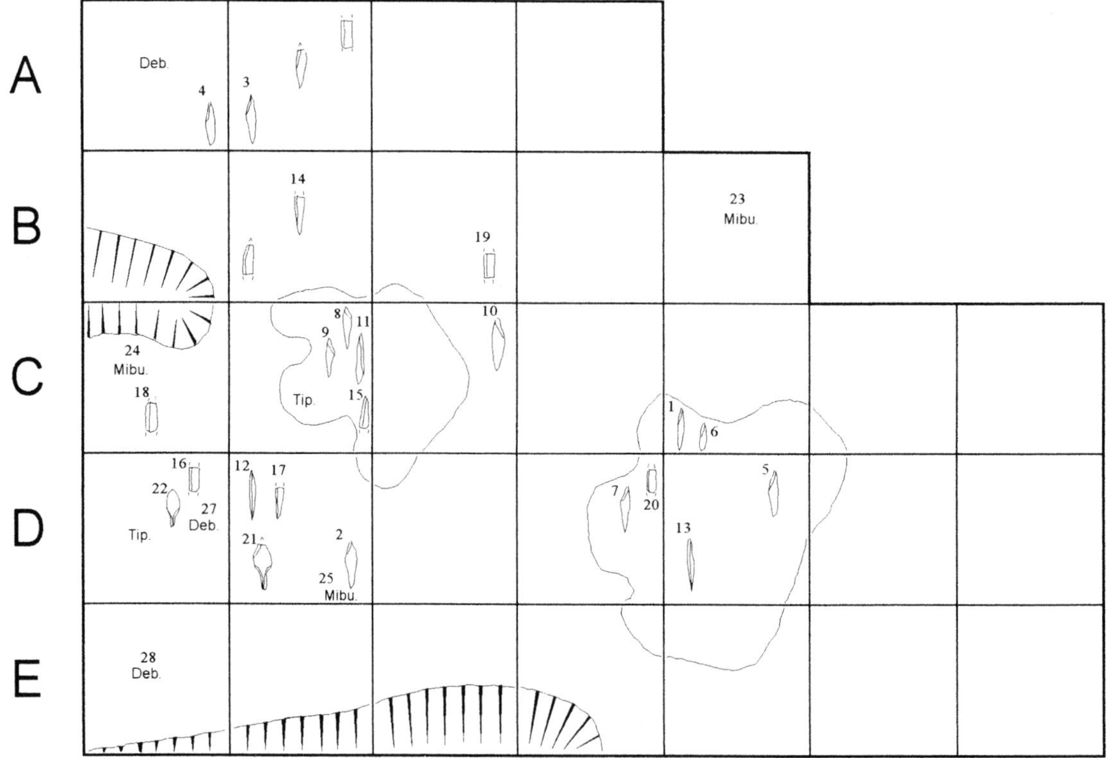

Figure 3.2 Avington VI: distribution of retouched points and microliths. The numbers correspond with those in Figure 3.1. Mibu. refers to a microburin; Deb. to other debitage

noticeable that Type A microliths blunted on the right side and described as A1c occur in the area of the major concentration in transects C19–20, but this is a small group. Superficially significant clusters of items appear in two other areas: transect A18–19 and transects D18–19. However, this might be no more than a function of the generally higher density of worked flints in these areas. There are many transects without a single representative from this group of artefacts but they are invariably transects with a generally low density of artefacts.

Endscrapers

Nine endscrapers were found within the Long Blade horizon and another above it. They divide between those made on blades or blade-like flakes and those made on flakes. Of the five made on blades or similar blanks (**Fig. 3.3**), one was found in the main Mesolithic layer but its patination and typology leave little doubt that it originated from the Long Blade assemblage. Three of the five appear to have been broken or, at least lack their proximal ends. In one case the missing end has been located and refitted, demonstrating that the scraper had originally broken approximately halfway along its length; the two pieces were found in neighbouring transects. The scraping edges are generally well-made and close examination reveals that some minute spalls, only 1–0.2mm long, have been detached, probably during use. The widths of the scraping edges vary from 13–28mm with four examples being 20mm or more.

The other endscrapers were made on flakes (**Fig. 3.4**). In two cases the proximal ends are missing but one of these two has been rebuilt, the missing fragment, approximately 33% of the artefact, located in the adjacent transect. As with the previous group, the scraper edge is generally well-made and in all cases exhibits at least some tiny scalar retouch or 'spalling' caused by use. The width of the scraper edge is larger in this group, the limits being 32–61mm with three between 37 and 40mm.

Measuring the angle of the scraper edge is both difficult and problematic. It is difficult because both the ventral surface of the blade or flake blank on which the scraper is made and the surface of the retouch scars forming the scraper edge, are curved surfaces which cannot define a precise angle. Furthermore, the removal of several spalls to construct a typical scraper edge generates its own set of angles, introducing further variability so that the angle changes from one part of the scraping edge to another. This variation may have been even further modified by edge damage caused by the angle and kinematics of use. Given this variability and the actual difficulty of measuring the angle a surprisingly consistent result was achieved. The minimum value was found to be 55° plus or minus 5° and the maximum value to be 60° plus or minus 5° for 9 of the 10 scrapers, the one exception producing a result of 70° plus or minus 10°.

The distribution of the endscrapers (**Fig. 3.5**) differs from that of the microlith element in that only one scraper was associated with a major concentration, the rest tending towards areas where the general density of artefacts was low. Four endscrapers, including one of the broken ones, were located in an area of little over 1m² centred on the intersection A, B 18, 19.

Burins

Burins constitute a minor element of the assemblage. Only three have been identified as deliberately produced. The largest of the three is a dihedral burin found in 1972 from a trial trench

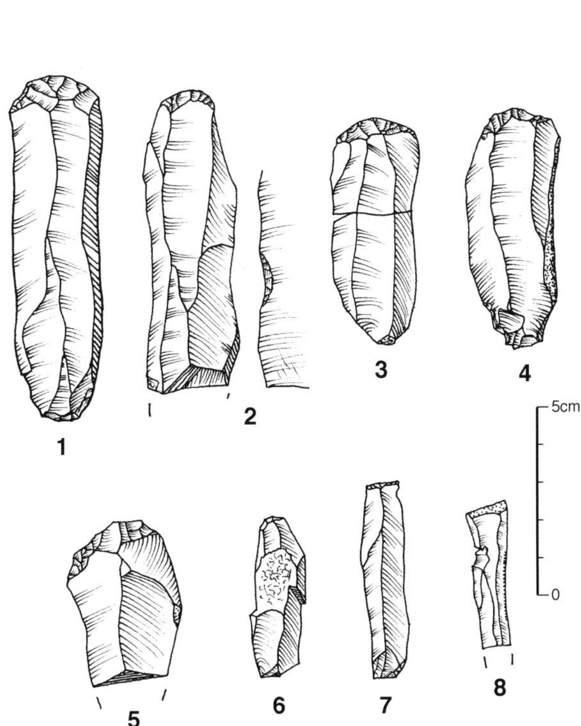

Figure 3.3 Avington VI: 1-5: endscrapers on blades; 6-8: retouched bladelets

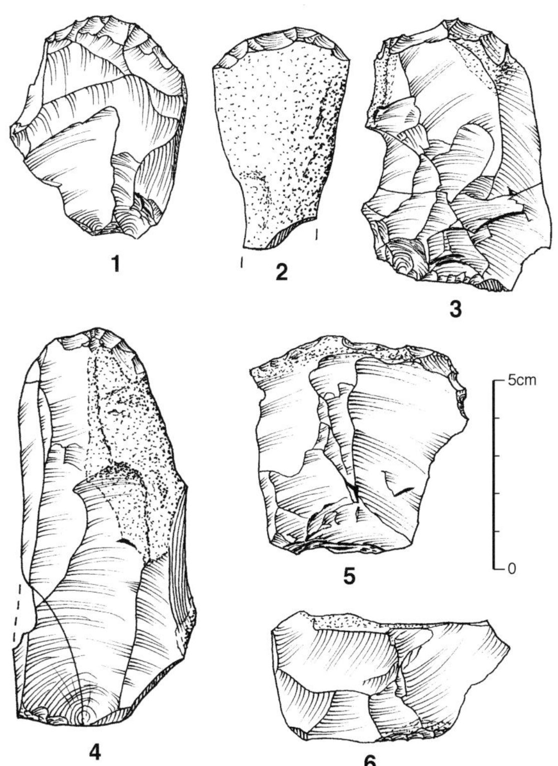

Figure 3.4 Avington VI: 1-3, 5: endscrapers on flakes; 4: endscraper found above Long Blade horizon; 6: utilised flake

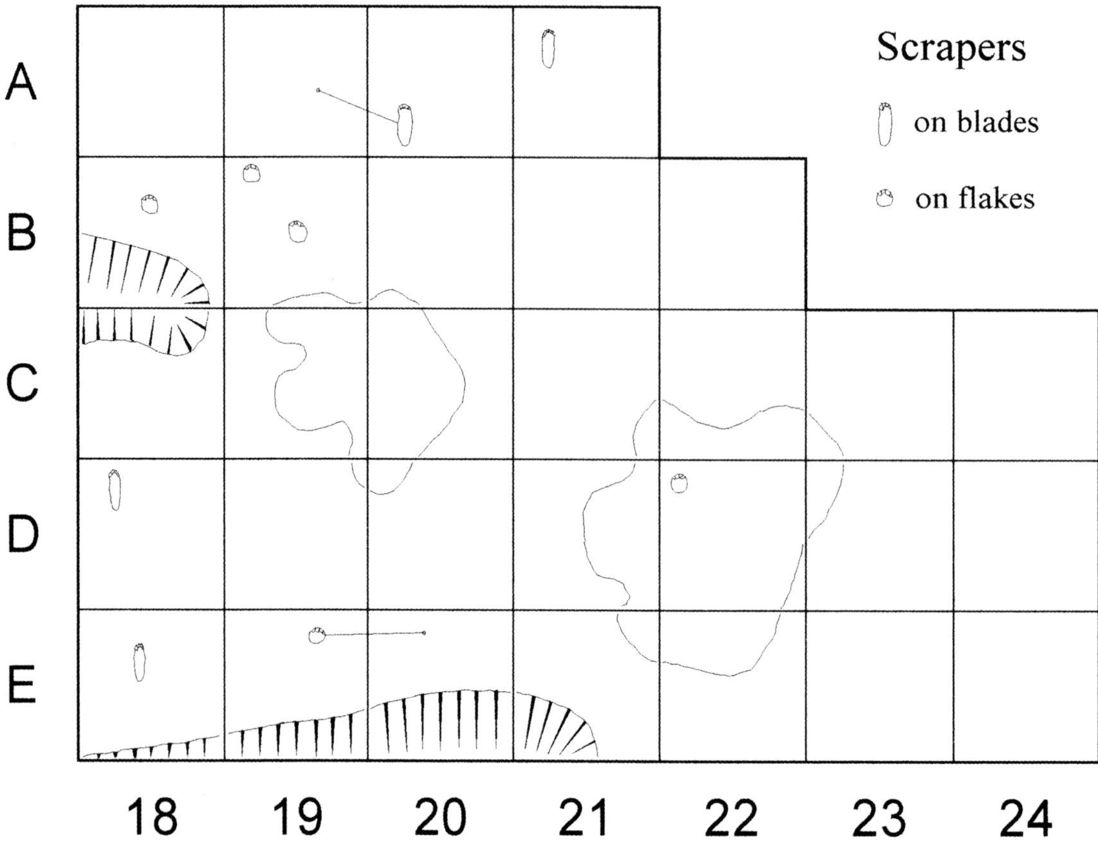

Figure 3.5 Avington VI: distribution of endscrapers

corresponding to transect A25, although found at a depth of only 0.5m. its character leaves little doubt that it is a Long Blade artefact; originally a large thick blade, the distal end has been transformed by the removal of opposing spalls and there is some additional abrupt marginal retouch along the left edge (**Fig. 3.6: 1**). The second example was made on a blade of rectangular outline from which a single burin spall has been removed from the distal end of the blade and there is some evidence of use across the end of the tool (**Fig. 3.6: 2**).The remaining piece is a small flake from which the butt has been detached to produce a transverse surface. This has then been used as a striking platform from which a burin spall was struck to form a small graving edge (**Fig. 3.6: 3**).

Utilized pieces

As with all assemblages of flint artefacts, there are a number of pieces which appear to have fulfilled some function, if only briefly, yet defy precise classification; these are appropriately described by some as 'tools of the moment'. It is probable that in the bulk of the debitage there are many pieces which were used and yet remain unrecognized, their use having left no obvious sign of such use. Obvious exceptions to this are the many pieces which have significantly damaged edges. These are described in French as *lame machûrées*, a term translated here as bruised edge blades, and are considered separately. Little purpose would be served by describing individually all the items set aside as utilised but a few warrant some mention.

One blade-like flake, retaining traces of cortex but lacking its proximal end, has a strong neatly made point worked on its distal end; both its form and the presence of use damage suggest that it may have functioned as an awl (**Fig. 3.6: 5**). Associated with the retouch there tiny scalar edge damage scars on one edge and half moon scars on the opposite edge; the difference and location of the scars suggest rotational movement against another material. Unfortunately, this artefact was found in the main Mesolithic Horizon but its character and above all its patination place it in the Long Blade assemblage. **Figure 3.6: 4** is similar in character.

A small blade, again lacking its butt, is notable in having some 23–25 tiny serrations along the mid-section of the right edge for a length of 16–17mm. (**Fig. 3.3: 8**); this microdenticulate was found just above the Long Blade surface.

Two blade-like flakes of similar size and shape, both broad-ended, are deeply notched by a single blow at their distal end. In both cases the notch has then been retouched, apparently with the intention of creating a point (**Fig. 3.6: 6**); however, this point appears to have broken away in use. What this use was is a matter for pure speculation. Both of these artefacts were recovered from the Long Blade horizon.

There are six other bladelets which exhibit evidence of use but there is no discernible pattern to the modifications observed within the set. One has been trimmed obliquely by typical microlithic blunting retouch to form a fine point whereas another (**Fig. 3.3: 7**) has been similarly worked but to a square end.

Two larger blades, approximately 100mm in length, have been retouched along the entire length of both edges: one has a pointed shape (**Fig. 3.6: 7**); the other is blunt-ended. The retouch is regular, scalar, unlike that found on bruised edge blades, and could either be deliberate or the result of damage during use. Such pieces are sometimes called 'fabricators' but their function is a matter of speculation.

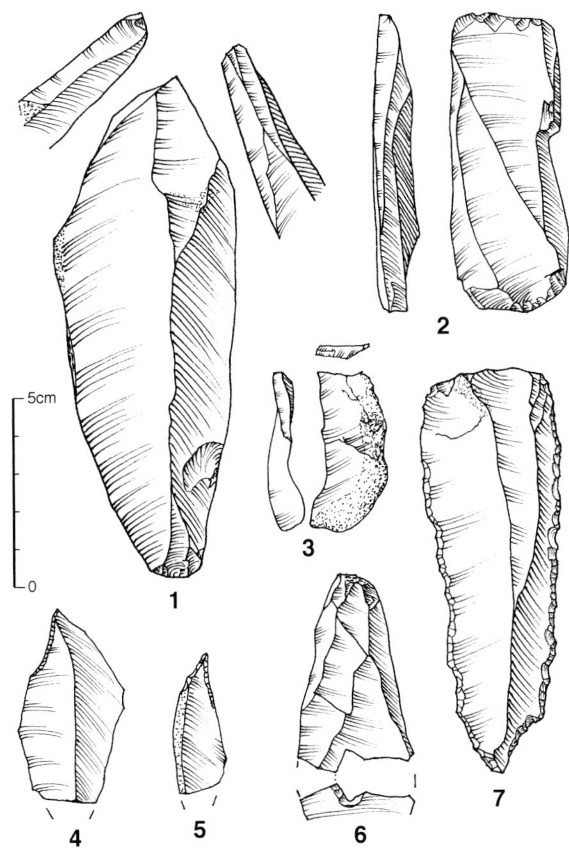

Figure 3.6 Avington VI: 1-3: burins; 4-5 awls; 6-7: retouched blades

Cores and associated pieces

As might be expected, cores are a major feature of the assemblage and all 50 of those described in summary in **Table 3.4** were found in the Long Blade horizon. These pieces are clearly and systematically worked to produce the blanks required for immediate use or further modification. There is only one example that could be said to be completely exhausted which suggests that the knappers required blanks of a certain size and nature and had an adequate supply of flint to meet their needs. The discarded cores tend to be large: 90% are between 75–175mm in length and between 35 and 75mm in width; the length:width ratio is broadly constant at 3.5. However, refitting has shown that some cores were initially as much as 300mm in length. Cores indicative of the use of comparatively small nodules are also present.

It is difficult to assess by superficial examination how much a core was used or to what extent it had been a successful source of blades but at least one has been identified as worked out or 'exhausted', that is to say nothing further could have been successfully struck from it. Refitting a core tablet or core rejuvenation flake to a core has shown that, on occasion, a considerable volume of flint has been removed from the working-face of the core albeit one of nondescript appearance. Equally, a core of elegant appearance may have produced comparatively few useful products. This raises the question of whether all of the artefacts were produced on site or whether aspects of their production and use took place elsewhere. A rough indication of this was obtained by calculating whether the number of identified cores is commensurate with the quantity of blades found in the Long Blade horizon. If the total number of

Table 3.4: Cores and associated debitage

	No.	Total
A. Large cores (length >70mm)		
Two platforms		
Group 1	17	
Group 2	24	
Single platform	4	
		45
B. Small cores (length<69mm)		
Two platforms	3	
Single platform	2	
		5
C. Core debitage		
Core, worked out	1	
Cores, abandoned early	6	
Core fragments	2	
Attempted core	1	
Shatter pieces	34	
		44

flakes and blades is set against the corresponding total of cores, an average value in the range of 60–70 may be obtained for the number of removals per core; a much higher value would result if the small waste was brought into the calculation. This is surprisingly high because the largest group of conjoined pieces currently contains only about 60 pieces and few refitted groups exceed 40 pieces; some series that are all but complete number less than 30. It seems improbable that substantial quantities of flakes and blades would have been transported any distance so it seems probable that some cores may be missing from the assemblage.

Table 3.4 also summarises other core related debitage.

The majority of the cores have two platforms. The nature of the platform is variable both in size and mode of formation: in some cases a single flake has been removed to form a plain surface whilst in other examples the platform has been facetted by the removal on a number of small flakes; both types of platform may occur on the same core. On occasion, as refitting has demonstrated, cores were drastically shortened by the removal of the end of the core as a chunk, (**Fig. 4.25**); other cores have been shortened by the removal of a number of core rejuvenation flakes.

TYPE I CORES

The large two-platform cores divide naturally into two groups based on the manner in which they had been worked at least in the final stages of the reduction sequence. Type 1 cores have a striking platform at opposite ends ('bipolar') of what is usually a cylindrical nodule. These cores range in length from 75–125mm. The shape and configuration of the cortex on several of these cores suggest that the original nodule of flint was usually not much greater in size than the core as found. This has been confirmed by the refitting as none of these cores were placed in reduction sequences from much larger nodules. Although these cores are all bipolar their geometry varies according to the position of the striking platforms. About 33% have bipolar opposed platforms that have been used to remove blades from the same working face; the latter then exhibits more or less parallel scars from both directions (**Fig. 3.7: 1–4**).

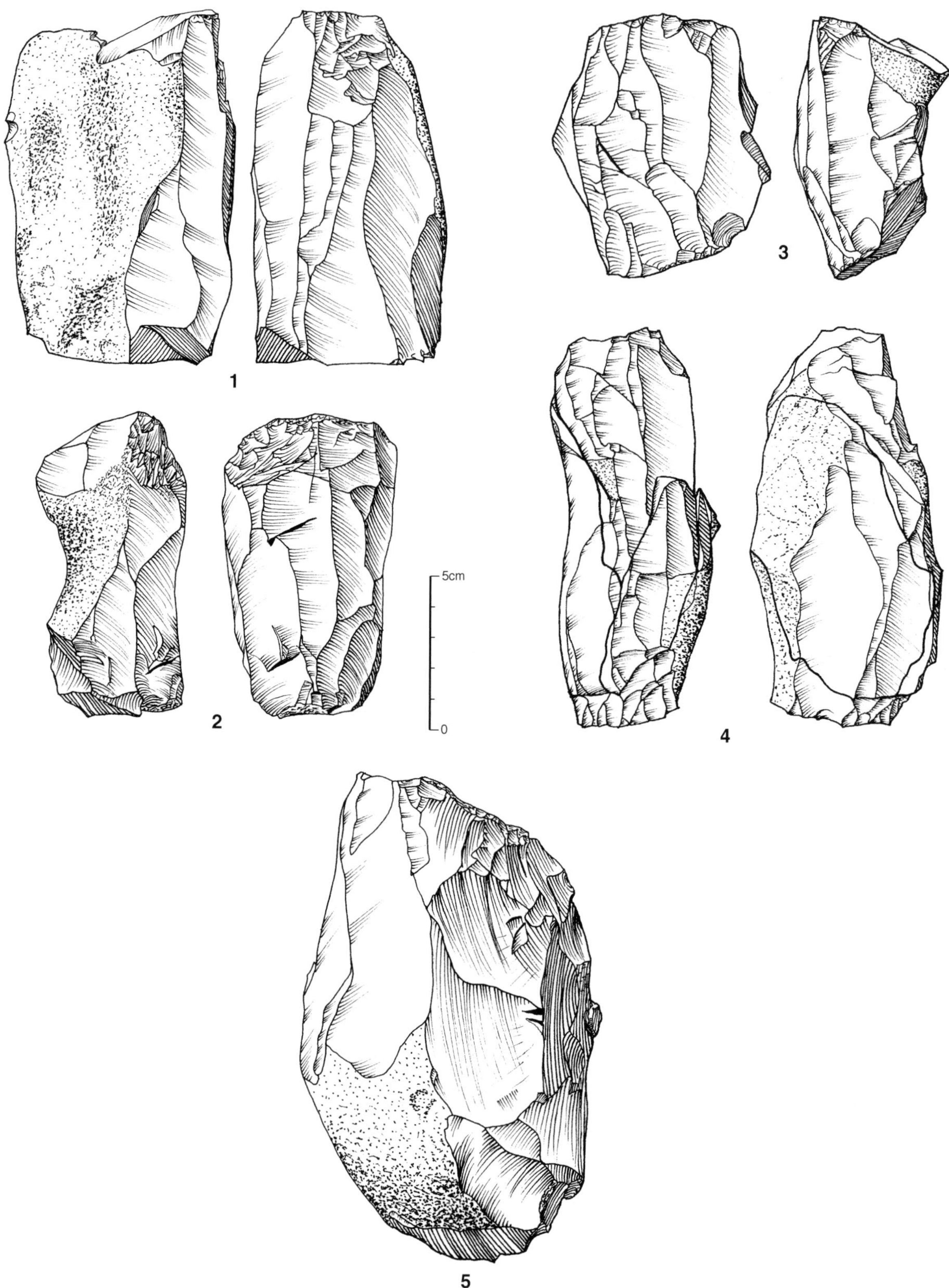

Figure 3.7 Avington VI: cores

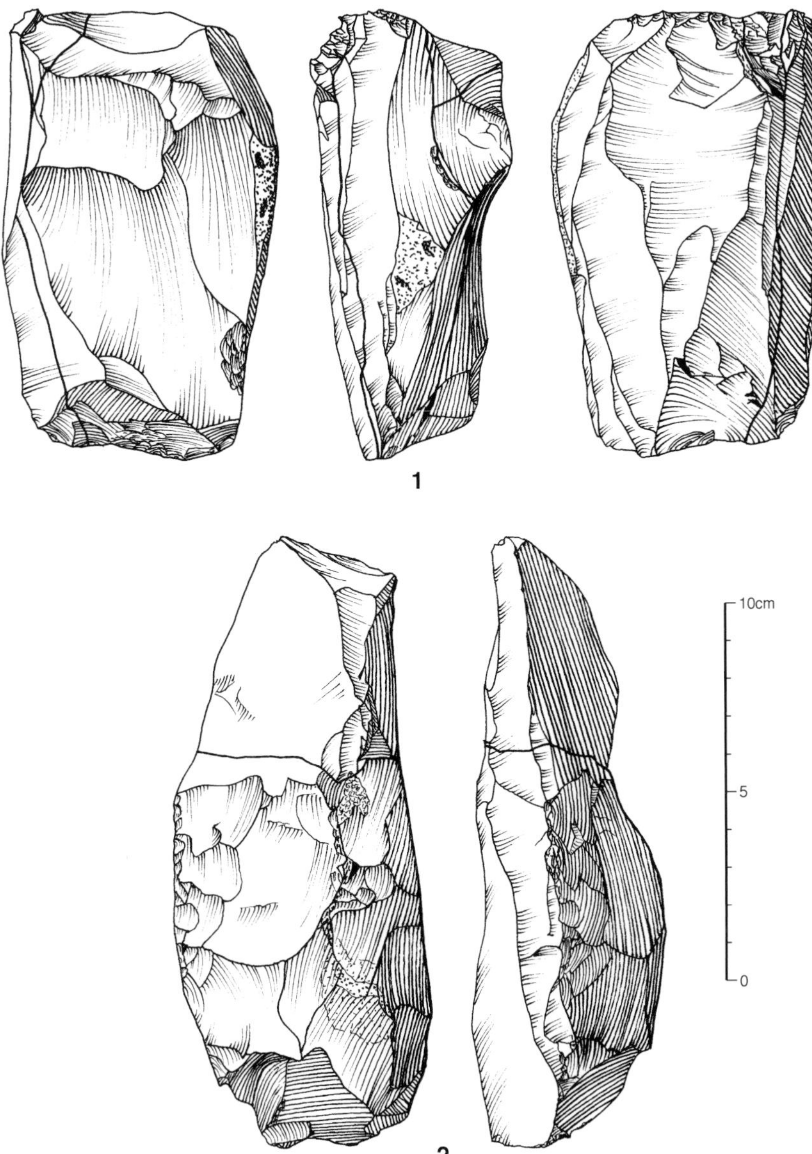

Figure 3.8 Avington VI:cores

Another third have bipolar platforms but instead of being directly above one another, one platform is rotated about the long axis by about 90°. As a result although continuous around the working face, the removals have been struck from different directions on each side (**Fig. 3.7: 5**). The remaining cores are intermediate between these two extremes, creating a continuous spectrum between them.

Type 2 cores

Type 2 cores differ from the group 1 cores in a number of ways; primarily they exhibit additional flaking beyond that necessary for the preparation of the striking platforms and the working face. **Figure 3.7: 5** is a typical example. This basic preparation took place at an early stage in the production of the core. These cores are much larger in size than the group 1 cores, ranging in length from 76–172mm; however, refitting has demonstrated that some of these group 2 cores were originally even bigger, approaching 300mm between their platforms. Their geometry also tends to be much simpler than that of group 1, in nearly all cases the two platforms are aligned to serve the common working face, which is thus struck bidirectionally. In cross-section, the group 2 cores divide into two distinct forms: 11 are broadly flat-backed giving an essentially rectangular cross-section (**Fig. 3.8: 1**) whereas seven cores are triangular in cross-section (**Fig. 3.8: 2**). Four of the latter group were found in the concentration in transects C19–20 and a fifth nearby in transect D19. In some cases at least, the triangular cross- section may represent preparation for the removal of a crested blade.

Single platform cores

Little can be usefully written about the large single platform cores, they are not extensively worked and two have had a large proportion of their removals refitted. In length they are 75–100mm and tend to be wider in proportion compared to the two-platform cores. Two were made on complete nodules and the others were made on fragments of flint.

Small cores

The small cores, less than 60mm long, constitute only 10% of all cores. Three have two platforms; the other two are single platform cores. These five cores are thought to be securely associated with the Long Blade horizon, there are several other small cores which could be considered but there is some doubt as to whether or not they are in fact Mesolithic cores which have become displaced. It is perhaps surprising that there are any small cores in the assemblage at all; refitting has demonstrated that even the largest cores produced some small blades and bladelets, 30–50mm in length, quite early in their productive cycles. Possibly rather than searching the accumulated debitage, it was quicker to prepare a small core in order to strike the required small blades.

CORE DISTRIBUTION

When the cores from groups 1 and 2 are plotted on a site plan, no distinction can be drawn between them; their distributions do not differ in any way (**Fig. 3.9**). There are, however, some features in the distribution diagram worthy of comment. As might be expected, cores occur frequently in and close to the major concentrations such as transects C19 and 20 where there were 11 cores and transect D22 where 12 were found. Less obviously, nine cores were found in an area of little more than 1m² in D18–19. Refitting has shown that this latter area was an active centre for flint knapping. The remaining nine cores were scattered about the site, often in transects with a low overall density of worked flints.

CORE FRAGMENTS AND SHATTERED PIECES

It is possible to envisage a variety of awkward practical situations arising during the conversion of flint nodules into flakes and blades. In addition to the generally well-made cores described above, there are various items in the assemblage which illustrate these eventualities. Occasionally, having produced one or more series of blades, a core has failed catastrophically and broken into a number of pieces. Where this has happened, and the core has been rebuilt, it has been included in the foregoing sections; there are few isolated fragments. On other occasions, reduction of the core has led to an unsatisfactory shape and one or more relatively large sections have been detached, subsequent rejuvenation of the platform making it impossible to refit such sections. Rather more frequently, a flawed nodule was unwittingly chosen and, as a consequence, the core has failed at an early stage either suffering total collapse or repeatedly failing to strike true. There are examples of both of these phenomena. One outstanding example of the first situation is shown by what was originally a large flat nodule, some 200mm across, which shattered into 12 or so fragments, mostly irregular in shape; three of the more major fragments exhibit some further flaking although none of them became fully developed cores. All these pieces were recovered from an area of a 1m² or so and the nodule rebuilt. Details of this example and others that failed or were otherwise abandoned early in the reduction sequence are to be found later in the section describing the extended refitting programme. Rather surprisingly, one or two of the cores abandoned at an early stage utilised small awkwardly shaped nodules, even had the core come to fruition, it would never have been very productive. A large flint nodule best described as an attempted core, 190 x 102 x 75mm, was found close to the concentration in transect D22, a few flakes had been detached at various points as if to test its quality. This suggests that it may represent basic raw material brought to the site ready for use.

Core rejuvenation flakes

The only type of core rejuvenation flake recognized by the writer is the basal disc form or core tablet which is a flake struck approximately perpendicular to the longitudinal axis of the core, removing all or part of an existing striking platform. It has proved impossible, in this assemblage, to identify with any precision the frequency of occurrence of this type of flake. At

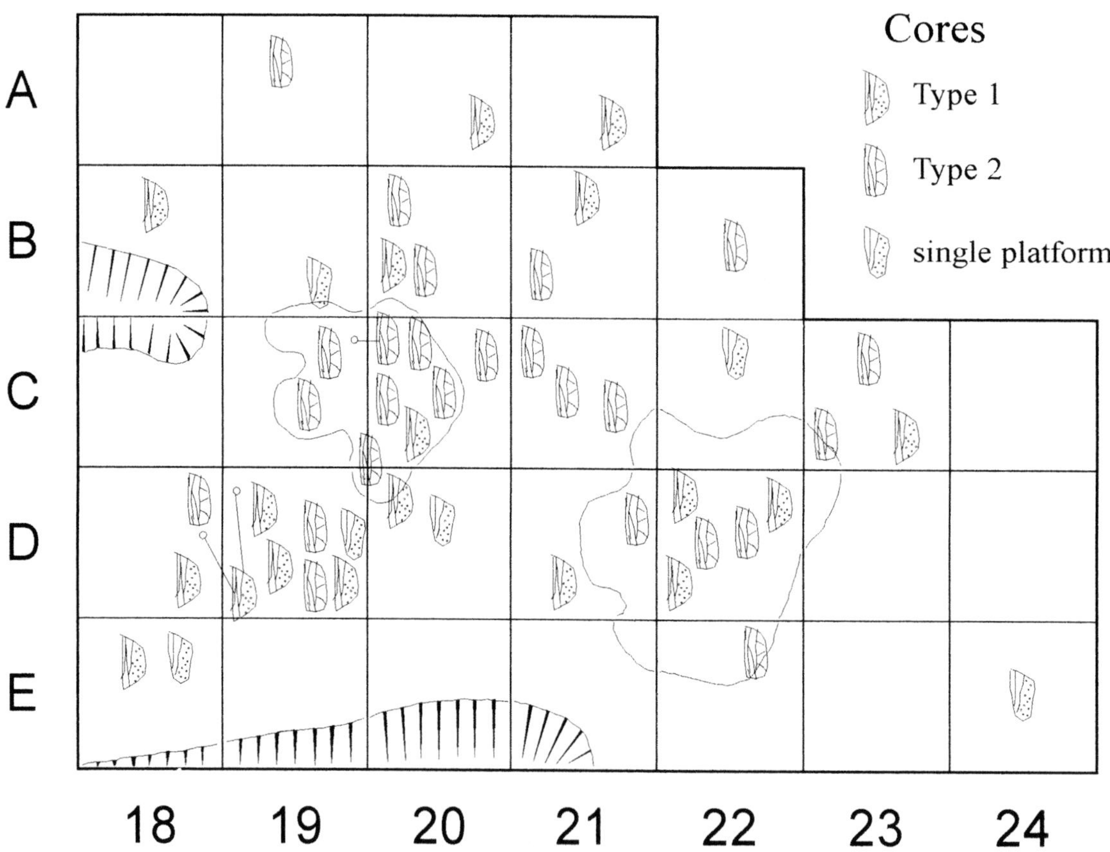

Figure 3.9 Avington VI: distribution of cores

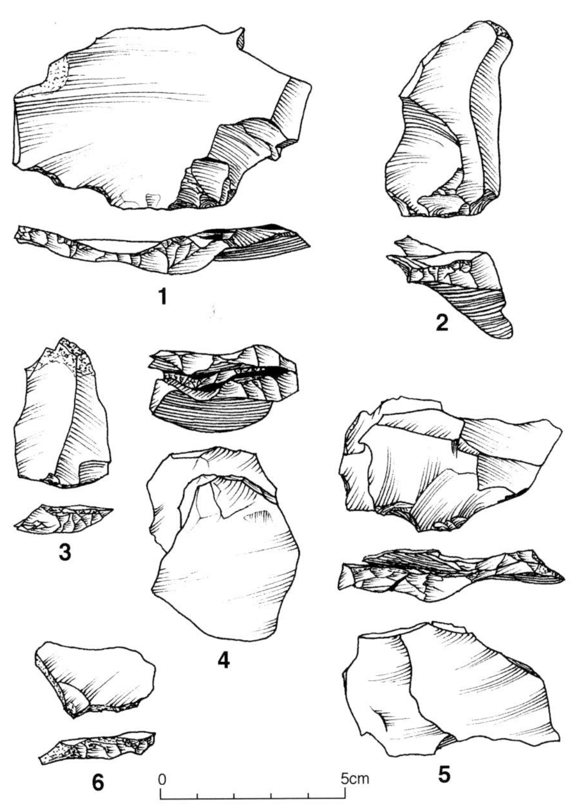

Figure 3.10 Avington VI: core rejuvenation flakes

one extreme it is instantly recognizable, part of the periphery of the flake retaining obvious traces of the upper end of the working face together with its striking platform (**Fig. 3.10: 1**). There are many such flakes in the assemblage. There are also many other flakes, often small in size, which appear to have been detached from across the ends of cores, often but not always by a blow aimed at the working face. These are functionally identical but less obvious having retained only a small amount of the working face (**Fig. 3.10: 3**).Their origin only becomes obvious when they are refitted to their parent core. The situation is made more difficult by the existence in the assemblage of crested blades of substantial size, where these were formed by initial bifacial flaking along a central ridge, the flakes so produced can be identical to the less extreme form of rejuvenation flakes just described. It is also possible that similar flakes were produced by the trimming of the sides of cores. The initial sorting of the assemblage separated 47 rejuvenation flakes, a subsequent revision taking into account the less obvious examples increased the number to 86. Refitting revealed further examples and, currently, approximately 100 core rejuvenation flakes have been identified but even this must represent a considerable underestimate. These numbers refer only to the Long Blade horizon; additional examples occur in the intermediate and higher levels.

When plotted on a length:width dispersion diagram, the core rejuvenation flakes form a well defined cluster; excluding the odd exception, lengths are in the range 20–65mm and widths in the range 20–65mm A line of gradient 1.0 broadly bisects the dispersion. About 80% of the flakes are between 3 and 12mm. in thickness but flakes as thick as 30mm or more have been recorded.

Plotting the distribution of the rejuvenation flakes reveals that the majority occur within the two major concentrations (**Fig. 3.11**). Indeed, their distribution is more marked in this respect than in the case of the cores. Few rejuvenation flakes occur outside the concentrations, several of those that do can be refitted to cores found close to them but there is additional evidence in the form of small patches of spalls and/or serial refits to suggest that there was active knapping in a small area away from the main concentrations. Core rejuvenation flakes do not appear to have been subject to dispersal in the way that some debitage has been.

Uncertainty concerning the actual frequency of core rejuvenation flakes means that the ratio of these flakes to cores or to core platforms cannot be estimated with any precision. Given that there are approximately 50 cores, nearly all with two platforms, and that there are approximately 100 rejuvenation flakes, then the two ratios are approximately 2:1 and 1:1 respectively. Taking into account that refitting has shown that several, even many, rejuvenation flakes can be associated with a single core, there is superficially at least some discrepancy between these results and those that might have been expected. This was consequently an obvious problem to investigate by refitting. In a small test involving less than 150 artefacts, refits were obtained but fewer than anticipated; it was noticeable that significantly more refits were obtained between core rejuvenation flakes and cores from the area of transects C19–20 than was the case with those from the area centred on D22. This proved to be the case in other refitting exercises. Of the 44 core rejuvenation flakes from the former area, 20 were refitted, yielding five pairs, two triplets and a quartet; whereas the 54 flakes from the area of transect D22 yielded just two pairs and two triplets: a total of 10 conjoining flakes.

When refits between the cores and the rejuvenation flakes were sought there was a measure of success but again more refits were found in the area of transects C–D 19–20 than in the area centred on D22 (**Fig. 3.11**). In the first area seven cores were refitted to a total of 14 rejuvenation flakes, the flakes in all cases being no more than 1m or so from their parent cores–often much less so. In contrast, only one core in D21 could be refitted to rejuvenation flakes (four in number)–this as part of an extensive series of refits; a second core from B22 can be conjoined to a pair of rejuvenation flakes from transect D22. In total, 11 cores and one core fragment were refitted to 24 core rejuvenation flakes, this includes two cores each of which had four rejuvenation flakes refitted. This refitting exercise confirmed the observation made earlier that the number of removals between the striking of core rejuvenation flakes could vary widely.

Examination of the conjoined rejuvenation flakes demonstrates a variety of knapping practices. On occasion, as many as four rejuvenation flakes were detached in succession without any intervening blade production; on other occasions the projection of one rejuvenation flake beyond the one that followed indicates that there were many removals between the two. There are also examples which show a change in the angle of the striking platform which enabled an extension of the existing working face or a new working face to be constructed. Several rejuvenation flakes suggest by their appearance that they were struck to remove imperfections that had developed around the edge of the platform.

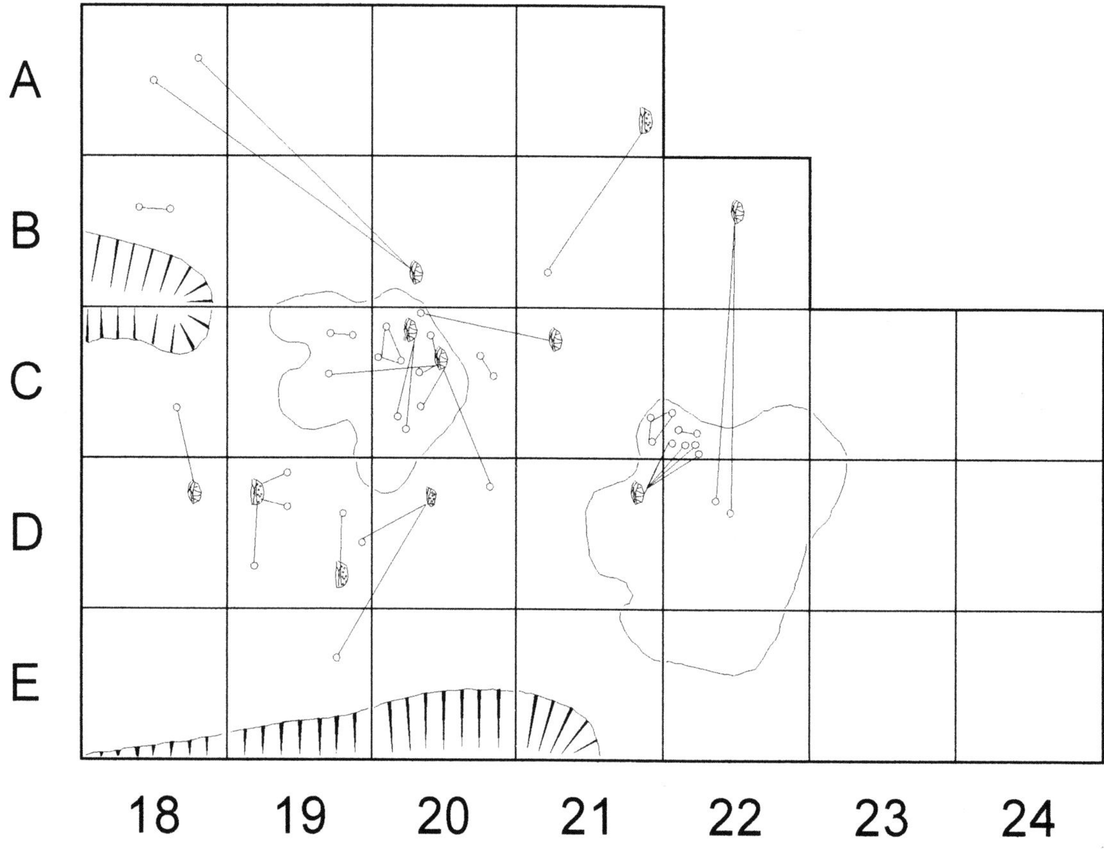

Figure 3.11 Avington VI: distribution of refitted core rejuvenation flakes and rejuvenation flakes/cores

Hammerstones

There are four pieces of flint which have been identified as hammerstones; in addition to these several cores have areas of battering which suggest possible use as hammerstones. The four identified as hammerstones are all nodules of flint which retain their cortex. One is round, smooth and regular in outline but somewhat flattened in cross-section, it is unmodified except for two areas, one major and one minor, which are battered; it weighs approximately 400g. The other three are slightly different. Although the smallest is broken, they are cylindrical and there is some flaking, possibly to prepare them for use as hammerstones. The best example measures 145mm x 60mm x 85mm and weighs approximately 850g; one end may represent an unsuccessful attempt to prepare a striking platform; the other end appears to have been shaped by the removal of several flakes from each side to form an edge approximately 60mm in length, this edge is heavily battered (**Fig. 3.12: 1**). The second example appears to have broken in antiquity, possibly during use. It was probably a cylindrical nodule weighing an estimated 300–400g; the surviving end has been flaked on both sides to produce an edge which runs across the end and some way up one side. As in the previous example, this edge is heavily battered (**Fig. 3.12: 2**). In the third example, a cylindrical nodule 180mm in length and 70mm in diameter and weighing some 1100g, the evidence for deliberate shaping is less convincing. Both ends show heavy battering resulting from percussion and this may have caused some flakes to be fortuitously detached. All of the four pieces described fit comfortably into the hand. Interestingly, three were found within the concentration in transects C19–20 and the fourth nearby in transect D20.

In addition to the examples described above, several cores appear to have served as hammerstones; the extent of their use for this purpose varies. There are four instances in which it is clear that cores were used as hammers and it is at least a possibility in five others. However, it is also possible that some of the battering observed on cores was deliberately applied to remove sharp edges for safer, more comfortable handling during knapping.

Crested blades

As with the core rejuvenation flakes, this term could encompass a broad spectrum of artefacts. Two principle types have been recognized. The most easily differentiated form was produced at an early stage in the preparation of a core: bifacial flaking along an edge of the nodule was applied to form a ridge or '*arête*' which would guide the force of a blow at one end to detach a comparatively long thick blade with a triangular cross-section. This blade was the first to be produced from the core and provided two new arêtes to guide subsequent blade removals. In an extreme case the whole of the upper surface of the blade bears witness to the initial bifacial flaking or 'cresting' applied by alternate removals from one side then the other. Where the crest is formed in this way, the pieces are described as double-sided. The flakes removed during this preparation vary in size from less than 10mm to as much as 30–50mm or even more on occasion (**Fig. 3.13: 1, 2**). In other cases the flaking may be somewhat less extensive but residual cortex is rare and of restricted extent (**Fig. 3.13: 3**). The second type is referred to as single sided; it differs from the first in that it only has flakes removed from one side of the arête; the other side often exhibits the scars left by the striking of earlier blades and flakes, less frequently it may a cortical or natural fracture surface (**Fig. 3.13: 4, 5**). In this assemblage the first or cross-flaked type

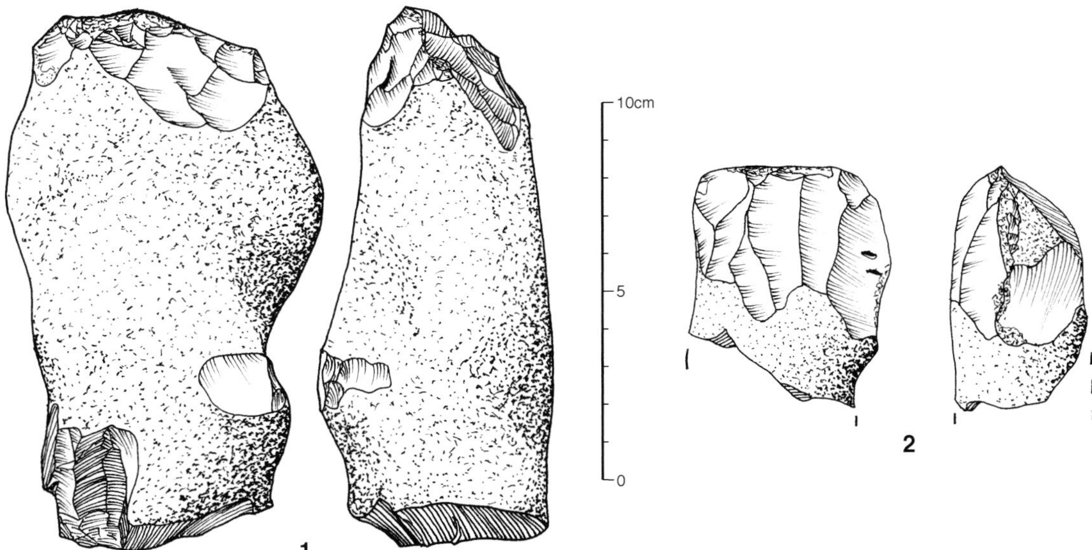

Figure 3.12 Avington VI: hammerstones

outnumbers the second in the ratio of nearly 2:1.

As well as the two types of crested blade already described, a significant number of blades and blade-like pieces exhibit removals struck at right-angles to the long axis, across the width of the blade. The distinction between these pieces and those described above, especially the second form, is somewhat arbitrary although the direction of the lateral or 'cross-flaking' is often towards the longitudinal axis rather than away from it as it is in the true crested blades. These less extreme examples, which tend to be wider in relation to their thickness, have been grouped with the majority of the blades and blade-like pieces described below.

Dispersion diagrams reveal that the crested blades range in length from 65–220mm providing further proof of the existence of very large cores; in width they vary from just under 20–*c*. 50mm. A line drawn through the dispersion has a gradient of 0.25, which indicates that on average the crested blades are four times as long as they are wide. When thickness is plotted against width, two results accrue; firstly, thickness was closely controlled and is invariably near to half the width; secondly, for the great majority of the examples the thickness is in the range 10–25mm.

In the complete examples and in the fragments that retain the bulb of percussion, inspection of the butt of these blades reveals that in nearly every case some retouch was applied to the edge of the striking platform prior to the blade being struck. Presumably this was to allow the force necessary to detach the crested blade to be applied with maximum accuracy.

Up to 20% of the crested blades have sections of one or more of their edges bruised or crushed, often markedly so (**Fig. 3.20: 2, 4, 5**). In a number of cases, where the artefact has snapped, the fracture truncates the bruising implying that the action that caused the bruising also caused the blade to fracture. Such bruising is not confined to the crested blades but occurs in the blades in general and, to some extent, in the flakes too and is discussed further in the section on bruised edge blades.

A number of crested blades have been incorporated into refitted groups. However, conjoining sequences which extend from the core to the outer cortical flakes also show that cresting was not a technique invariably used on every nodule.

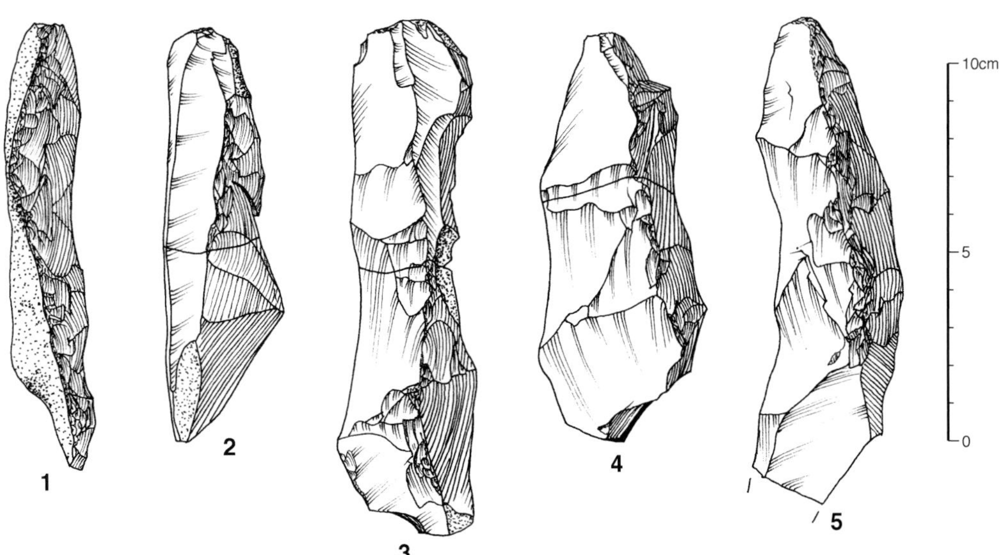

Figure 3.13 Avington VI: crested blades

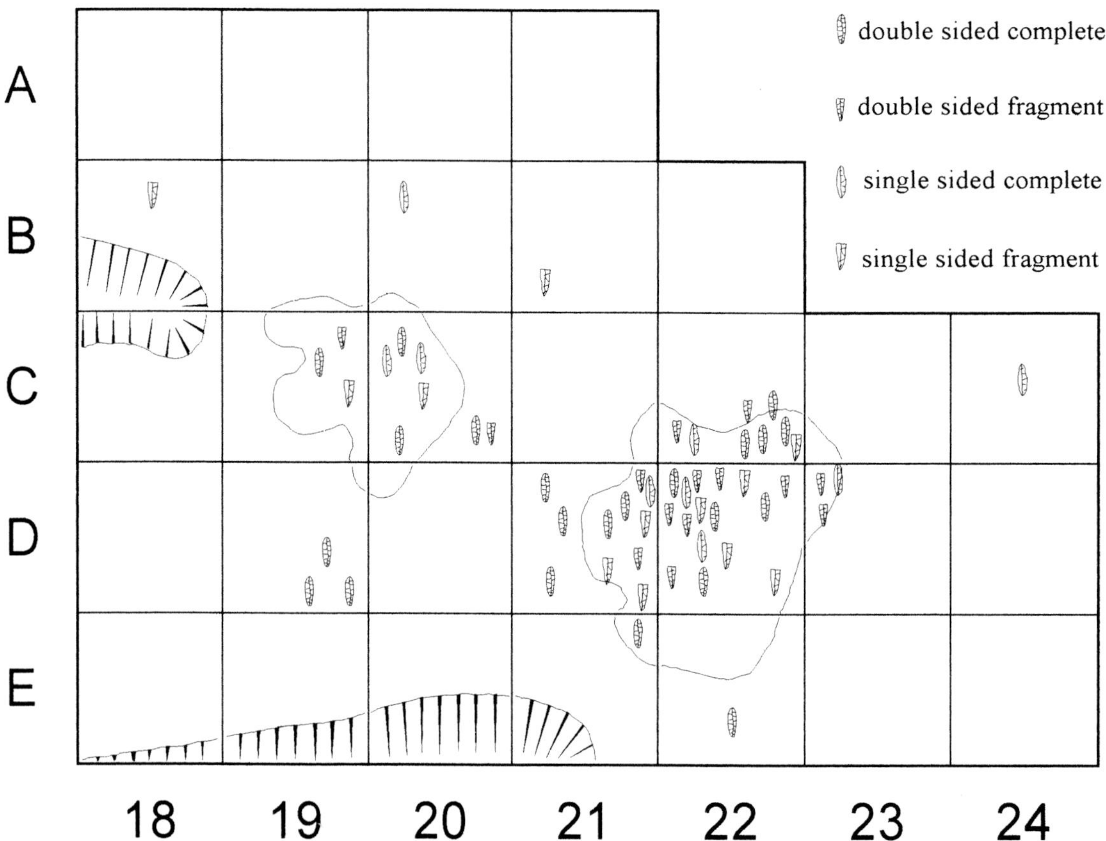

Figure 3.14 Avington VI: distribution of crested blades

DISTRIBUTION OF CRESTED BLADES

In total, the more narrowly defined forms of crested blade number 59; 27 of these are fragments and several of the complete examples are conjoins. Numerically they are thus broadly equal to the cores, representing about 1% of the assemblage. However, their distribution appears to vary significantly (**Fig. 3.14**). Although in general the crested blades are closely associated with the major concentrations and the areas immediately adjacent to them, they are not evenly distributed between the two areas. The crested blades from the area of transects C19–20 amount to 0.66% of all worked flints whereas those from the area around transect D22 represent 1.9% of the total number: thus crested blades are relatively three times more common in this second area. Other indications that these two concentrations have a degree of separateness and independence will be described later (p. 39–40).

Blades

In numerical terms, the blade element is the most important aspect of the Avington VI assemblage, representing approximately half of all the artefacts other than small pieces and spalls. In transects A–E 18–20 blades constitute as much as 57.8% of the artefacts whereas in transects A–E 21–24 the proportion is 49.2%, resulting in an overall value of 53.9%. For this reason and because this element also includes the defining artefact of the Long Blade Industry, it is considered in some detail.

Blades are basically defined as blanks of regular character with more or less parallel sides which are least twice as long as it is wide. In this assemblage they are usually struck from two-platform cores; some have triangular or trapezoidal cross-sections although on many examples the cross-section may vary from triangular to trapezoidal along the blades length reflecting the manner in which blanks have been detached from the working face of the core. Blades retaining variable amounts of cortex are also included in this group. During the initial sorting of the Avington VI Long Blade assemblage, the blades were separated by eye and, as a consequence, a few have a width:length ratio which a rigidly applied metrical definition would exclude from this category. The blade element has been divided into two primary units as follows:

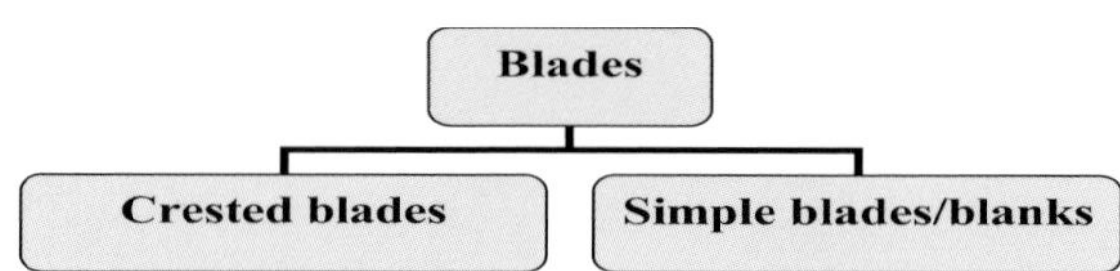

The crested blades have been described above as debitage and the simple unmodified blades may be waste pieces, or blanks intended for the manufacture of retouched tools or for use unmodified. Both groups have been further sub-divided into complete or fragmentary.

Breakage

Breakage is a notable feature of this element of the assemblage. A considerable number of blades broke either during separation from the core or as a result of some subsequent operation. In total, blade fragments represent some 31% of all of the recorded artefacts. There is some variation in the proportion of broken blades between the two major concentrations C19–20 and D21–22: the former includes 33.2% and the latter 28.8% but this relates more to variation in the relative frequency of simple

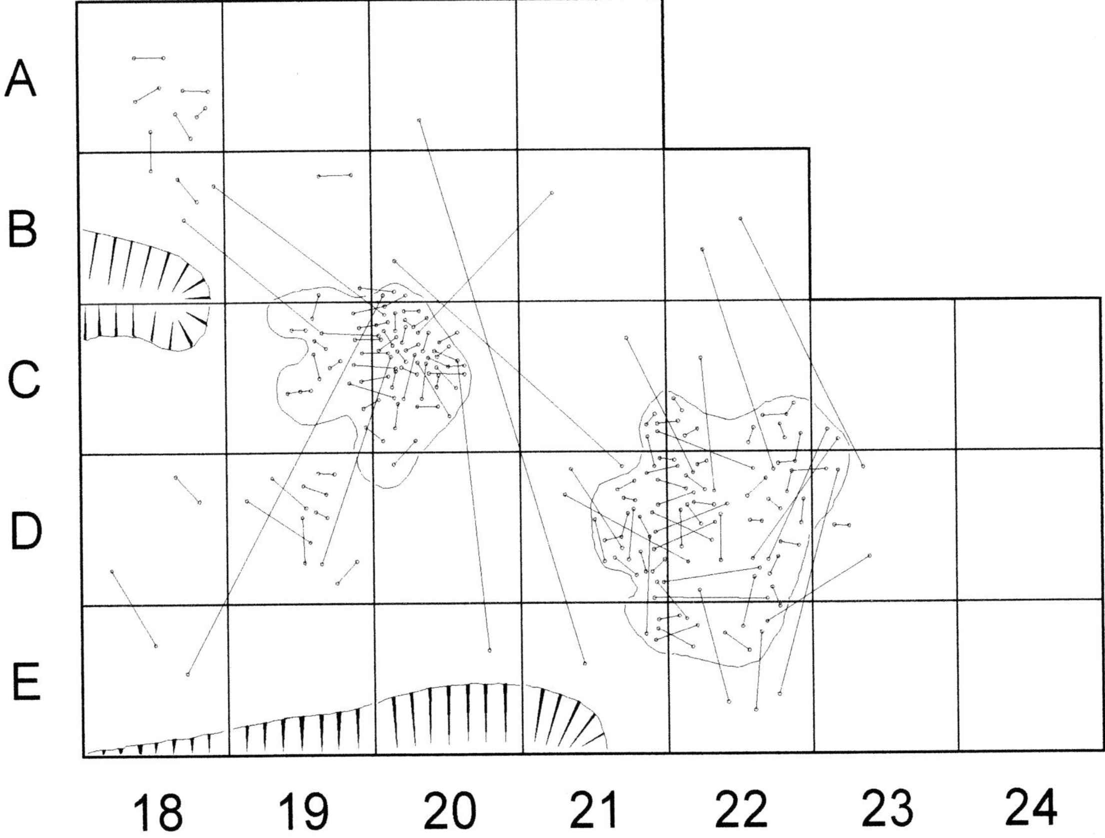

Figure 3.15 Avington VI: distribution of refitted blades

waste flakes than to factors intrinsic to the blade element. An estimate of the minimum number of broken blades was obtained by counting the number of proximal end fragments that are complete with butts. When the unbroken blades are compared to the blade butts of the fragmented blades, the numerical ratio is commonly close to 2:1. Taken at face value, this would imply that 33% of all blades are broken. This could mean that one strike in three failed to successfully produce a complete blade. However, this calculation does not take into account the possibility that the blade was fragmented after it had been struck from the core, either deliberately or as a result of use. It has also been noted that there are sections of large blades for which no conjoins could be found; indeed, this is true of blades of all sizes. Ultimately, there is no way of differentiating with absolute certainty in every case between blades that fragmented when they were initially struck and those that were broken subsequently. Several of the extended series of refits include blades composed of two or more sections; in at least one series virtually every blade is fragmented, all the fragments having been found in an area of only 1m² or so (**Fig. 3.15**). It appears highly probable that at least a large proportion of the blade fragments are the result of blades failing to separate from their parent core in one piece. Why so many blades should fragment on striking is largely a matter for conjecture but the writer has noticed on a number of occasions that on conjoining two pieces together when for example replacing a blade on a core, the fit achieved is not absolutely exact although they clearly did belong together. Careful observation has revealed that one or other or possibly both of the pieces have undergone subtle changes in shape subsequent to striking. A similar effect may sometimes be observed in a modern workshop, a piece of cold rolled steel bar if machined asymmetrically to its major axis will distort during the next day or so as unbalanced internal stresses become relieved. It may well be that during the formation and subsequent history of some of the original flint nodules, zones of stress came into existence which interfered with the knapping process. It is even possible to speculate that it was the exhaustion/disappearance of sources of large nodules of stress-free flint that led to the extinction of the Long Blades themselves. This is perhaps a trend which can be seen to run through the Early Mesolithic into the Late Mesolithic, subjectively there may be said to be a steady deterioration in the general quality of the flint assemblages together with demonstrable reduction in the size of the blade element and an increase in the relative frequency of shatter-pieces.

Description

In the context of this section, and to avoid needless repetition, the term blade will be used to include all pieces with a general blade-like character, all items which can reasonably be supposed to have resulted from the application of blade technique will be included. The results presented here are based on both the unbroken blades and those that have been completely rebuilt by refitting their constituent fragments. Together they represent between 25% and 30% of all of the recorded flints. General analyses were conducted on the whole group but the more detailed analyses were restricted to the blades from transects C19–20 and transects D21–22. This procedure was adopted on the grounds that the background scatter could well be an amalgam of many if not all of the occupations whereas the two concentrations might represent more discrete time intervals. There is some evidence to suggest that this was the case. Each pair of transects represented about 55% of the total sample available for study from that part of the site.

When viewed collectively, the artefacts in the blade element have a uniform appearance, reflecting the definition applied and give the impression of being well-made. The majority appear broadly parallel sided although slight convexity is common; mostly they have rather square as opposed to pointed ends; occasionally convex sides combined with a pointed end creates an elliptical outline. The best of the most regular blades are elegant artefacts but these are relatively infrequent as shown by an analysis of the number of arêtes per blade on large samples from concentrations 1 (C19–20) and 2 (D21–22). Less regular blades have fewer arêtes and the analysis showed the majority of Avington VI blades (85%) have just one or two arêtes. Of the remaining 15% just a few had more than two and up to four arêtes on the dorsal surface. Slight differences were also noticed between the concentrations. Concentration 1 was found to contain more regular blades, 208 out of 340, than concentration 2 where there were only 83 out of 289. Differences in the quality of the raw material in use at each concentration have also been noted and may be the cause of this variation.

For the purposes of detailed analysis, the unbroken and rebuilt blades were sub-divided into five groups as summarized in the chart below.

As the chart shows, all the products resulting from blade production technique have been included. The primary division of the blades has been made on the basis of whether they retain cortex or not. Cortical blades have been identified as those on which more than 10% of the dorsal surface is covered by cortex and these constitute some 20–25% of all the blades. The two major groups of cortical and non-cortical blades have then been further sub-divided to include simple and cross-flaked, and cross-flaked, regular and irregular forms respectively. Simple blades are those which show more or less parallel unidirectional or opposed removal scars. Cross-flaked blades have been defined as blades exhibiting evidence of previous removals (flakes) more or less at right-angles to the longitudinal axis of the blade but excluding the true crested blades as described above. They constitute less than 10% of the blades as a whole. In the majority of the blades the dorsal surface exhibits little or no cortex and no evidence for lateral flaking; such blades have been produced from simple working faces struck either parallel or opposed. However, as a result of both human error and imperfect raw material, the blades present a varied appearance ranging from neatly regular to irregular examples. It is probable that many blade-like flakes were actually struck solely to remove accumulated irregularities from the working face of the core and can properly be classed as debitage.

In this report the simple non-cortical blades with more or less parallel unidirectional or opposed removals scars have been separated into those with regular and irregular shapes. This was an entirely subjective separation but, nonetheless, it was felt to be a worthwhile exercise. Some confirmation for this may be found in **Table 3.5** which presents the analysis of some metrical data for these categories; those blades classified as irregular are seen to be relatively thicker and wider. Separating the unbroken and rebuilt blades from transects C19–20 and from transects D21–22, concentrations 1 and 2 respectively, into these divisions also revealed some differences between the two concentrations (**Fig. 3.16**). The frequency of cresting is similar in the two concentrations but the proportions of simple cortical blades are significantly higher in concentration 2. **Figure 3.16** also highlights the fact that the two concentrations contain differing proportions of irregular and regular blades, fine regular blades being relatively rare in 2. This is probably related to variation in the raw material. The types of flint observed in concentration 2 vary in size from those found in 1 and it would appear that better quality and more types of flint were available to the knappers working in the former area. Differences in the source of supply for the raw materials may well have caused the variation observed here in quality of the end products.

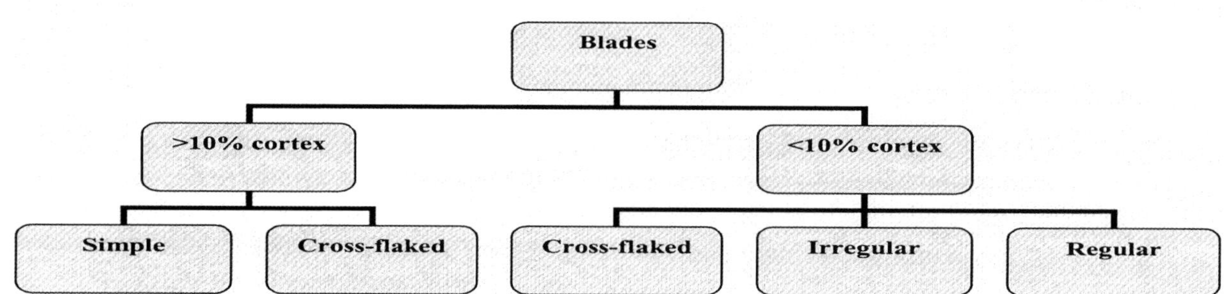

Table 3.5: Triangular co-ordinates for blades

Function	Simple cortical	Cross-flaked cortical	Cross-flaked non-cortical	Irregular non-cortical	Regular non-cortical
l/(l+w+t)	0.719	0.744	0.711	0.664	0.736
w/(l+w+t)	0.217	0.185	0.218	0.274	0.212
t/(l+w+t)	0.064	0.071	0.071	0.062	0.052

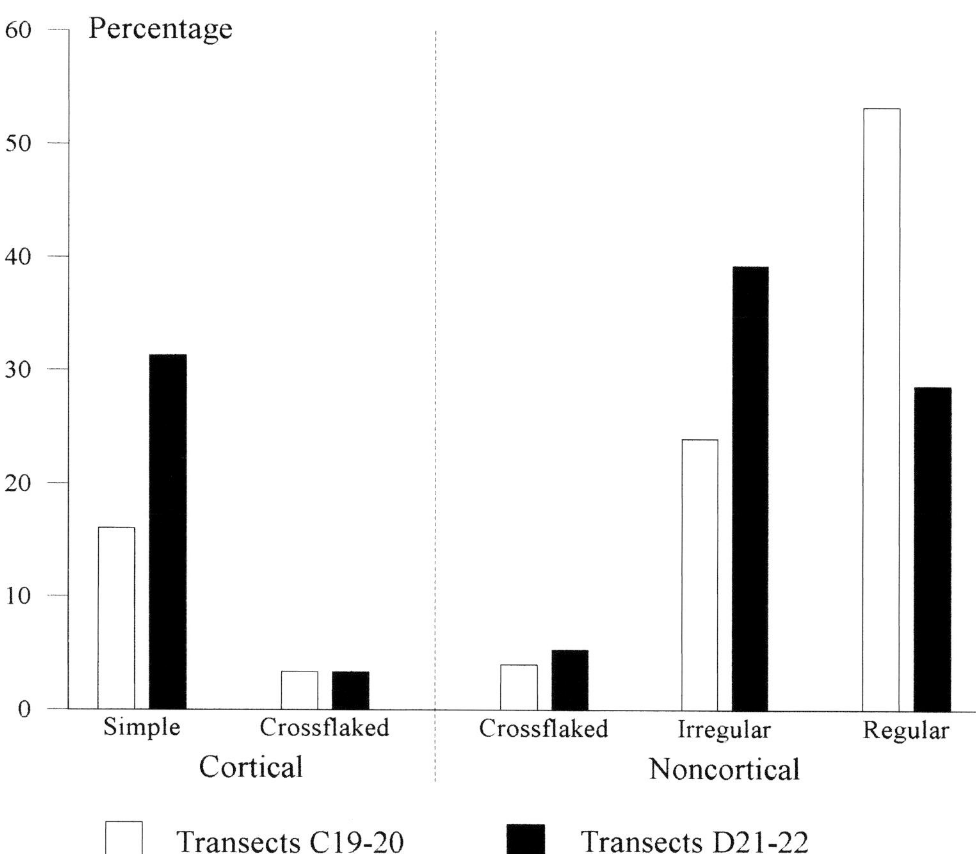

Figure 3.16. Avington VI: relative frequencies of blade types in concentrations 1 (C19-20) and 2 (D21-22)

Size

The size and relative proportions of the complete blades were examined in some detail; the length and width were measured to the nearest millimetre and thickness to the nearest 0.5mm. **Figure 3.17** shows the bar charts used to investigate the distribution of length. The separate charts for the two samples from concentrations 1 (C19–20) and 2 (D21–22) show much in common; both are bimodal, each having a maximum in the region 30–60mm and a second much less pronounced maximum at about 100–130mm. These maxima represent the 'Long Blades'. Not surprisingly, many of the larger items are cortical. In detail, the blades from concentration 2 tend to be longer than those from concentration 1. When the length:width data is plotted, the dispersion diagram obtained indicates that generally the blades are distributed about a line with a gradient of approximately 0.25; that is, the length of a blade is commonly about four times the width. This is particularly true of the fifth group, the regular non-cortical blades; the less regular blades tend to be somewhat wider in relation to their length. No distinction was observed in the length:width data when comparing the two samples, suggesting that no differences had been detected in the material from transects C19–20 and D21–22. Further similarities were found by transferring the metrical data into triangular co-ordinates in order to show the relative length, width and thickness of the different blade types. **Table 3.5** shows results which indicate that the thickness of the blades is between 25%–33.3% of the width and that length is from three to four times the width. Once again, this analysis revealed no distinction between the two major concentrations.

Blade butts

Data relating to the characteristics of the proximal blade ends were recorded for the samples from transects C19–20 and D21–22. Observation of the bulbs of percussion showed that they are invariably diffuse. Such bulbs are often associated with indirect percussion or soft hammer technique. Bulbar scars are often present. Particular attention was paid to the butts which are fragments of the striking platform detached from the core. Initial observations indicated that virtually all the blades had at least some retouch associated with the edge of the striking platform as the original core. Quantitative investigation confirmed this initial impression showing that the frequency of this retouch was 95% across the whole sample and that the same frequency obtained in C19–20 (95.6%) as in D21–22 (94.5%). Inspection of the cores produces a much lower value, suggesting that the preparation was often carried out immediately prior to striking of the particular blank rather than immediately after the detachment of the previous sequence of removals. In this case the retouch would serve to adjust the angle and height of the platform so that the blow could be precisely applied before each detachment. The retouch has been variously applied: it may be directed just across the platform, only down the working face and sometimes in both directions. These three types of platform preparation are referred to as types i, ii and iii respectively and their frequency in transects C19–20 and D21–22 are expressed in **Table 3.6**.

Table 3.6: Platform retouch

Transects	Number of Observations	Type i (across butt)	Type ii (down face)	Type iii (both directions)
C19 - 20	282	20%	49%	31%
D21 - 22	240	12%	62%	26%

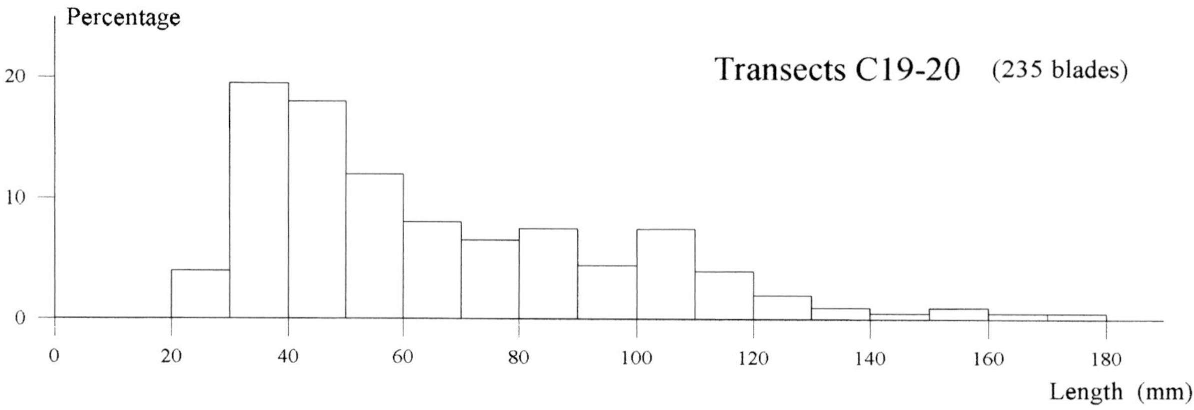

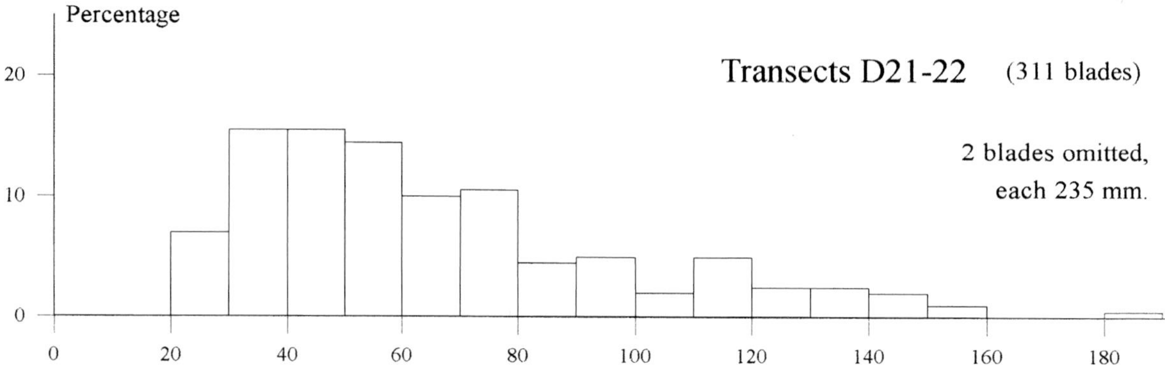

Figure 3.17 Avington VI: summary of blade lengths in concentrations 1 and 2

These data seem to indicate some difference between the two transects. In both concentrations it was noted that the type of retouch was distinctly related to the length of the artefact involved, the majority of types i and iii occurred on the longer blades whereas with the shorter blades type ii retouch was by far the more dominant. This is an intriguing observation and presumably relates to the flint-knapping technique.

In order to assess the amount of the original striking platform retained by the blade, the butts were measured. Initially, the general practice of taking two measurements at right-angles was adopted but this is unsatisfactory because the edges of the residual platform may not be sharply delineated. To improve on this, it was assumed that the area of striking platform retained would relate to the size of the blade, the latter could be represented by previous measurements viz. width and thickness of the blades. Thus a quantity, the Striking Platform Quotient (SPQ), can be defined as:

Striking Platform Quotient = (a x b) / (w x t)

where a and b are the dimensions of the residual striking platform or butt, and w, t are the width and thickness of the blade.

Although neither the shape of the remnant platform nor the cross-section of the blade are rectangular, the area of each will be proportional to the product of the two quantities identified and it was felt that the constants of proportionality so introduced would be similar in magnitude, thus cancelling from the equation given. The actual values obtained covered a wide range: the minimum value noted was 0.0045 but values less than 0.025 were rare; the maximum value recorded was 2.1 but this was exceptional, values greater than 1.0 were again rare. This quantity is of course dimensionless. It was observed that to a degree the SPQ was a function of the length of the blade: the longer the blade the smaller the quotient or, in other words, the SPQ was inversely proportional to the length of the blade. When the data were set out separately for the two concentrations, in general terms there was considerable similarity. In both cases some 50–55% of the determinations fell in the range 0–0.3 and 80% of the values were less than 0.6. However, in detail there may be some observable differences: the blades from transects D21–22 retain marginally less striking platform than those from transects C19–20, although it is questionable whether the analytical technique was itself sufficiently accurate to justify such small variations as being real.

Bruised edges

The proportion of blades exhibiting bruised edges was variable, the overall value (including the crested blades) was 2% for transects A–E 18–20 whereas for transects A–E 21–24 it rose to 6%. The correlation between the occurrence of bruised edge blades and areas of apparent knapping activity was high. As previously noted, the proportion of crested blades exhibiting bruising was also high at about 20% and this may relate to the observation that a large proportion of the longer simple cortical blades are also bruised; the common factor being that both are early products from their parent core.

Blade fragments

Numerically, this is an important element in the industry, 31% of all the sizeable worked flints fall into this category. However, this is a somewhat false impression since each fragment represents only a part of an artefact. Generally, the blades have fractured transversely and oblique fractures are rare. The nature of the fractures varies, ranging from clean simple fractures to more complex forms, for example, some may exhibit thin protruding lips, others have a rounded or 'hinge' nature, in the odd case a third minor component or splinter was created together with the two main sections. Although the three categories of blade fragment have much in common, there are some differences in detail. The blade butts (proximal fragments) represent varying amounts of the original blades although the majority probably represent about half or less, only occasionally do they appear to represent a large fraction of the original blade. In contrast, the middle sections (medial fragments) are less inclined to the extremes, most have a length:width ratio from 2:1–3:1 with a few about 1:1; many are broadly rectangular in outline. The tip sections (distal fragments), as with the other two types, represent varying amounts of the original blades but tend to be relatively longer, some could well be blades that have been separated from little more than the bulb of percussion.

Some reference to the blade fragments has already been made when examining the question of the frequency of occupation (**Fig. 3.15**). Further, when discussing blade breakage generally, attention was drawn to the fact that approximately 33% of blades fractured into two or more pieces during or after manufacture. Further data on these fragments are presented in **Table 3.7** below.

Table 3.7: Frequency of blade fragments

Transects	Proximal ends	Medial segments	Distal ends	Total
A - E 18 - 20	328	156	396	880
A - E 21 - 23	279	80	287	646

These data show that distal fragments are the most numerous. This might seem rather surprising as it might have been supposed that proximal fragments would be the most frequent since butts may separate from the core leaving the rest of the intended blade behind. There are a number of possible explanations for this apparent discrepancy; for example, the larger butt sections would lend themselves to the production of tools such as scrapers and could have been removed for this purpose; again, refitting has confirmed that in some cases only a short length of a blade incorporating the bulb separated from the rest of the blade, such short fragments are to be found in the small waste and did not come into the analysis. The frequency of medial sections is notably lower than the other two types; this would suggest that blades tended to fragment into two rather than three or more sections unless the middle sections were removed to somewhere outside the excavated area. This frequency also varies between the two areas, being relatively higher in transects A–E 18–20. If the preceding analysis is carried out using data from concentrations 1 and 2 only, no significant difference can be detected; the relative frequencies remain essentially the same. As previously shown (**Fig. 3.15**), where the blade fragments have been refitted together, generally they were separated by no great distance.

Table 3.8 summarizes the data from a second line of enquiry which was designed to examine the complete and partially reconstructed blades in order to establish how many sections some blades had broken into, using the data from the initial refitting exercise.

Table 3.8: Number of fragments in rebuilt blades from transects A - E 18 - 20, 21 - 23

Area	Rebuilt from two fragments	Rebuilt from three or more fragments	Ratio
A - E 18 - 20	76	14	5.4:1
A - E 21 - 23	74	24	3.1:1

In detail, analyses of the fragmentation evident from the conjoined blades from the two areas show different results but both indicate that the majority of the blades suffered a single fracture rather than the two or more required for true segmentation. The subsequent extended refitting exercise, during which further blades were rebuilt, tended to offer confirmation of this result. However, whereas the first analysis suggested greater frequency of blades having been separated into three or more sections in the area A–E 18–20 compared to the area A–E 21–23, the second analysis gave the opposite result. The second analysis could be regarded as the less reliable since it was based on a much smaller number of artefacts. Nonetheless, both analyses indicate that less than half of the blades which were broken separated into three or more sections. Logically, full segmentation would require both proximal and distal sections (the more irregular sections) to be removed in order to isolate the most regular section of the blade, thus at least two fractures are necessary. On balance, it seems reasonable to suppose that some of the blades were deliberately separated into three or more sections but these may have been in the minority. It was also noted, as a result of the extended refitting exercise, that the frequency of blade fragmentation was core-dependent, the removals from some cores exhibiting a much greater degree of fragmentation compared to the removals from other cores. This could indicate differences in the quality of the raw material although this is not the only possible explanation.

Flakes

These are virtually self-defining and are, broadly, the residue left after the extraction of the blade element and the other more specialized forms of debitage. In the absence of clearly defined variables it cannot be supposed that an objective separation has been achieved and a degree of overlap between various types is inevitable. There is also a tendency for the simple flakes, especially in the smaller sizes, to degenerate into miscellaneous fracture pieces including shatter pieces and 'bashed lumps'. The point at which flakes become spalls is again purely arbitrary, in this assemblage any unspecialized item less than 15–20mm tended to be classified as small waste. When viewed collectively, the simple flakes exhibited no particular shape.

Within the assemblage, the simple flakes represented 35.3% of all the indexed pieces; however, there was significant variation across the site, irrespective of whether it was calculated on a general or particular basis. This may be summarized as follows:

Transects A–E 18–20 frequency = 31.2%

Transects C19–20 frequency = 30.4%

Transects A–E 21–24 frequency = 40.2%

Transects D21–22 frequency = 40.6%

As the figures show, simple flakes were significantly more frequent in and around concentration 2 centred on transects

D21–22. As has been noted above, regular blades were a less frequent component in the blade element from this area. These two observations taken together would fit the hypothesis that locally available nodules of raw material were worked into cores destined to be used to produce blades elsewhere. Certainly the ratio of cores:flakes appears to be anomalous, in and around transects D21–22 there are 13–15 cores (some cores could equally well be assigned to either concentration), thus yielding a core:flake ratio in the range 1:55–1:65, as an average value this is much too high. Even in the other half of the site the ratio is about 1:30 which again appears too high. The cores present at the site generally do not exhibit sufficient flake scars to account for the number of flakes in the assemblage. It is accepted that large or giant cores could have been worked down in size, indeed refitting has shown this to have been the case; even so, it is felt that there are too many flakes and to some extent too many blades, for the number of cores recovered. However, this aspect is made more complicated by the observation made during the extended refitting programme that several of the rebuilt nodules were incomplete because they lacked cortical flakes that could not be located in the assemblage, these flakes having presumably been removed elsewhere.

A major feature of the blade element was the extent to which pieces were fragmented, in contrast the simple flakes were observed to be generally unbroken. The proportion of broken flakes was effectively constant across the site; samples drawn from the two concentrations yielded the results: transects C19–20, sample 279 flakes, broken 9.0% and for transects D21–22, sample 256 flakes, broken 8.2%. This relatively low degree of fragmentation could be a reflection of several factors, acting singly or in some combination. Such factors might include the technique used to detach the flakes, the size of the flakes which tend to be significantly smaller than the blades, and the quality of the outer layer of the flint nodule which might be more homogeneous and/or less stressed.

The simple flakes were not subjected to the same detailed metrical analysis as the blade element; nonetheless, samples were measured for length and width and other observations

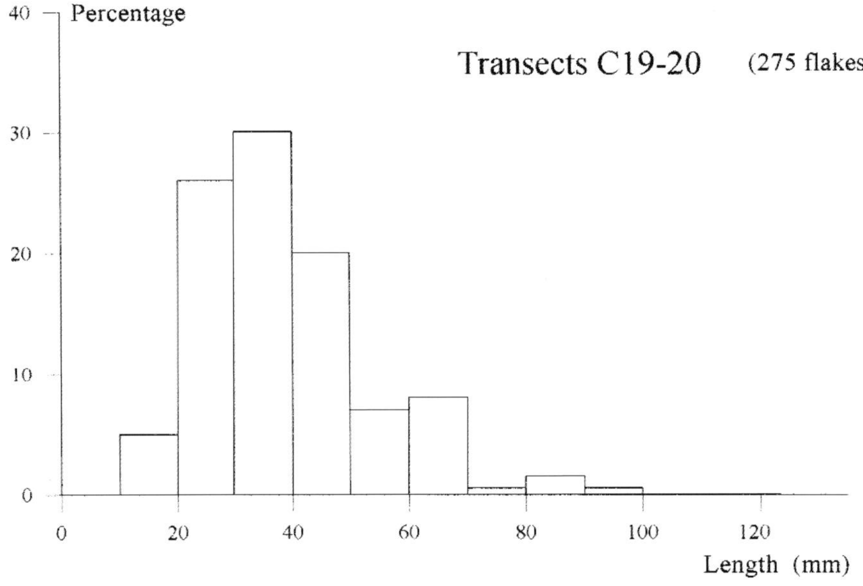

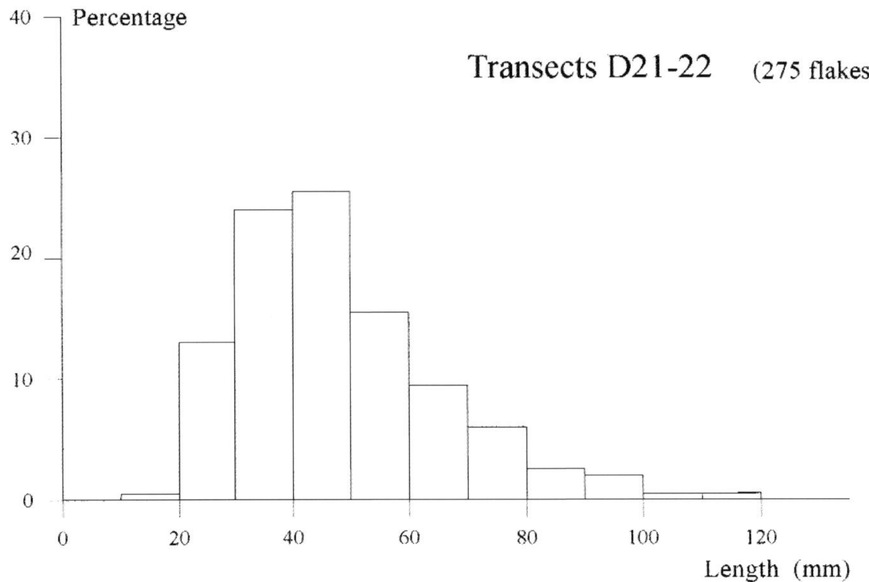

Figure 3.18 Avington VI: summary of flake lengths in concentrations 1 and 2

were made. Unlike blades, the length of a simple flake is not always obviously defined; as far as possible the length axis of the flake was determined by reference to the bulb of percussion and its associated striking platform, the width was taken at right-angles to this axis, these two axes in effect defined a rectangle which enclosed the flake. These two dimensions were measured to the nearest mm. It was felt that no useful purpose would be served by measuring thickness. Compared to the blade element, the simple flakes are relatively short, few exceed 70mm in length and a large fraction is less than 40mm. There is a significant difference between the samples drawn from the two major concentrations: flakes from transects D21–22 are longer than those from transects C19–20 (**Fig. 3.18**). The length-width dispersion diagrams for samples drawn from the two concentrations are similar, the distribution is fairly evenly spread either side of a line of gradient 1.0, which means that the number of flakes on which the width exceeds the length is broadly equal to the number of flakes in which the width is less than the length; flakes with a width greater than twice the length are rare. There is just a suggestion that the flakes in the sample from transects D21–22 tend to be narrower in relation to their length than is the case with the flakes from transects C19–20.

The amount of cortex present differed slightly between the two concentrations; in transects C19–20 44.8% of the flakes exhibited no cortex at all whereas in transects D21–22 the proportion exhibiting no cortex reduced to 33.5%, rather more flakes in transects D21–22 had more than 25% cortex than was the case with transects C19–20, (**Fig. 3.19**). The nature of the cortex also differed in detail between the two halves of the site. Comparing the simple flakes from transects A–E 18–20 those from transects A–E 21–24 revealed that although in general the same types of cortex occurred, the balance was different in the

Table 3.9: Platform retouch on flakes

Transects	Number of observations	Type i (across butt)	Type ii (down face)	Type iii (both directions)
C19 - 20	111	15%	75%	10%
D21 - 22	148	15%	74%	11%

two groups of flakes. In the first area, the dominant cortex is thin, smooth and often a shade of grey in colour although a sandy coloured variant is present. Thick cortex is comparatively rare, even rarer is thick cortex which has a rough and pitted surface. The second area, centred on transects D21–22, is much less dominated by the thin greyish cortex, the thin sandy coloured cortex is relatively more common and, perhaps most significantly, thick cortex often with a rough and pitted surface is much more common. The different types of cortex presumably reflect different sources of raw material.

Examination of the bulbs of percussion on the simple flakes reveals some variation. Some flakes have prominent bulbs and appear to be the product of hard hammer technique; such flakes retain appreciable amounts of the striking platform, which may be wholly cortical or modified. In other cases the bulbs of percussion is less prominent and much less of the platform has been retained by the flake; these examples closely resemble the blade element in such respects. Possibly they were detached using the same technique. As with the blade element, there was modification to the edge of the striking platform and/or the upper part of the working face before striking; the frequency of this platform retouch varied between the two concentrations, in transects C19–20 47% of the flakes have some form of such retouch whereas in transects D21–22 the proportion is 57%. However, separated into the three types as shown in **Table 3.9**, the two samples are remarkably similar.

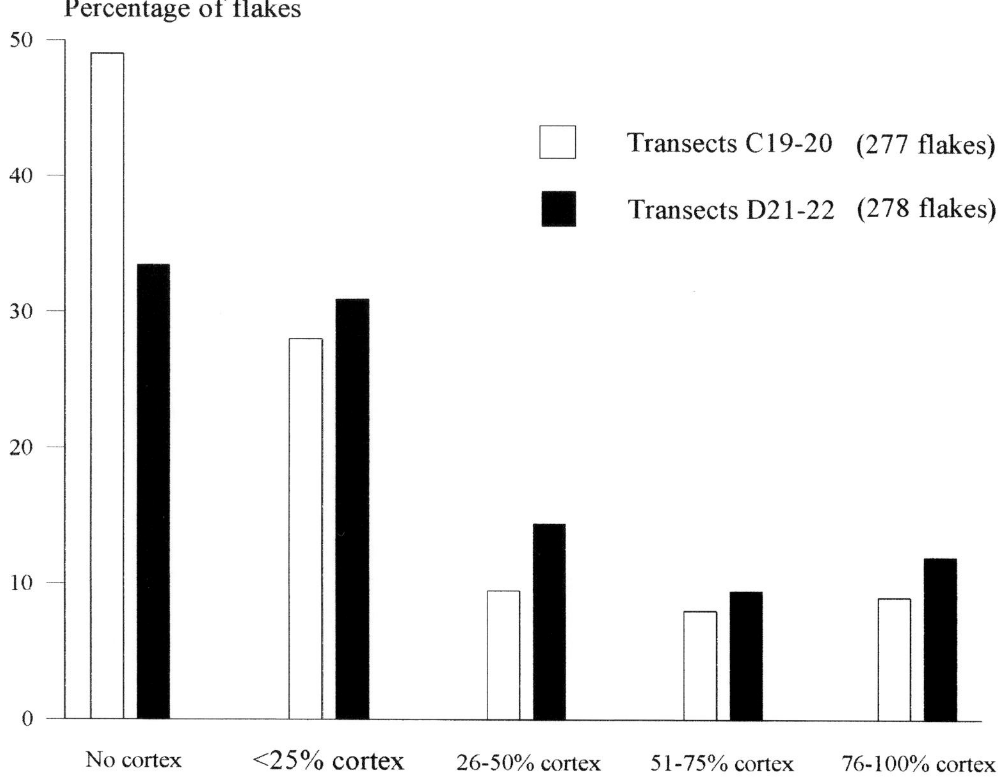

Figure 3.19 Avington VI: cortex on flakes in concentrations 1 and 2

Comparison with the data for blades shown in **Table 3.6**, suggests significant differences although the general pattern is much the same for both. Further, with the flakes there does not appear to be any correlation of the type of retouch with the size of the artefact as there was with the blades.

The presence of bruising is not a significant feature of the flakes, there are examples with varying degrees of bruised edge but they are comparatively rare, in fact there are none at all associated with the concentration centred on transects C19–20 and its surrounding area. In the area defined by transects A–E 21–24, 1.1% of the flakes were bruised. This correlates with the fact that more of the blade element in this area was bruised than was the case with the blade element in the area of transects A–E 18–20. Thus bruising generally appears to be more of a feature of transects D21–22 and the immediate area.

Bruised edge artefacts

Bruised edge pieces are by far the most common artefacts showing evidence of use at Avington VI. **Table 3.2** shows that bruised edges mainly occur on blades or blanks which are blade-like in character; bruised edge flakes are comparatively rare, the ratio of bruised blades:bruised flakes being is approximately 5:1. As the ratio of blades:flakes for the entire assemblage is approximately 1:1, this would suggest deliberate selection. The incidence of bruising is relatively higher on crested blades than on the plain blades being approximately one in five for crested compared to one in 20 for plain blades; it has also been noted that bruised edge blades are often cortical. The common factor could be that these pieces are associated with the earlier development of the core. Further comment on this point will be found below. The incidence of bruising appears to vary across the site being approximately twice as prevalent in the area A–E 21–24 as it is in the area A–E 18–20.

Metrical analyses of these pieces focussed on length and mass. In the sample of 49 pieces for which these attributes were recorded, the length varied more or less continuously from 80mm–237mm. As might be expected, crested blades tended to the longer lengths. Analysis of their mass disclosed that whereas the great majority were in the range 30–110 g, five had masses in the range 230–300g and there were no examples between 140g and 230 g. This shows a dichotomy with respect to mass which may reflect variation in function.

Examination of the bruised edge pieces suggests that the working life of these pieces was very variable. In the simplest case only a single short length of bruising is observable, typically 15–20mm; in other cases a single but more extensive length of as much as 40–60mm is present, (**Fig. 3.20: 1**). However, the majority of the bruised-edge pieces exhibit more than one zone of bruising, commonly two (**Fig. 3.20: 2, 3**) but there are examples with three (**Fig. 3.20: 4, 5**) and occasionally four such zones. The bruising may follow the general outline of the original blank but in many cases, especially the more intensively used pieces, the edge has been worn back forming a concave outline which in extreme cases takes on the appearance of a notch. In the writer's view, the nature of the bruising fits into a spectrum; in the early stages of use some discrete spalls are detached, often 3–5mm in size but larger, up to 10mm and more, can be observed; further use results in a degree of battering/micro-crushing with consequent broadening of the edge although the edge-like quality is still present to some extent; finally, after much use, a zone of heavily battered edge appears which in cross-section is much rounded (**Fig. 3.20: 3**), this is commonly well back from the original edge of the blank. By this stage any cutting quality that the edge once possessed had long since disappeared.

Uses

Having described the character of the bruised-edge pieces, it is appropriate to speculate on their possible use or uses: there is no *a priori* reason why they should have had a single use although this might be inferred from the fact that they do appear to be a reasonably coherent group of artefacts. The nature of the edge damage suggests two hypotheses concerning the use of these pieces. The first is as knives which require a cutting edge that would have been used in a to and fro motion; the second is as hammers or choppers which would involve a percussive action that would affect more restricted lengths of edge.

The possibility that these blades may have been used as knives or saws does not fit well with nature of the edge damage. Those with intense damage had lost their ability to cut long before they were finally abandoned and show neither wear nor edge damage consistent with the kinematics of sawing or cutting. Indeed, the edge damage spalls that were detached during use appear to result from forces acting more or less perpendicularly to the long axis and there does not appear to be any horizontal component involved.

Damage caused by force applied more or less perpendicularly suggests a percussive use as a hammer or chopper. The former seems more probable in this case as the damage is not randomly positioned along the edge of the blades, in general being neither in the middle nor towards the extreme ends. This is to be expected if they had been used as hammers. When an elongated object of uniform composition is used to deliver an impulse force, there is an optimum zone where contact should occur, as in the everyday examples such as hitting a ball with a bat. This phenomenon is susceptible to physical analysis and details may be found in intermediate level physics textbooks often in sections dealing with simple harmonic motion. The ideal point of contact is identified as the centre of percussion. It is possible and quite easy to calculate the location of the centre of percussion for objects of uniform shape and composition. However, flint blades do not have such a regular shape so, for example, derivation of their moment of inertia or radius of gyration is not a simple matter. A further difficulty is that there is no way of knowing exactly how the blades were held. Nevertheless, by making some reasonable approximations, it can be shown that the Centre of Percussion is likely to be some 66.6% the length of the blade or 0.67L. An alternative, perhaps more subtle analysis produced the result 0.60L. Thus the hypothesis that the bruised edge blades were used as hammers may be tested by measuring the overall lengths of the blades (L) and measuring the length along the major axis at which the centre of the bruising is located (l) and for each occurrence of bruising evaluating the ratio l / L (**Fig. 3.21**). The results of this analysis, involving 88 observations, showed that only in 4 cases did the value exceed 0.75; in 49 cases the values were in the range 0.60–0.75. This means that 56% of the observations were close to the value 0.67L; the remaining cases, 35 values or 40%, the range was 0.50–0.59. Given that the variation in the three-dimensional shape of the

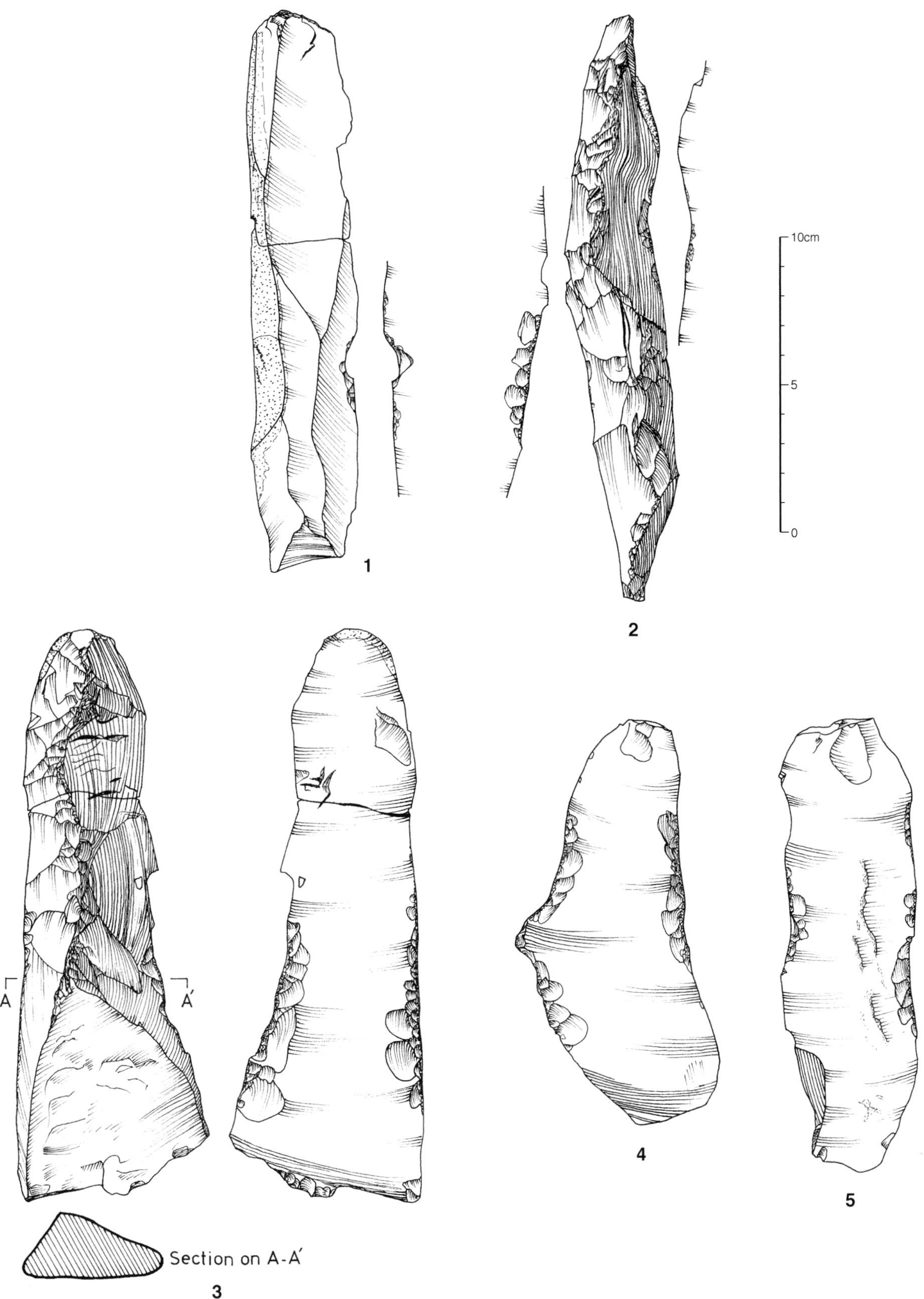

Figure 3.20 Avington VI: bruised edge blades

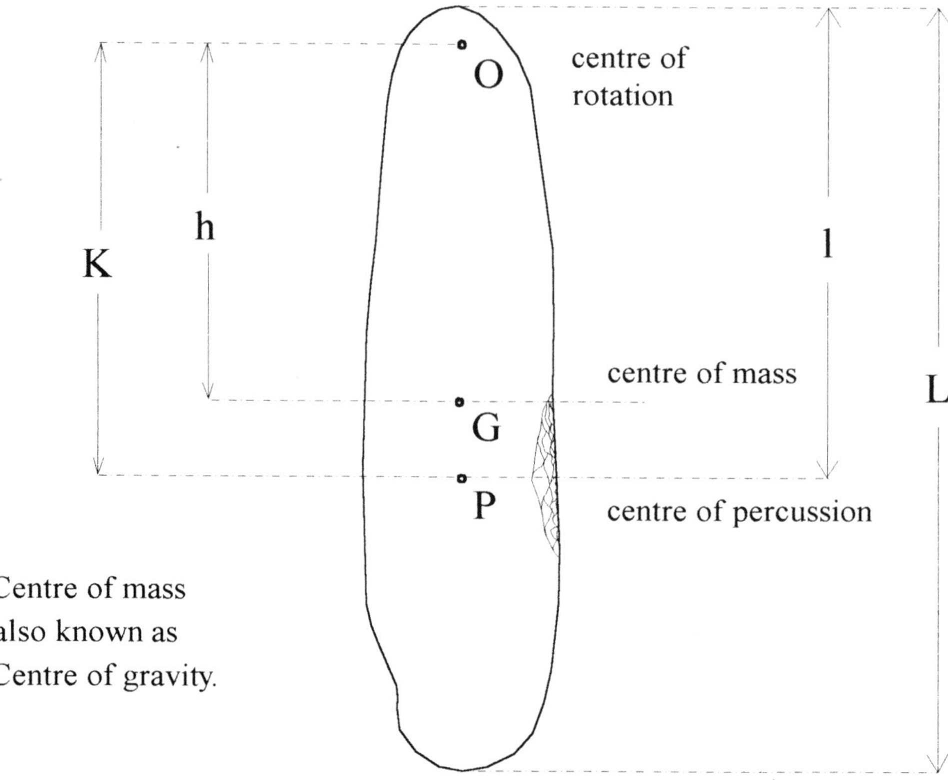

Rotate about O, blow at P, for no rotation about O

(i.e. maximum efficiency for the transmission of energy and no 'kick' to the hand)

with respect to the blow at P

$$\text{then } OP = \frac{h^2 + K^2}{h} \qquad \text{where } K = \text{Radius of Gyration.}$$

Alternative treatment :

$$\text{Centre of Percussion} = \frac{\text{Moment of Inertia}}{\text{mass} \times h} \qquad \text{if blade held at one end.}$$

Figure 3.21 The physics of the centre of percussion

blades makes the mathematics of the theoretical derivations of the centre of percussion more difficult to calculate, the fact that 65% of the values fall between 0.55 and 0.75 is taken as strong support for the hammer hypothesis.

The foregoing analysis leads logically to the question as to what was being struck. It might be expected that the wear characteristics would depend on the nature and shape of the object being struck. In order to explore this aspect the writer conducted some experiments. In the first series, sharp edged flints were used to strike larger pieces of flint, aiming at the edges of pieces with included angles similar to those observed on the striking platform and working faces of the cores. Experiments involving varying numbers of blows and blows of different force were carried out. These replicated the damage patterns on the original material closely. One hundred blows were enough to generate a zone approximately 20–25mm in length in which the original edge of the hammer was worked back into a distinct concave outline which in cross-section was well rounded and exhibited the fine battering so typical of the bruised edge blades. In the early stages of use in particular, small spalls, 3–5mm across, were commonly detached. The effect on the flint being struck was the removal of small spalls some 5–15mm or so in length, depending on the force of the blow. In the second series of experiments, similar sharp edged flints were used to strike bone (pig femurs from a local butcher). Attrition of the flint edge was certainly observed but its character exhibited differences, the damage pattern of the bruised edge blades and flakes in the assemblage was not replicated, most notably there was little sign of crushing and rounding of the edge; again, the detached spalls appeared to be relatively wider than those detached in the flint-on-flint series. It is not difficult to understand why these differences occur, flint is hard and not very elastic, flint-on-flint contact will be a point contact with locally high impact forces, the force of the blow will be concentrated in a small area; in contrast, bone is much softer and more elastic, flint-on-bone contact will lead to the flint cutting into the bone and with the much greater area of contact between the flint and the bone, the force of the blow will be dissipated over a much larger area (and to some extent in time too), in particular this might be expected to reduce the crushing/battering effect, as observed. It could be argued that further experiments are needed involving other materials. However, two likely materials, wood and antler, are not unlike bone with respect to hardness and elasticity and might reasonably be expected to behave in much the same sort of way, wood more so than antler. Results obtained in experiments by Barton (1986) tend to confirm this (ibid fig. 37) although massive damage is illustrated on a blade used to chop softened antler (ibid fig. 36).

If it is accepted that at least the majority of the bruised edge flakes and blades were the product of flint-on-flint contact, that they were used as hammers, then the question arises as to the context. The most obvious explanation would appear to be that they were used to adjust the edges of the striking platforms of the cores; as has been noted previously, 95% of the blades and approximately half of the flakes show evidence of such adjustment of the core prior to their removal. This trimming- could easily be achieved using the bruised edge pieces given their physical dimensions; used edge-on, as they clearly were, they would have allowed accurate positioning of the blow and the mass range of 30–110g would have allowed blows of the appropriate force.

Examination and replication of the bruised edge blades suggested that the natural way to hold them for use as hammers was between the thumb and crooked index finger, the flat ventral side of the blade against the finger and the thumb against the ridged face of the blade. Indeed, some blades only felt comfortable when held in this particular manner and invariably exhibited only a single zone of bruising at the appropriate point as determined by the likely centre of percussion. Other blades could be held comfortably in two or more orientations, including in some cases being held from either end, these blades commonly exhibited two or more zones of bruising. Such kinematics would also explain the more extensive zones of bruising sometimes observed; if the blade had been used and then put down and then subsequently picked up for further use, it is quite possible that it would not have been held in exactly the same position and consequently the second series of impacts would not have occurred at the same point as the first, lengthening the initial zone of bruising: changing the radius of gyration will change the centre of percussion. Experiments by the writer, referred to earlier, demonstrated that even a lengthy series of blows, in excess of a hundred, tended to produce a zone of only 15–25mm in length.

At the beginning of this section, it was noted that nearly all of the bruised edge blades were in the mass range 30–100 g, which would be appropriate to the percussive use presented above. However, there is another heavier group of bruised edge blades with a mass range of 230–300g. These weightier pieces could deliver a much heavier blow and, therefore, could have been used to generate much larger removals.

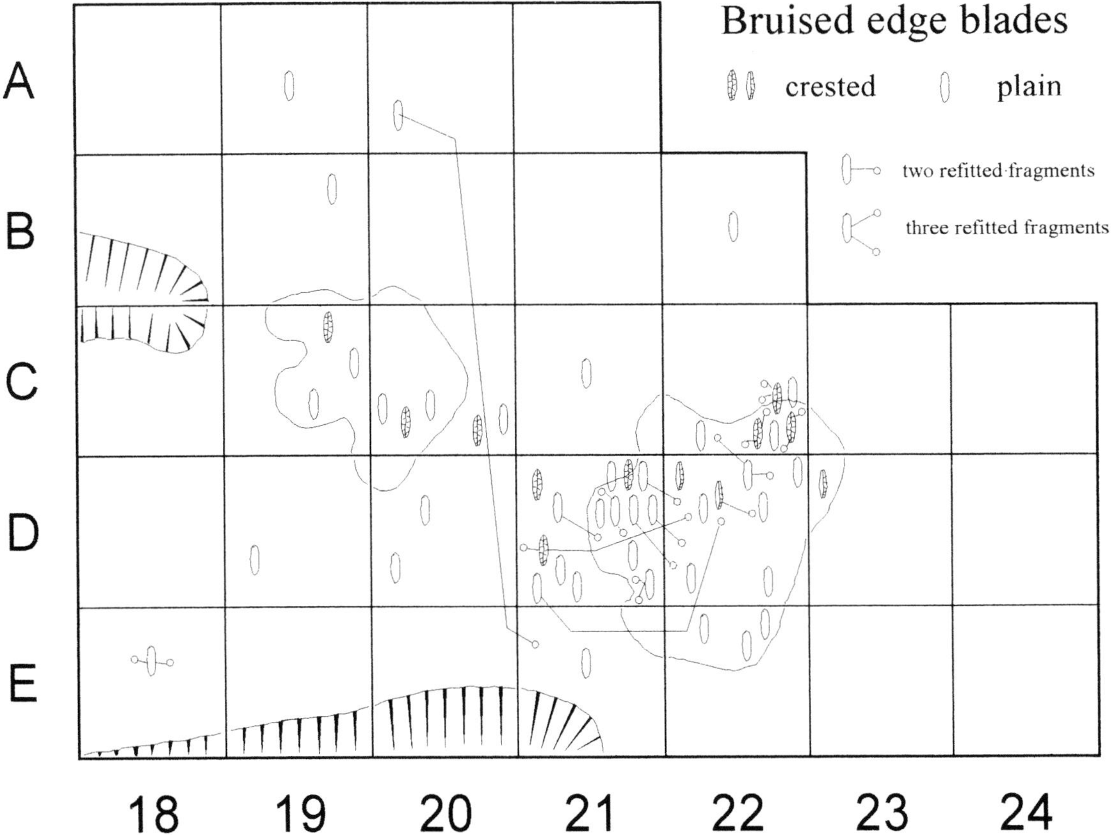

Figure 3.22 Avington VI: distribution of bruised edge blades

In conclusion, it is suggested that the bruised edge pieces were, in modern terminology, a form of cross pein hammer, various forms of which are to be found in current tool catalogues. However, where such blades occur at Sproughton, Suffolk it has been suggested that they may have been used for butchery or repairing bone and antler equipment (Barton, 1986b). At Avington VI an additional piece of evidence in favour of their use as hammers is their distribution: they are all clearly associated with areas of the site that are demonstrably centres of flint knapping activity (**Fig. 3.22**). In the case of the broken examples, the dispersal of the fragments could conceivably be influenced by such factors as a fragment flying off as a result of fracture or having been tossed away in a fit of irritation resulting from the breakage. Similar conclusions have been reached in a study of bruised edge blades from sites in the Somme Valley. In this research Fagnart and Plisson (1997) note that such pieces consistently occur in association with knapping debris on sites where the exploitation of flint resources appears to be the main activity. Following experiments using blades on various materials and observations of the edge damage associated with experimental and the archaeological pieces, they conclude that bruised edge blades and flakes were used as hammers on stone (ibid. 105). In the light of this function they further suggest that such pieces should be regarded as indicative of a particular type of knapping activity that is notable during the Late Glacial but not necessarily exclusive to this period.

Summary

The Avington VI Long Blade horizon contains a high proportion of Long Blades produced from two-platform cores. Although retouched tools are relatively rare (**Table 3.2**) they include several obliquely blunted points, two tanged or 'Ahrensburgian' points and a Blanchères Point. The obliquely blunted and tanged points have previously been found with Long Blades both elsewhere in Southern Britain and in the 'Tanged Point Complex' (Taute, 1968) of Germany, Holland and Belgium. Like the Blanchères point, a type found in Late Magdalenian and Epipalaeolithic assemblages in France (Bodu *et al.*, 1997) and in Germany (Waldmann *et al.*, 2001) they are diagnostic of the Late Glacial/Late Upper Palaeolithic. In common with other Long Blade sites in Britain and northern Europe (Barton, 1992), the assemblage contains a significant proportion of bruised edge blades resulting from percussive utilisation of both blades and crested blades. The large quantity of debitage indicates that knapping took place on the site. As the Long Blade horizon was largely undisturbed when discovered, the distribution of the artefacts may be said to reflect the use of the site. However, more detailed evidence about spatial organization, the selection, quality and use of flint, as well as the knapping methods, techniques and technical procedures of the reduction sequence or chaîne opératoire has been obtained from the refitting work described in the next chapter.

Chapter 4

Refitting the Avington VI Long Blade Assemblage

Introduction

Whilst the typology, metrical and non-metrical attributes of the artefacts in the Long Blade assemblage remained to be described only a limited number of conjoins could be made without interfering with the need to measure and describe individual pieces. However, it was clear from this preliminary process that a large proportion of the assemblage would go back together and that by refitting the artefacts much would be learned about the technology and spatial organization at the site. Consequently, once the preliminary part of the report had been completed, a major programme of refitting was carried out. Nearly 1,000 hours were spent on this and, although in all probability there are still many refits still to be assembled, it can be said with some confidence that these will not alter or substantially add to the information gained to this point. In general the refitting was confined to pieces larger than 15–20mm; to have included the smaller waste would have trebled the number of pieces involved and enormously increased the magnitude of the task without being informative. The description of each group of refits involves discussing the methods, techniques and technical procedures used by the knappers, as well as the planning and decisions these indicate, leading to the broader issues to which these data contribute.

Vertical disturbance

Several of the refitted groups contain artefacts recovered above the Long Blade horizon. Most commonly these come from the zone just immediately above and were recovered during the final clearing and cleaning of the Long Blade horizon and, in some cases, could be regarded as technically undisturbed. Generally, the horizontal distribution of these pieces falls within the boundaries established for the concentrations on the main surface. Other pieces were found in the intermediate zone between the main Mesolithic and Long Blade horizons; as might be anticipated, some of these pieces also exhibit a greater horizontal dispersal, lying outside the boundaries established for the main group in that series. A small number of artefacts, such as in the group refitting to core 154, were recovered from the main Mesolithic Horizon yet conjoin within major groups. The most extreme example of a dispersed artefact is the section of a large blade found well above the Mesolithic Horizon, at least 50cm above the Long Blade horizon, during the initial cutting of the 1979 trench. This fragment refitted into a major sequence securely located in the main Long Blade horizon. The cause of such vertical dispersal has already been noted in the description of disturbance caused by burrowing animals evident in the stratigraphy. Such animal activity may well have gone on for millennia, until comparatively recently in fact.

Horizontal dispersal within the Long Blade horizon

Examination of the horizontal distribution of the artefacts within the refitted groups located in the Long Blade horizon has yielded interesting results. Their dispersal is commonly somewhat restricted, even in a sequence of some 40 or 50 pieces. Generally, although the excavation was organised using $1m^2$ transect system, artefacts were normally recovered and recorded in terms of quadrants, that is to say most artefacts can be assigned to an area of 500 x 500mm, these sub-units have been designated according to the points of the compass, for example C20SW, D21NE. Plotted on a transect diagram artefacts from a given reduction sequence are often enclosed in an area of at most 1.0 x 0.5m (**Figs 3.14; 4.4; 4.7**). This includes those sequences extracted from the two major concentrations each of which occupy much larger areas. The recovery of an entire group from areas as small as 1.0 x 0.5m suggests that these probably represent the scatters produced during single knapping operations. The dispersal of the debitage created during a knapping operation depends on a number of factors including the exact technique employed by the flint knapper. The dispersal will be greater if debris is allowed to fly off than if removals are trapped under the knappers' hand and then allowed to drop. Similarly, the dispersal will be greater if the knapper worked while standing rather than kneeling or squatting. Generally, the refits made from these tight groups consist of pieces 20mm or larger, the smaller spalls no doubt often flew beyond these limits.

Generally, most of the items in a given refitted sequence can be referred back to the main Long Blade horizon as excavated and photographed; the larger items at least can often be identified in the photographs. Finds that came from immediately below that horizon were separately bagged and recorded. The number of these slightly deeper items which figure in the various conjoined series is variable but they are frequently present. The vertical dispersion of these series is often therefore approximately 150mm. This observation poses questions with regard to the dynamics of the large piles of worked flint that constitute the two major concentrations.

In some of the refitted sequences there are odd items which were recovered well away from the main scatter. Examination of these artefacts often reveals that they have an attribute that could well have made them of use, for example a blade with a length of clean sharp cutting edge. Occasionally, the artefact may exhibit signs of damage but whether or not this has accrued subsequent to its initial deposition, perhaps as a result of use, is open to question. As previously noted, where the sequence includes bruised edge blades, these invariably remain with the sequence as a whole; they are not more widely dispersed.

Another aspect of the various refitted series is their location within the excavated area. Several are clearly associated with one or other or, occasionally both, of the two major concentrations. However, there are sequences, including one extensive one, which are clearly located away from either concentration. Although the two concentrations were obviously considerable centres of knapping activity, they were not exclusively so. It has been previously noted that some knapping left only a small area of spalls all other items of consequence apparently having been removed. One such area was noted in transect C18 well away from any concentration.

Patination

An earlier observation that was confirmed and illustrated by the refitting programme was that the patination of artefacts could vary significantly across conjoins found in close proximity. Artefacts within a conjoined group can sometimes exhibit quite different patinas, even the different fragments of the same removal. In the latter case, refitting has clearly demonstrated that patination has reflected subtle differences in the composition of the raw material: for example, a series of conjoined removals may exhibit in one area a blue-white patina whereas the adjacent area is a dense white, the boundary between the two patinas being continuous from one removal to another. This phenomena has been previously noted as for example by Worthington Smith over a century ago (Smith, 1894) and is a reminder that patination is not simply an aging process but is caused by variable interactions of the soil chemistry of the immediate burial environment on the equally varied intrinsic physico-chemical nature of the flint.

The main artefact concentrations

The sheer quantity of material in both of the major concentrations suggests that they represent many knapping operations. Most of the refitted groups contain only 20–50 artefacts of any size and are found scattered within restricted spaces of about 1.0 x 0.5m. By contrast, the concentrations contain approximately 1,500–1,800 such pieces over an area of *c.*1.5 x 2.0m². This suggests that each concentration represents some 50–100 knapping operations.

Analyses of the debitage set out in this report show certain differences between the two major concentrations. It is therefore interesting to note that there are six groups which have conjoining sequences recovered from both concentrations. Most but not all of these sequences were initially worked at concentration 2 (C–D 21–22) and then moved to concentration 1 (C19–20). This suggests that both the major concentrations were broadly contemporary or at least 'open' at the same time but it does not preclude the possibility that although overlapping in time, one of the concentrations may have been somewhat younger than the other. It was noted more than once during the refitting programme that achieving refits was easier with material from concentration 1 (C19–20) than it was with material from concentration 2 (C–D 21–22). It might be expected that the later material on the site might have suffered less dispersal and thus be easier to refit.

It is clear that the two major concentrations were primary centres of knapping activity, although as has been shown knapping did take place elsewhere. Furthermore, it seems improbable that these concentrations of debitage are merely 'dumps' of material, the result of some 'tidying-up' operation. During excavation it was observed that the flints seemed to be *in situ* and this has been confirmed by the refitting of reduction sequences from restricted areas which would not have survived in such discrete scatters had they been tidied up and/or dumped. It would appear that commonly but not always the flint knappers chose to work in identifiable and comparatively restricted areas of the site. The reason for this is not apparent. It is equally difficult to say why so many good quality blades were apparently left unused in the debris. The usual explanation advanced is that a tool blank of a particular size and character was required, perhaps to fit an existing handle or haft. That so much good material was left in the concentrations may also provide an explanation for at least some of the vertical dispersal of artefacts as people sorted through selecting suitable pieces for expedient use rather than deliberately knapping for the purpose. This would also tend to alter the profile of the material left behind giving it a cruder character and this has indeed been noted in the description of the blades from both concentrations (see p. 28). In relation to this speculation it is perhaps worth noting that although the two major concentrations contain approximately the same numbers of worked flints, concentration 2 has a significantly larger area than that of concentration 1 but there could be many explanations for this.

Knapping methods

The refitted groups are described individually below but there are a number of general observations which may be drawn together to yield an overall picture.

Most of the groups are sufficiently complete for the size and shape of the original flint nodule to be deduced. In size, nodules commonly varied in length from smaller ones of approximately 100mm or less to nodules as much as 300mm or more. The shape of the original nodule also varied considerably: some were rounded; others were more cylindrical, whilst some were pieces of tabular flint sometimes of a highly irregular nature. In the case of tabular flint, it was not unusual for the flaking to begin with an edge rather than at a more extensive face. In terms of blanks, the refitting has shown that even the largest cores, capable of producing Long Blades in excess of 150mm also produced much smaller blades of 50mm or less. The latter were detached sequentially with the larger blades; they result from adjusting the proximal end of the large blade before it was detached from the core.

Several of the reduction sequences clearly show that some earlier phase or phases of working have not been recovered despite thorough searching of the assemblage. Whether the missing sequences are present in an un-excavated area of the site or exist at a totally different site is a question that cannot be answered. However, there are cores which are complete to the point where the crested blade(s) have been refitted but some outer flakes are missing, again despite careful searching of the assemblage. In these cases the most likely explanation is that some preliminary flaking was done at the point of extraction of the original flint nodule, possibly to verify its quality and reduce its weight.

Examination of the refitted groups confirms and extends the observations concerning the nature of the striking platforms on the cores. These were commonly formed from several flake scars, frequently subjected to further modification by the removal of what were small flakes even on the largest cores. The removal of a complete platform, generating what is variously called a 'core tablet' or 'basal disc rejuvenation flake', characteristic of Mesolithic assemblages, is comparatively rare.

Several of the refitted sequences extend to include the outer cortical flakes and in some cases these clearly demonstrate that crested blades were not always prepared and struck. Blade production began immediately following the initial preparation of the core and the cortical flakes themselves often present a strong blade-like aspect. There are examples in which the cresting first prepared has been approached from both platforms and two crested blades have resulted, sometimes these overlap conjoining 'head to tail' as in the case of group 175. Not surprisingly, refitting has demonstrated that the two platforms, present in most of the cores, were worked essentially simultaneously, a few removals from one platform followed by further removals from the other; although in some cases it is apparent that one platform tended to produce longer removals than the other. Ultimately, of course, the knapping of the core was strongly influenced by the quality of the flint; there are many examples in the sequences described below where flaws in the flint have severely distorted the working and the quality of the flint has already been suggested as a probable cause of the variable degree of fragmentation observed in the assemblage. This can vary from as low as one in five in some sequences to as high as three in four in others. The refitting shows that that the transverse fractures which sometimes divide the removals into two or more pieces often cluster together into one or more groups, this clustering could be taken to indicate the existence of one or more fundamental flaws in the material of the flint nodule.

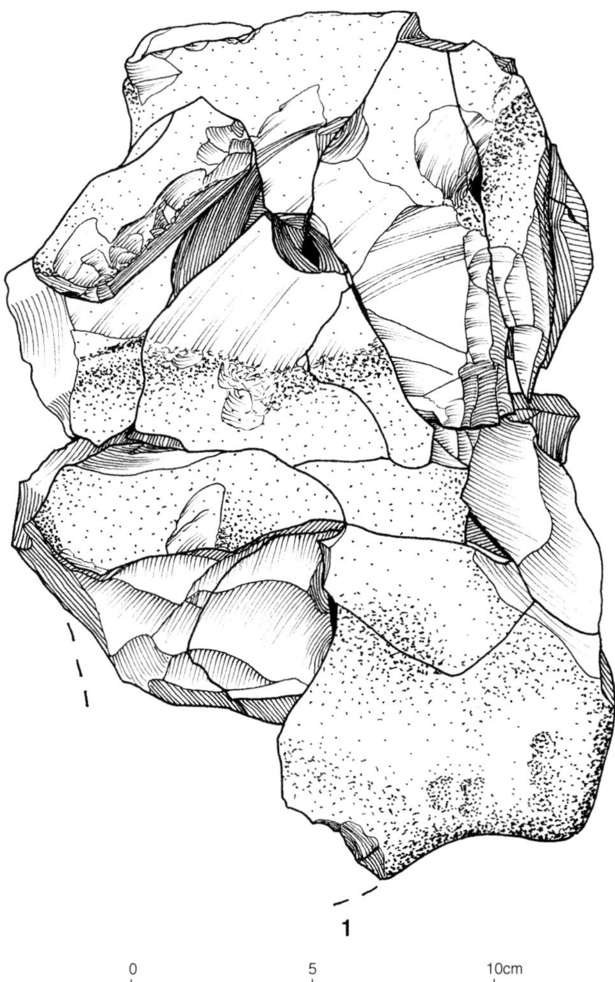

Figure 4.1 Avington VI: refitted nodule incorporating core 158 (top right)

The refitted groups

In the description of the selected refitted sequences that follows, groups including a core are identified by the index number assigned to the core. In the drawings, the usual convention of using a heavier line to indicate the conjoined edges of individual artefacts has been observed.

Group 158

The majority of pieces in this group (**Fig. 4.1**) were found in a small area clearly associated with concentration 1 (**Fig. 4.2**). The core constitutes only a small fraction of a largely reconstructed original nodule, currently about 80% complete. Most of the missing pieces originated from the lower left-hand side as figured. A few flakes have been omitted from the drawing in order to keep it within the page limits. The original nodule was broadly tabular but irregular in shape, 230 x 90 x 170mm in size, with thin sandy coloured cortex and some very ancient fracture surfaces. These characteristics suggest that it could have come from a clay-with-flint deposit.

There are features of the refitting which indicate that the nodule was of poor quality. At an early stage in the reduction sequence it appears to have failed catastrophically, collapsing into possibly two or three major fragments, these in turn were the subject of further working but they also failed and the nodule was reduced to many, largely useless, fragments. The problem was that the central zone of the nodule was dominated by many intersecting planes of weakness probably caused by an incipient frost fracture which resulted in extremely irregular and unpredictable fracture. Only part of the outer zone of the nodule was of better quality and allowed the striking of some quite well-controlled flakes. It is possible that the first working of the nodule, on the right-hand side as figured, was intended to set up a crested blade but almost immediately a major failure occurred, the nodule separating into two or more pieces. The part shown in the top right of the figure was more extensively worked than most fragments and was clearly intended to be a blade core but this too proved to be unsatisfactory and was abandoned: this is core 158. There is no definite evidence to indicate that the nodule was subjected to any test flaking prior to being worked as described and this might suggest that it was sourced near to the site.

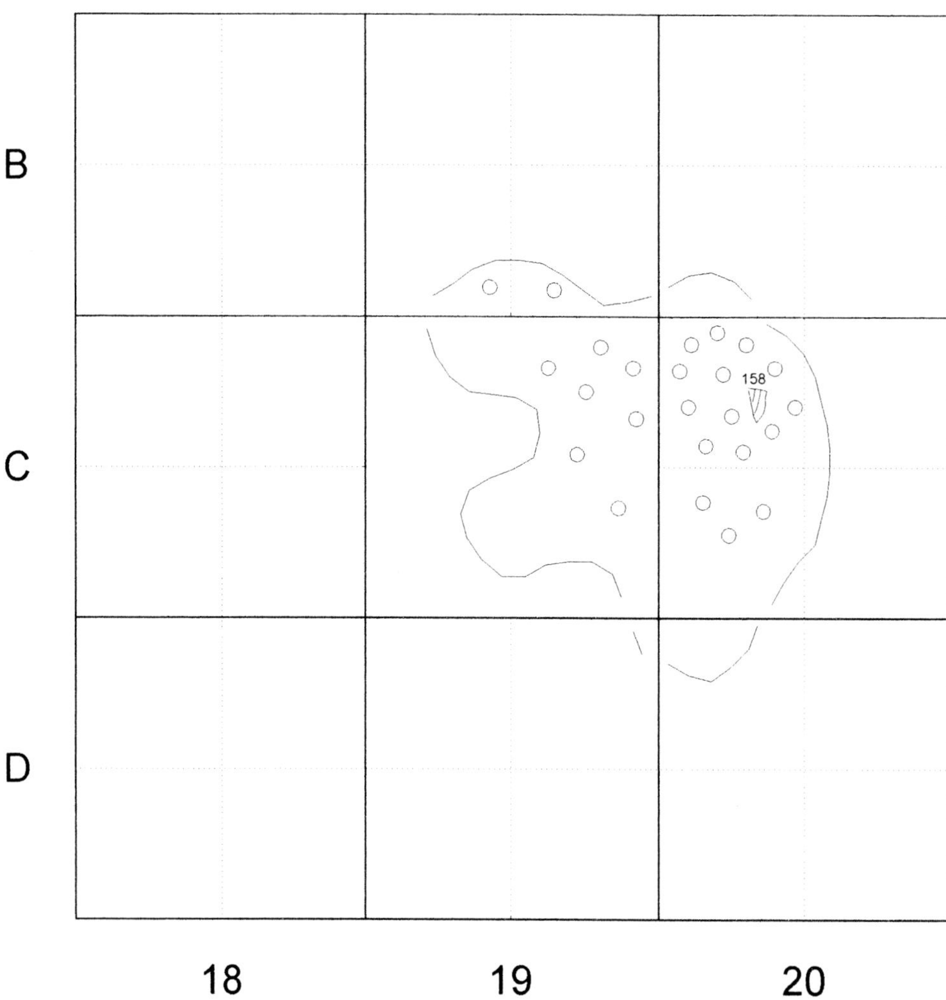

Figure 4.2 Avington VI: distribution of the artefacts in refitted group 158

Group 264

It is estimated that between 80% and 90% of the original nodule is represented in group 264 and that this would have been approximately 200mm in length and probably about 90mm in width. The third dimension, because of the asymmetry of the nodule varies from 90–130mm (**Fig. 4.3**). The cortex is thin and smooth and exhibits occasional fine surface detail. Although the nodule incorporated a fundamental flaw which seriously disrupted the knapping, few of the refitted removals are fractured; in this respect the flint was of at least reasonable quality. However, as with group 158, catastrophic material failure is the dominating feature of this group. There is evidence to suggest that a typical long blade core, intended for the production of blades 120–150mm or more in length, was the objective but in the event the only useful product was a small core yielding a few blades 50–80mm in length. This demonstrates that small cores were produced at least expediently and that whether or not the knapper intended to produce Long Blades when beginning work, s/he was capable of adapting to the constraints of the nodule to obtain a variety of blanks.

The conjoined pieces suggest that the likely first stage in the reduction sequence was the removal of a series of flakes from the left-hand side of the nodule (**Fig. 4.3: 1**); none of these flakes has been located which may indicate that this operation occurred elsewhere. These initial removals revealed a serious flaw in the flint which was to become critical. The original intention at this stage may have been to produce a crested blade from the left-hand side. Following this initial work the second major sequence involved the removal of the cortex adjacent to the initial series of flakes together with the protuberance, it is interesting to note that this latter objective was achieved not by the removal of one or two large thick flakes but by a comparatively long sequence of about 12 flakes, mostly thin pieces, which were often quite small (**Fig. 4.3**). This may have been a less risky procedure than detaching the projection in one hit. Thirdly, flakes were struck from the right-hand side as drawn including two comparatively large flakes. As the drawings show, there are some flakes from the lower part of the nodule that have not been located and refitted, they may have been detached elsewhere or they may have been converted into finished forms, such as scrapers and thus removed. At this stage there appears to have been an attempt to form a platform (upper end as drawn), but the first flake detached was irregular and the next attempt, the removal of a much thicker flake, resulted in catastrophic failure: the embryonic Long Blade core shattered into four fragments. One of these became core 264 (**Fig. 4.3: 2, 4, lower left**).

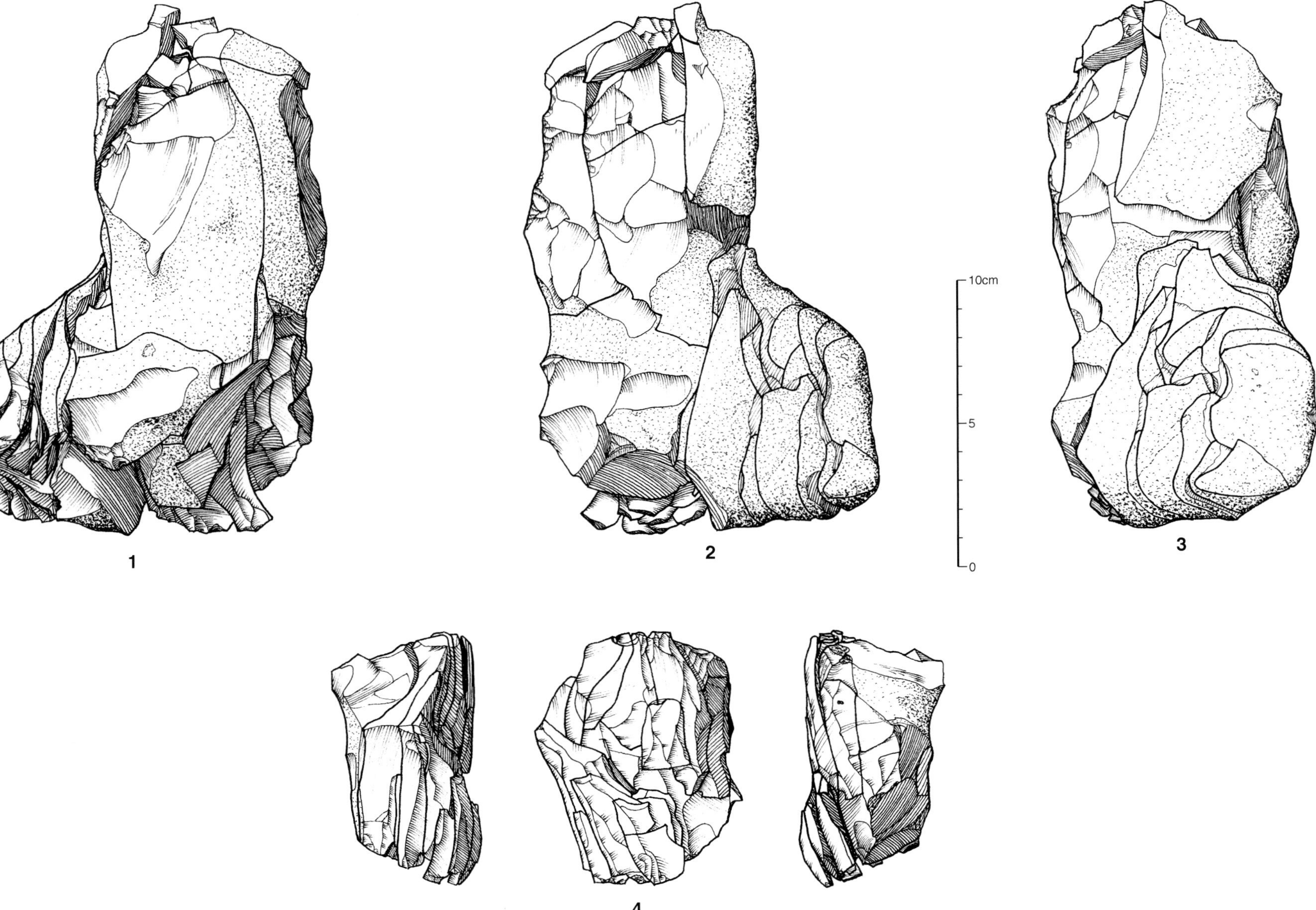

Figure 4.3 Avington VI: refitted group 264. 1-3: maximum extent of refitting; 4: core with last stage removals refitted

As a result of the previous irregular fracture, embryonic core 264 was distinctly asymmetrical (**Fig. 4.3: 3, 4**). To regularize the shape a series of small blades 30–60mm in length was removed from the lower platform as drawn and most but not all of these have been refitted. Following this initial shaping and trimming of the core, a series of blades was struck using both of the platforms; again not all have been refitted. It is likely that some 3–6 blades, varying in length between 50–80mm, were the products retained for use. When tested, none of the microliths refitted into this series. The upper platform refits perfectly to the other fragments indicating that it was never rejuvenated; the blades refitted to the lower platform also indicate that this platform was not rejuvenated either. Both platforms were retouched prior to blade removal, the retouch being down the face of the core rather than across the platform.

The detailed distribution of these refits is shown in **Fig. 4.4.** As is often the case it is approximately 1m across although the great majority of the refitting pieces were found in a much smaller area. The distribution is clearly associated with one of the major concentrations. The fact that core 264 and its 17 refitted removals were found in the same small area as the rest of the removals from this nodule supports the contention that the initial working of the nodule and the subsequent development of core 264 were consecutive aspects of a single unified knapping sequence. The alternative scenario, that a shatter piece was retrieved from a pile of debitage and developed into a core on a separate later occasion, is unlikely since it might be expected to have given rise to a different distribution from that observed: two at least partially separate scatters might have resulted if this had been the case.

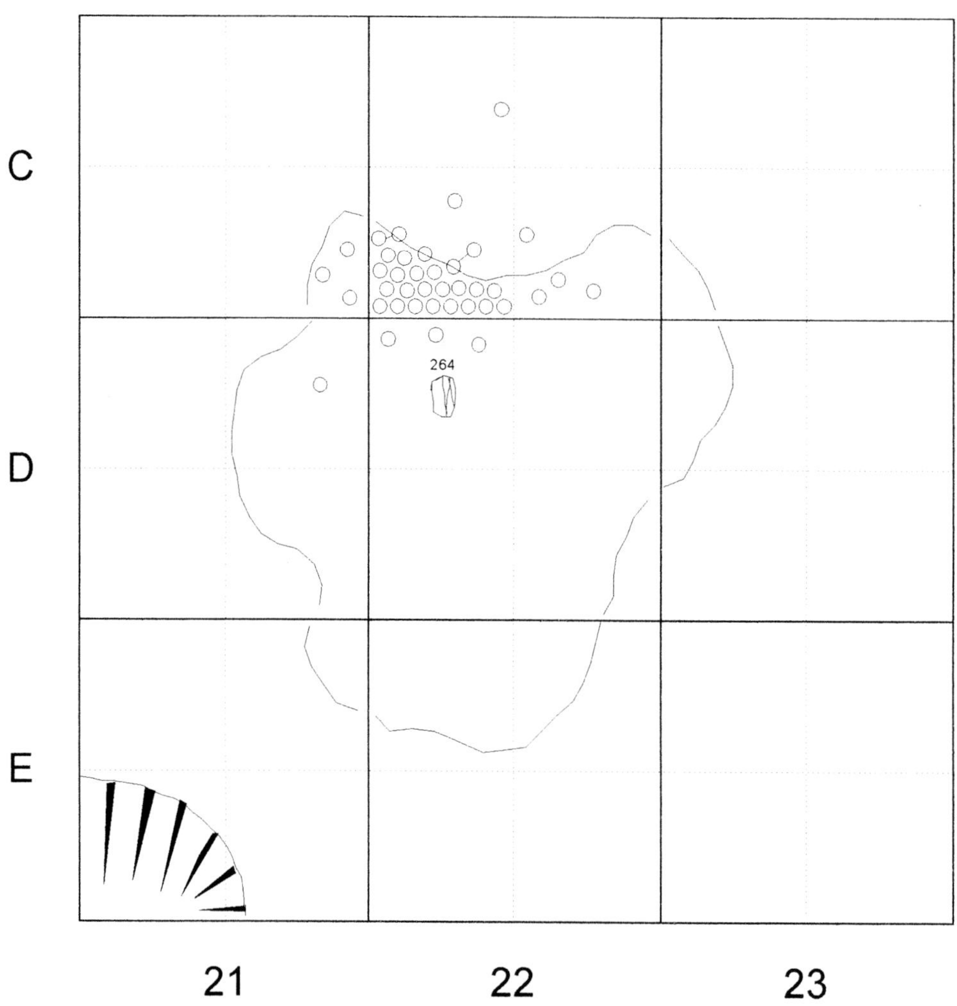

Figure 4.4 Avington VI: distribution of the artefacts in refitted group 264

Group 137

This sequence is essentially complete except for spalls (**Fig. 4.5: 1**). The refits make up a nodule that was 105 x 45 x 80mm in size, of regular shape and had thin smooth sandy coloured cortex.

The refitting shows that the reduction sequence started with the removal of a large flake which broke in two. The irregular ventral surface of the flake suggests that this fragmentation was caused by stress in the flint but its removal formed the platform from which the remaining six mainly cortical flakes were struck; two of these broke as they detached. These removals formed the working face of the core. Two final removals then followed including a small blade, both of these fragmented. The edge of the platform was then retouched and there is evidence of an unsuccessful attempt to strike one or more blades from the left-hand side (**Fig. 4.5: 1**). At this point the core was abandoned; there is no sign of any attempt to form a second platform. If anything of use was produced it did not leave the immediate area. It may have been that the flint was recognised as having an intrinsically unsatisfactory nature.

The core was recovered from the south-east quadrant of transect D19, of the 12 fragments representing the 9 removals, 11 were found in transect E19 and the remaining piece in transect E20.

Group 199

The refitting of this group shows that it was reduced from a relatively small nodule, approximately 110 x 40 x 50mm, which has bipolar faceted platforms, neither of which yielded flakes of any length (**Fig. 4.5: 2**). One large flake, which broke in two, has been refitted. After this flake had been removed some rather desultory attempts were made to work the embryonic core further, including some lateral flaking possibly to form a small crested blade. However, the core was quickly abandoned. Nevertheless, the group is of interest because it illustrates that on occasion quite small nodules were selected for blank production.

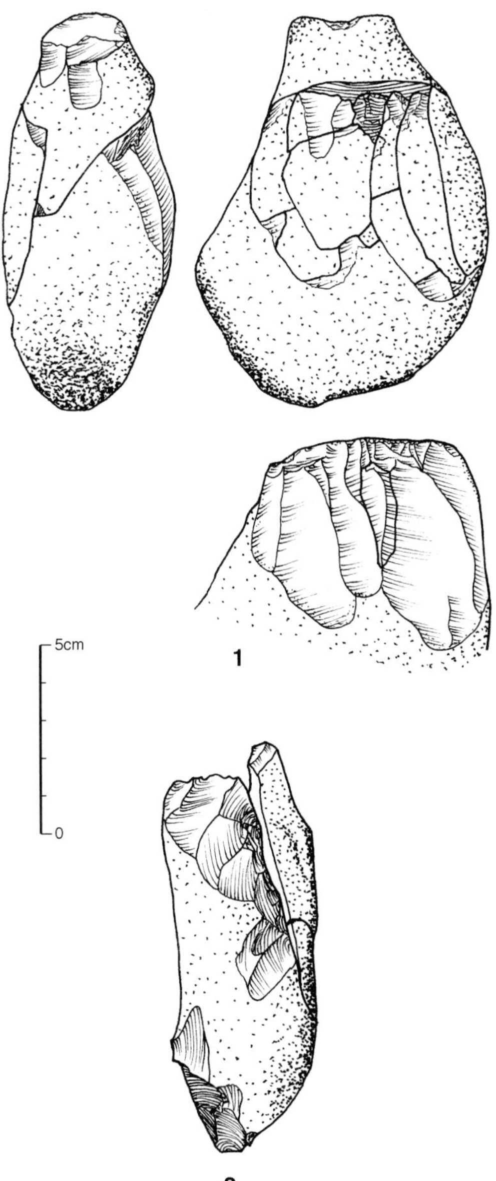

Figure 4.5 Avington VI: 1: refitted group 137. 2: core 199 with broken flake refitted

Group 150

Core 150 which resulted from the reduction sequence described from the refitting group it carries has already been mentioned in chapter 3 (p. 21 and **Fig. 3.7: 5**); despite considerable expenditure of effort, it has only been partially refitted, (**Fig. 4.6**). The original nodule is likely to have been at least 250mm in length and some 100–120mm in diameter, it was comparatively regular and rounded in shape; the cortex is thin and smooth.

The earliest stages of the reduction sequence have not been reconstructed, despite careful and extended searches for refits; these stages involved the formation of a striking platform (upper as drawn) and what appears to be the preparation for a crested blade (**Fig. 3.7**). This initial flaking revealed the somewhat intractable nature of the flint: an edge was crested but could not be detached despite several unsuccessful attempts which resulted in short abruptly terminated flake scars. Following this failure a second crested blade was prepared almost diametrically opposite the first (**Fig. 4.5** top right), this was essentially worked on one side only, the other side formed by a single large removal. This cresting was removed in two stages: a small crested blade which broke in two was detached first, the proximal end of this flake has not been recovered; secondly a much larger crested blade was struck off. At about the same time a large blade-like flake was struck from the same platform (**Fig. 4.6** left-hand side). A series of removals followed, again from this platform, most of which have not been refitted; of the two which have, one came from the same scatter as the majority of the refits but the other was found some distance away.

During this second phase, the core was significantly shortened (**Fig. 4.6**). Most of the removals from this part of the sequence are also missing but two core rejuvenation flakes have been refitted to the upper platform as drawn. This second phase may well have involved more than one set of removals with the core moving between the two major concentrations. Attention also seems to have been given to the lower platform (as drawn), possibly at some point in the second phase outlined above, and a series of largely cortical flakes were detached before a modest volume of flint was worked away but exactly how cannot be determined since the removals have not been refitted. This sequence also yielded evidence for the rather intractable nature of the flint which is possibly why the core was abandoned whilst a large volume of flint still remained.

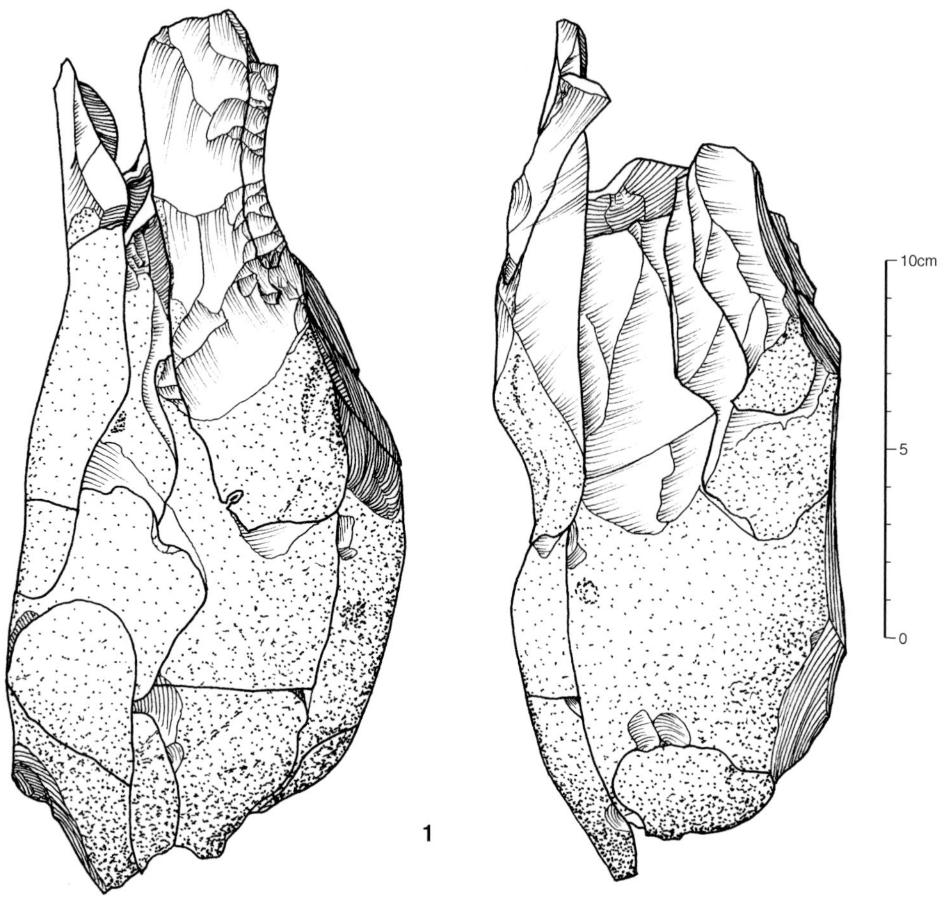

Figure 4.6 Avington VI: refitted group 150

The spatial distribution of the artefacts refitting in this sequence is interesting. Core 150 was recovered from the north-west quadrant of transect B20 and one fairly large blade-like flake refitting in part directly on the core from transect C19, this removal fits part way through the sequence identified as the second phase. All of the remaining 14 items, representing 10 removals several of which must have been broken into two or three fragments not all of which have been recovered, came from a small area centred on the north-west quadrant of transect D22 (**Fig. 4.7**).Thus the history of the core would appear to be its initial acquisition as a nodule of raw material and the preparation of an unsuccessful crested blade, away from the excavated area; a second, successful, crested blade and further reduction then occurred in the vicinity of transect D22; a second platform then allowed further removals which were detached and left in part at least in the area of transect D22. Finally, further reduction from the first platform occurred in the vicinity of transects C19–20.

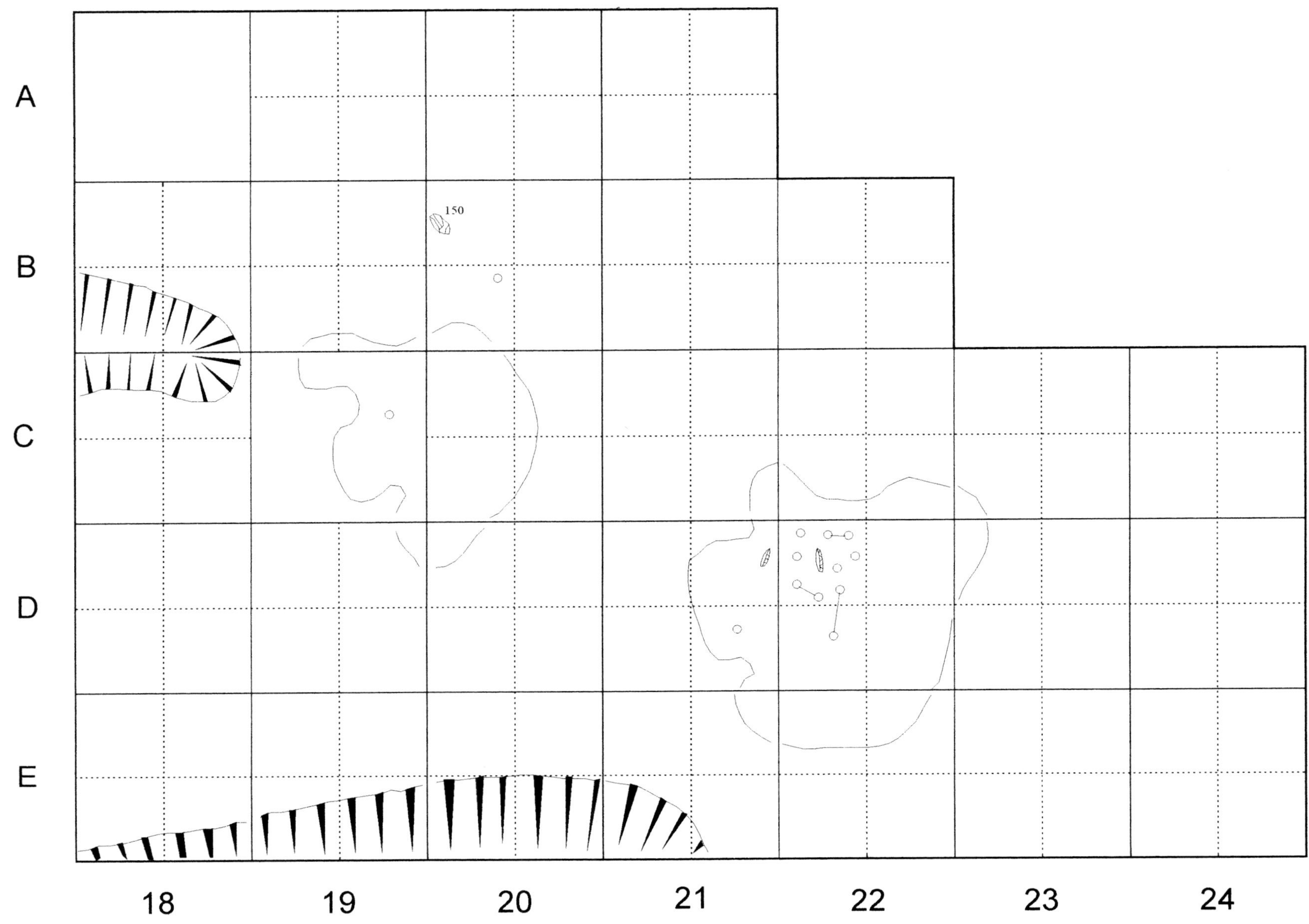

Figure 4.7 Avington VI: distribution of the artefacts in refitted group 150

Group 195

Considerable effort was expended on this group which has been extensively rebuilt. The original nodule was 140 x 90 x 80mm, pear shaped and with a thin smooth cortex (**Fig. 4.8**). Initially, cortical flakes were struck from either side of the apex to produce a small platform. One or two flakes were then struck from the face of the core but these have not been located. The platform was then extended by the removal of two rejuvenation flakes; a series of flakes could then be removed from it, extending the working face of the core and removing cortex from it (**Fig. 4.8, right-hand side**). From this face several blades appear to have been struck; two of these fragmented and have been recovered and refitted. The centre of **Figure 4.8** shows the working face with the two flakes refitted; one is lacking its distal end. The scars of the associated blades which have not been recovered are shown shaded, those scars not shaded correspond to the outer flakes refitted and shown in the right-hand drawing **Fig. 4.8**. Finally, the platform was once again extended and its edge retouched but no further reduction took place and the core was abandoned. It is noteworthy that of the 15 removals refitted, 10 were broken into two or more fragments, presumably during the reduction process. This suggests that the quality of the flint was unsatisfactory and this may have been the reason for the abandonment of the core. There is no evidence for an attempted second platform although battering indicates that the core was subsequently used as a hammerstone.

The core was found in the north-west quadrant of transect D20, the majority of the removals in transect D19 (**Fig. 4.9**).

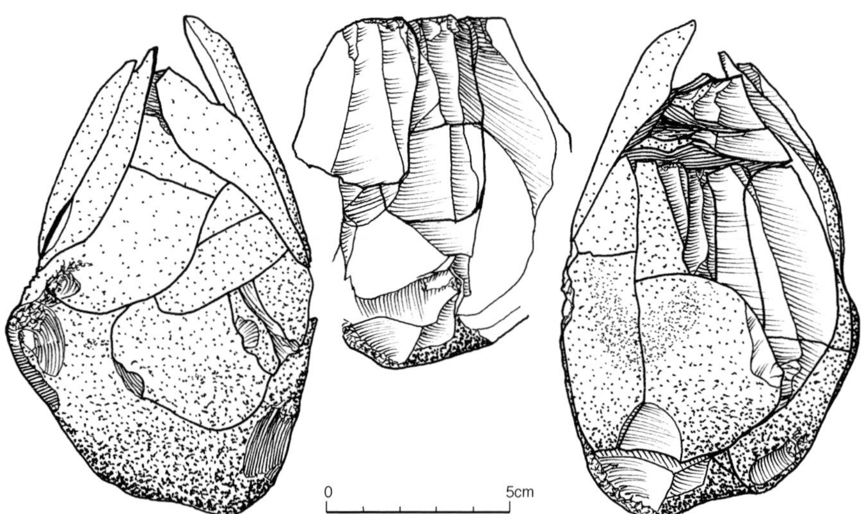

Figure 4.8 Avington VI: maximum extent of refitting on group 195 with a later stage of the working face of the core shown centre

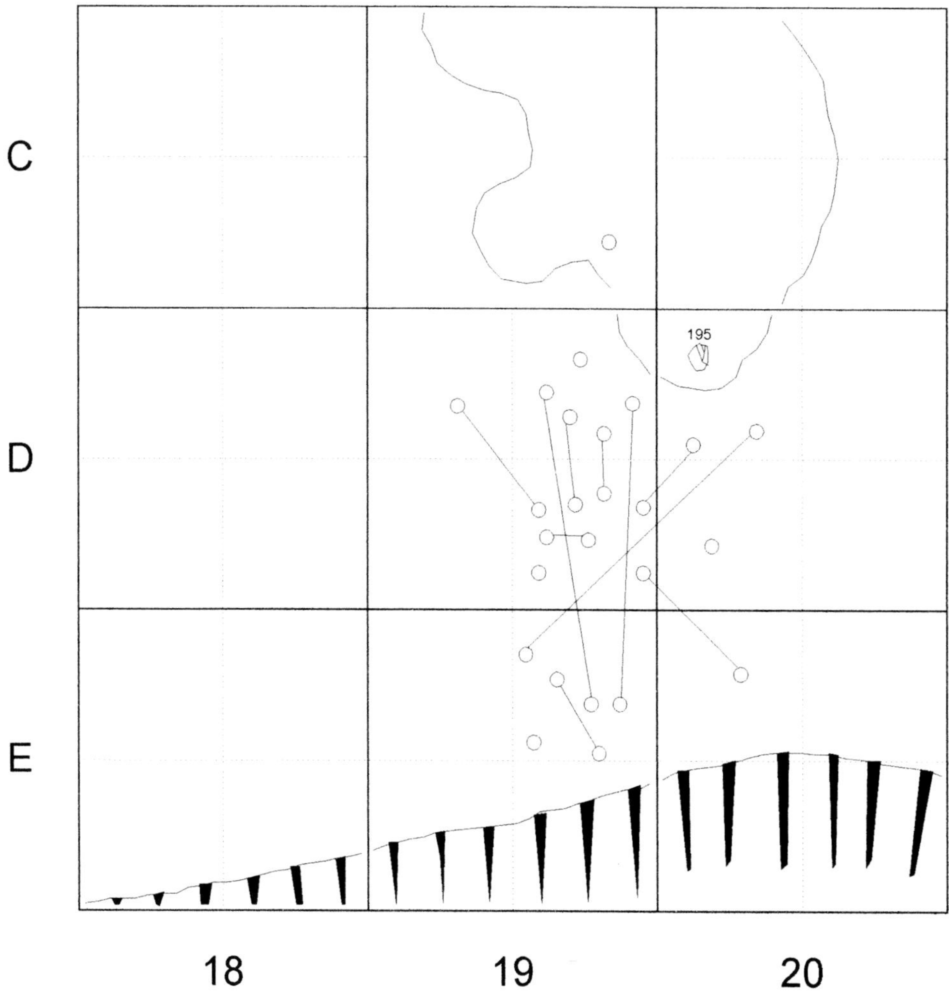

Figure 4.9 Avington VI: distribution of the artefacts in refitted group 195

Group 154

This group has been extensively rebuilt and reveals a great deal about the reduction sequence. The original flint nodule appears to have been about 300 x 100 x 120mm in size; in shape it was generally regular with only minor protuberances and other irregularities, the cortex is thin and greyish in colour. It would appear to have originated from a chalk outcrop or from associated weathered chalk deposits given the relatively fresh appearance of the cortex and the absence of ancient fracture surfaces. Despite this, the quality of the flint was poor and few of the knappers' products were removed for use elsewhere. Many of the removals either fragmented during the reduction process or stopped short of their intended full length, ending either in hinge or step fractures (**Fig. 4.11: 2; 4.12: 2**); of the 35 'blades' refitted no less than 16 are conjoined from fragments and there are some 8–10 cases of blades terminating in hinge or step fracture. These failures are not distributed at random but occur in well defined regions of the nodule (**Fig. 4.10–4.12**).

As with several of the extensively refitted cores, the initial removals have not been located. However, as the majority of the elements were found in transects A18 and B18 it is possible that the missing pieces exist at the site in the immediately adjacent unexcavated areas. The missing removals include those detached to form one or both of the striking platforms together with several large flakes from the back and sides of the core, as well as some smaller flakes. The earliest removal refitted is a lateral flake with an entirely cortical butt, struck midway along the left-hand side of the core (**Fig. 4.10**). This was followed by a short series struck from the lower platform (as drawn) which may have included a crested blade. None of these elements have been found and, as they have a blade character, this may indicate that they were of use and were moved elsewhere. From this point on, the recovery and refitting is all but complete; nearly all the removals of any size are represented by at least a major fragment. The reduction sequence is well documented. It began with the removal of several blade-like flakes with varying amounts of cortex, mostly from the lower platform but also a few from the upper platform, the end of this stage is shown (**Fig. 4.10**). Once the cortex had been removed and the face of the core fully defined, there was progressive reduction, the majority of the removals, 25 of the 34 refitted 'blades', were struck from the lower platform; this ratio is maintained if allowance is made for missing pieces, more having been struck from the lower platform. The heavier use of the lower platform is also reflected in the number of refitted core rejuvenation flakes: 11 of these have been refitted to the lower platform but only three to the upper. Blades of all sizes were produced, from less than 70mm–more than 170mm in length. As previously noted, blade fragmentation and/or terminating short was frequent, the final removal was a particularly extreme example of this (**Fig. 4.12**) and probably led to the abandonment of the core despite the volume of flint remaining.

This major reduction sequence is illustrated in **Figures 4.11–4.13**. As stated above, the lower platform was frequently rejuvenated (**Fig. 4.10**) and this may have stabilised it and reduced the necessity of further adjustment by more faceting. This is evident from the blade butts (**Fig. 4.13**) which show that minor trimming was carried out removing comparatively small spalls of a centimetre or two across, probably to facilitate the striking of a particular blade. The blades from this lower platform (**Fig. 4.13**) appear to fit into five principal series. Both the blade butts and core rejuvenation flakes show that the edge of the striking platform was adjusted by a little retouch down the working face and across the platform (**Fig. 4.12**). On occasion at least, this retouch was confined to the area from which a blade was to be struck: some rejuvenation flakes conjoin in a perfectly simple manner (**Fig. 4.10**). None of the removals from this core exhibit any sign of bruising and bruised blades are generally rare in this area of the site.

Core 154 was found in the south-west quadrant of transect B20, all but three of the larger removals came from transects A18 and B18 (**Fig. 4.14**). The vertical distribution is also of some interest. During the 1978 excavation, a group of long blade artefacts was encountered in transect B18 at a higher level than expected, subsequently the Mesolithic pit in transects B18, C18 was recognised and the displaced artefacts were assumed to have been carried with the clay spoil dug from the pit. Whether or not these artefacts were identified by the Mesolithic pit diggers is impossible to determine and we can only speculate on what they might have thought about artefacts which included blades 10 times larger than anything they themselves produced. No less than thirteen items refitted to core 154 come from this displaced group; a further nine items from core 154 were recovered from the main Mesolithic horizon of transect B18. In some cases the items are fragments and these have been reunited with other fragments, usually from the main Long Blade horizon as in the case of a blade rebuilt from three fragments, the middle from the main Mesolithic Horizon and the other two fragments from the Long Blade horizon.

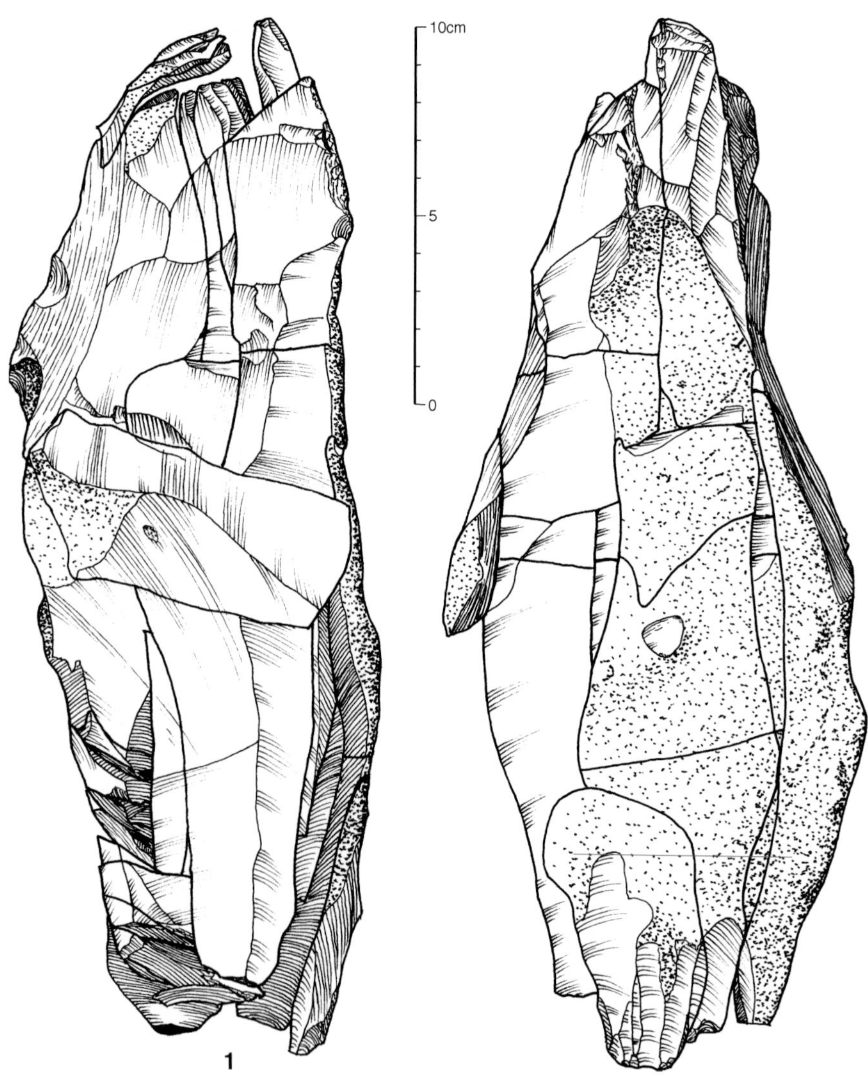

Figure 4.10 Avington VI: maximum extent of refitting on group 154

Figure 4.11 Avington VI: intermediate stage in the reduction of core 154 showing fragmentation of some of the removals

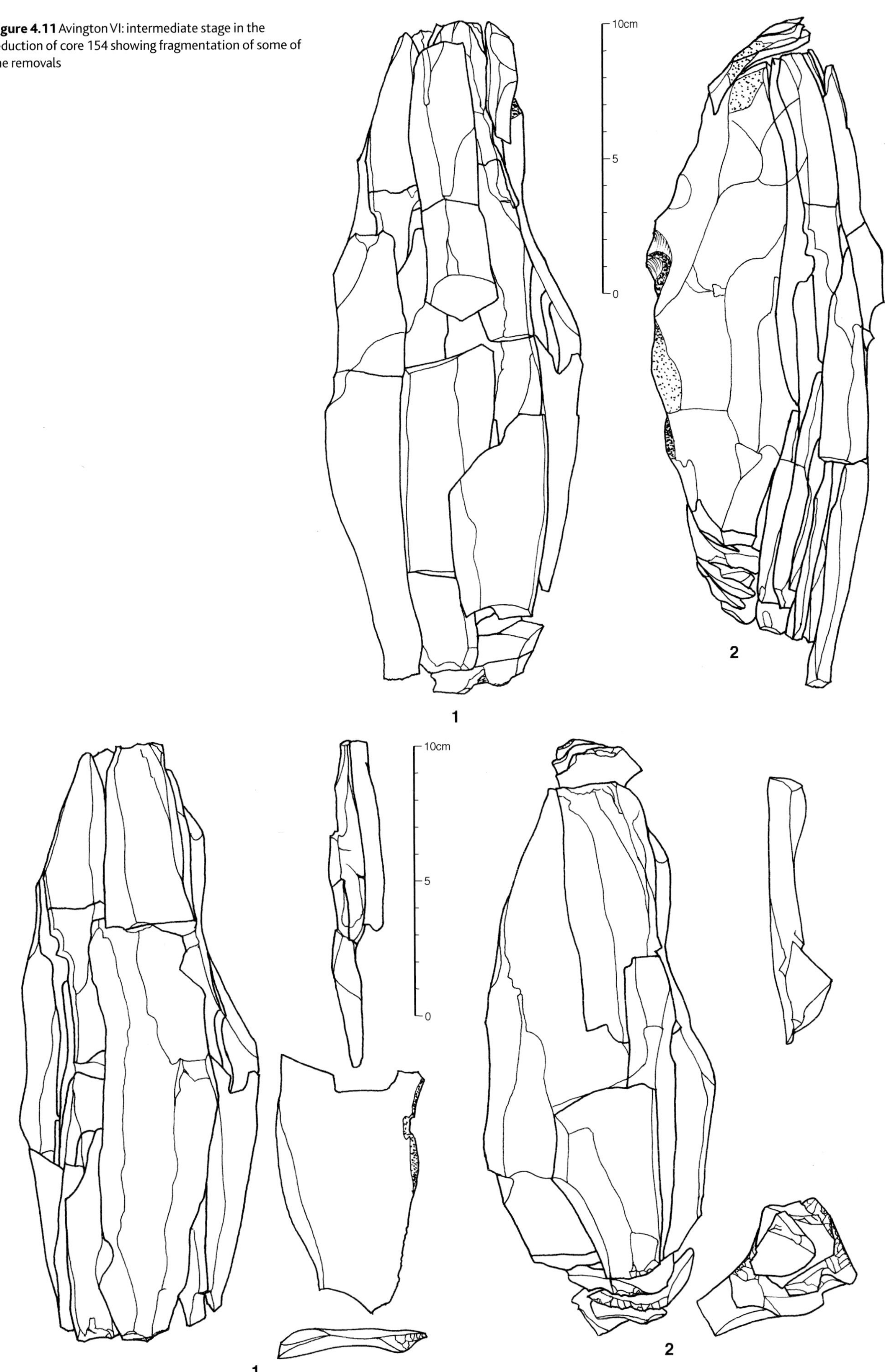

Figure 4.12 Avington VI: later stage in the reduction of core 154. 1: showing step, hinge and normal but short terminations of some blades and 2: retouch of the lower platform

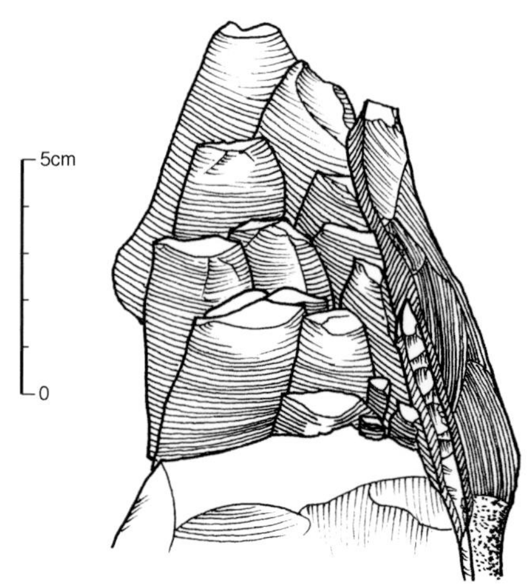

Figure 4.13. Avington VI: butts of blades refitted in group 154 indicating several stages of core rejuvenation.

Group 118

Although extensively rebuilt, there are notable gaps in the reduction sequence represented by this group. It is likely that some of the initial removals included several large flakes which are not in the assemblage, probably because they were detached elsewhere. Scattered through this reduction sequence are blades of varying quality which have not been found, the most probable explanation in these cases is that they were removed for use even though in some cases they retained cortex on their upper surface. Finally, unlike core 154, despite repeated attempts it has proved impossible to rebuild the striking platform sequences: there are no refitted rejuvenation flakes. There is no reason to suppose that these were ever anything other than simple waste and therefore they should be, and almost certainly are, present. However, as core 154 demonstrates, striking platforms were subject to constant trimming, commonly by the removal of small flakes and spalls; locating such small items among a mass of similar such small pieces is a hugely time consuming and arduous process. Whereas core 154 was worked in an area where the density of worked flint was low, core 118 is principally associated with the dense concentration in transects C19–C20; thus the task is different in the two cases.

Estimating the size of the original flint nodule is problematic because of the missing removals, especially the cortical flakes, but it is likely to have been 280–300mm in length and 90–100mm in diameter. There is evidence that although generally regular in shape, one end swelled somewhat. The cortex is thin, comparatively smooth and greyish in colour. It may well have been sourced from a primary context.

As noted, the earliest part of the reduction sequence is missing; this includes, among others, several large flakes (**Fig. 4.15**). However, it should also be noted that in order to keep the drawings of this group within page limits and provide maximum detail some removals have been omitted from the figures in a somewhat arbitrary manner. The first removals recovered were struck from the lower platform (as drawn), the largest of these three flakes is bruised; these were followed by a short series of blade removals from the same platform, none of these has been found (**Fig. 4.15: 1, 2**). Attention was then transferred to the upper platform and several removals followed, some of the refitted pieces fractured; not all the pieces in this series have been found (**Fig. 4.14: 2–4**). At this point the reverse side of the nodule was exploited and this yielded a far greater number of removals, 34 from a total of 41 recovered. Throughout this particular part of the sequence there are pieces missing, including most of the cortical removals (**Fig. 4.15: 3, 4**). Of the 34 removals, 20 were struck from the upper platform. The butts of the blades from the upper platform indicate three main phases of rejuvenation; in the initial phase of working three layers of blades were removed, then rejuvenation followed by a single layer of blades, then further rejuvenation and another layer of blades and a final rejuvenation quickly followed by abandonment (**Fig. 4.15: 1**).

Examination of the lower platform suggests a similar, if slightly simpler, series of events; the first platform from which existing refits originated probably yielded two layers of blades, this was followed by at least one rejuvenation operation but missing removals make it impossible to be certain of the detail on this point; the next layer of refits document a platform some distance away from the first identified above, this second (?) platform appears to have yielded a single layer of blades, finally rejuvenation formed the platform to be seen in the drawings (**Fig. 4.15: 2**). There is evidence of an attempt to strike from the existing platform but the removal terminated short and the core was abandoned. Towards the end of this reduction sequence two large blades were produced, one was recovered (**Fig. 4.16: 4**) and the other may be visualized by reference to the surrounding refits and the core (**Fig. 4.16: 3**), they appear to have been similar to each other but possibly the missing blade more nearly fitted requirements and was taken away for use. During this reduction sequence at least 21 out of 41 removals fractured. Although the upper platform produced the majority of the removals, work alternated continuously between the two platforms as the interleaving of the two sets of removals documents. Various stages of this sequence of 34 removals have been drawn (**Fig. 4.16**); as may be seen from the drawings, the blades are generally neat in appearance. The swelling of the nodule noted in the description given at the beginning contributed a series of blades and several of these have been separately drawn (**Fig. 4.17**), there are at least four blades missing from this part of the sequence. In length the blades vary from 40mm (**Fig. 4.16**) –<140mm (**Fig. 4.15**). By the end of its life, the original nodule of some 300mm in length had been reduced to a core approximately 140mm in length.

The missing removals from the initial stages of the core leave some uncertainties about the knappers' intentions. As noted, one of the flakes was bruised, it has already been observed that bruised blades tend to be large, often cortical, and therefore represent early removals so it may be that the incidence of bruising is underestimated in this case. However, it has also been suggested that bruised blades were commonly discarded at the point of knapping and so should have been recovered. Crested blades were also produced early in the sequence but there is no unequivocal evidence for the existence of a crested blade from core 118, although a fragment of an outer blade does exhibit some small lateral removals (**Fig. 4.15**) but this may be nothing more than localised trimming (as in **Fig. 4.15**) and so doubt remains.

Of the 41 refits located, seven came from the area of concentration 2 and are comparatively widely dispersed, these represent the earlier stages in the working of the core; the remaining 34, from the principal reduction of the core, are associated with concentration 1 and are more tightly grouped (**Fig. 4.18**).

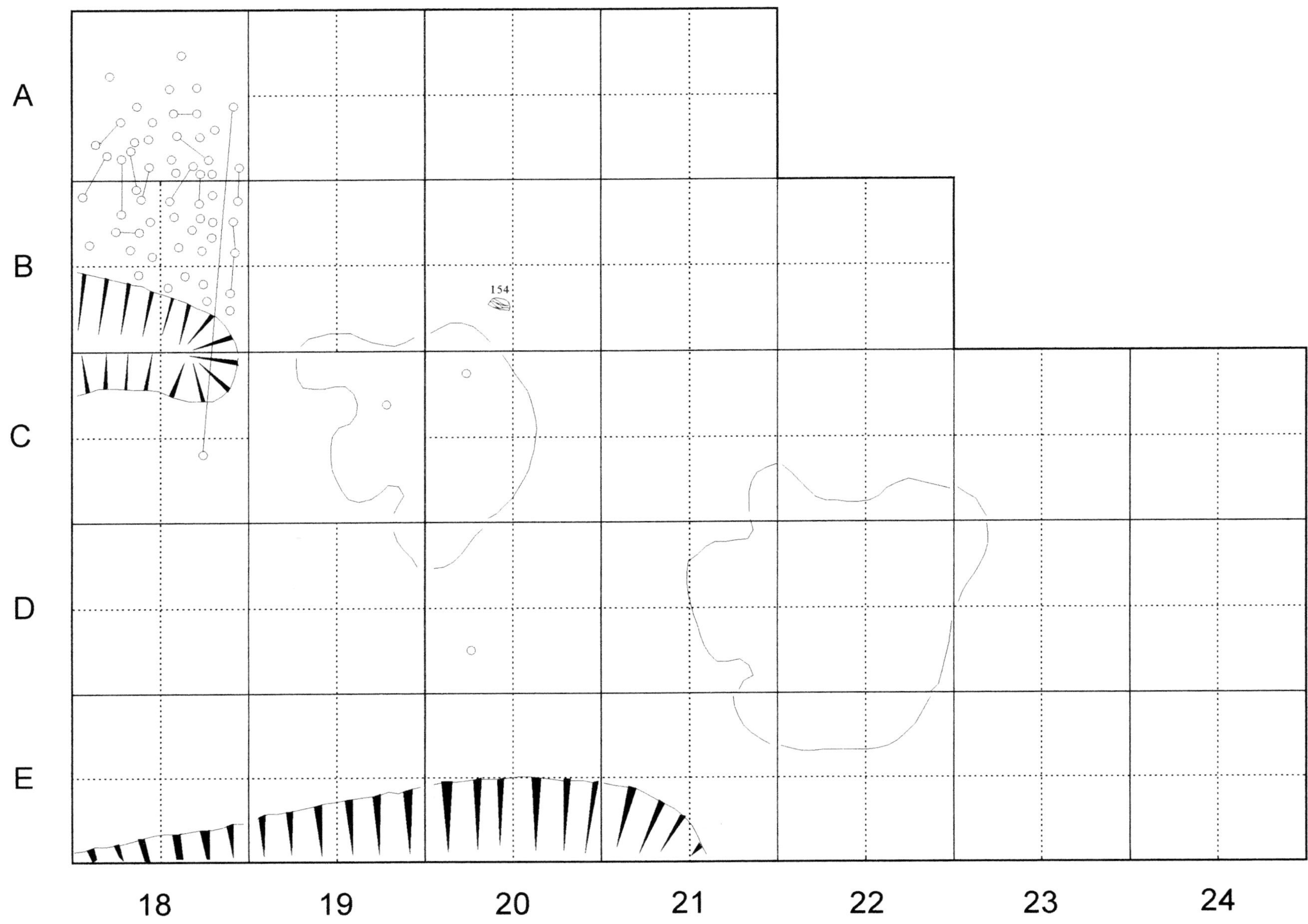

Figure 4.14 Avington VI: distribution of artefacts refitted in group 154

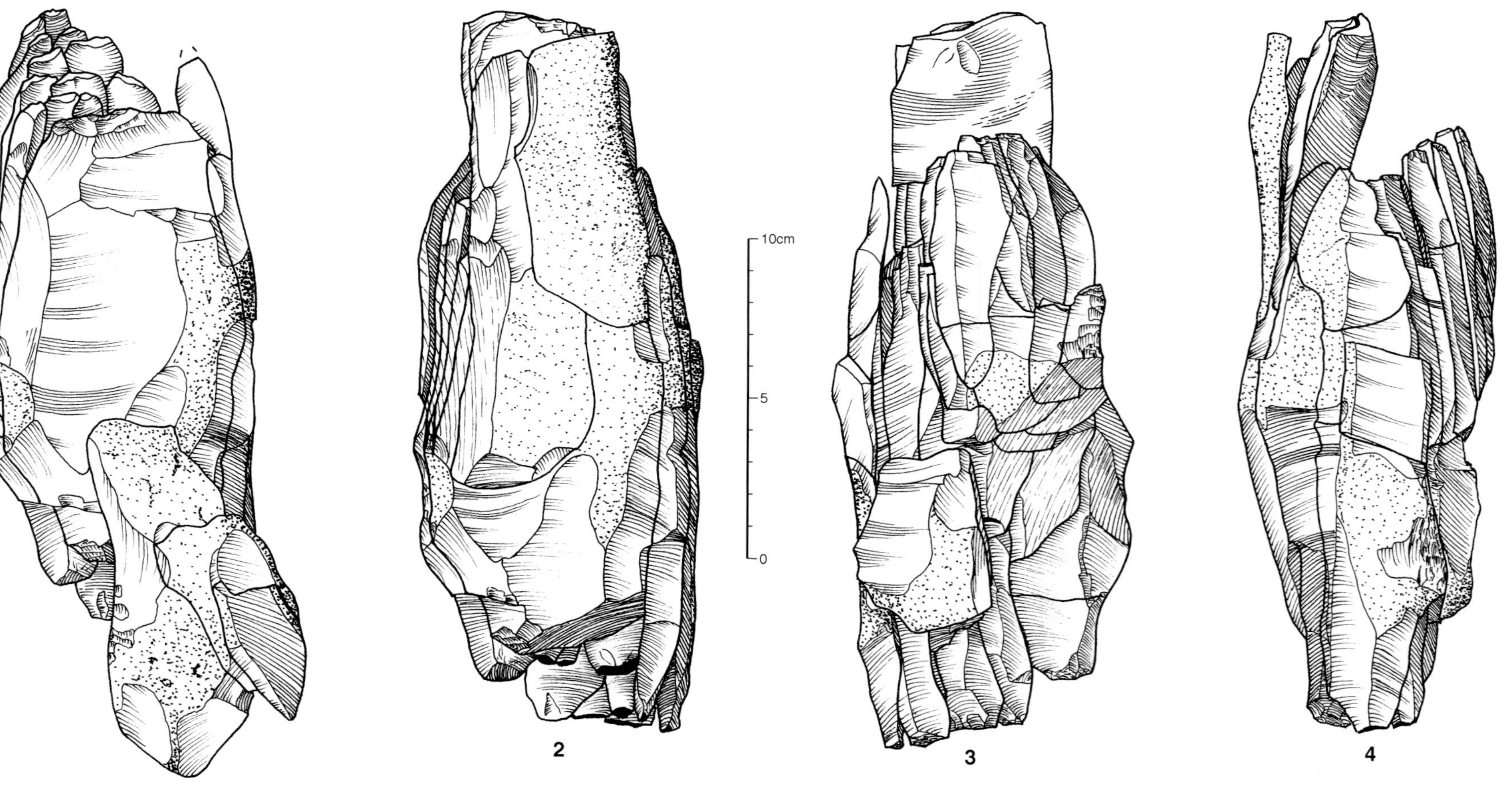

Figure 4.15 Avington VI: maximum extent of refitting on group 118 showing views of an early stage in the reduction sequence

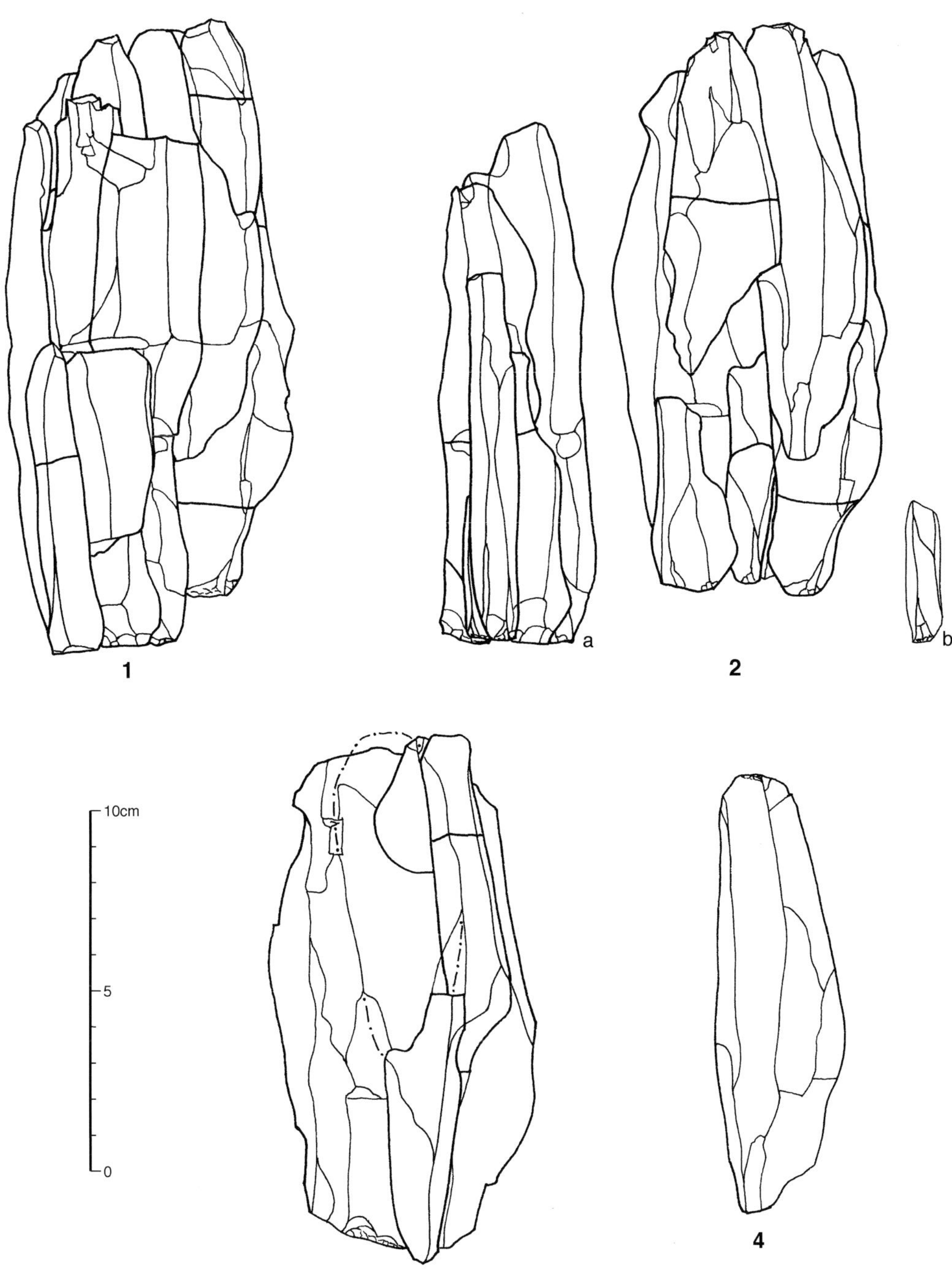

Figure 4.16 Avington VI: refitted group 118 at a later stage of reduction

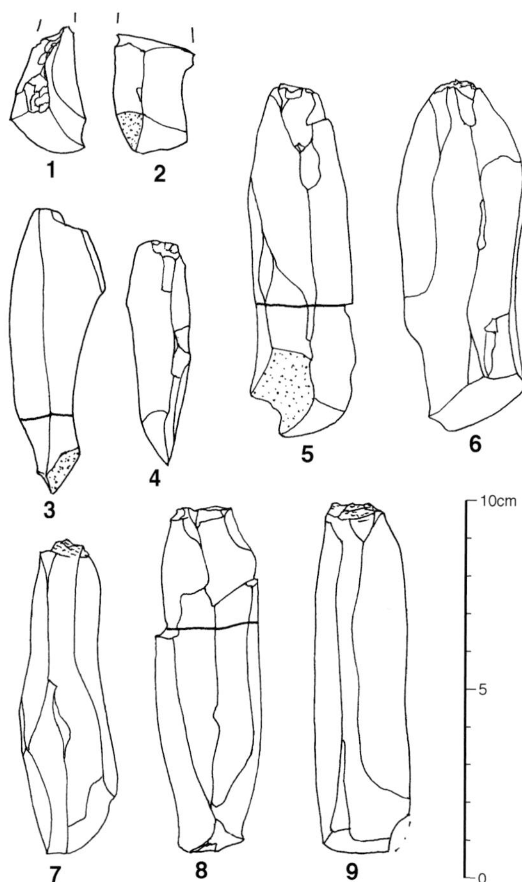

Figure 4.17 Avington VI: flakes and blades detached to reduce the convexity in the working face of core 118 as shown in 4.15:3, 5 (upper right)

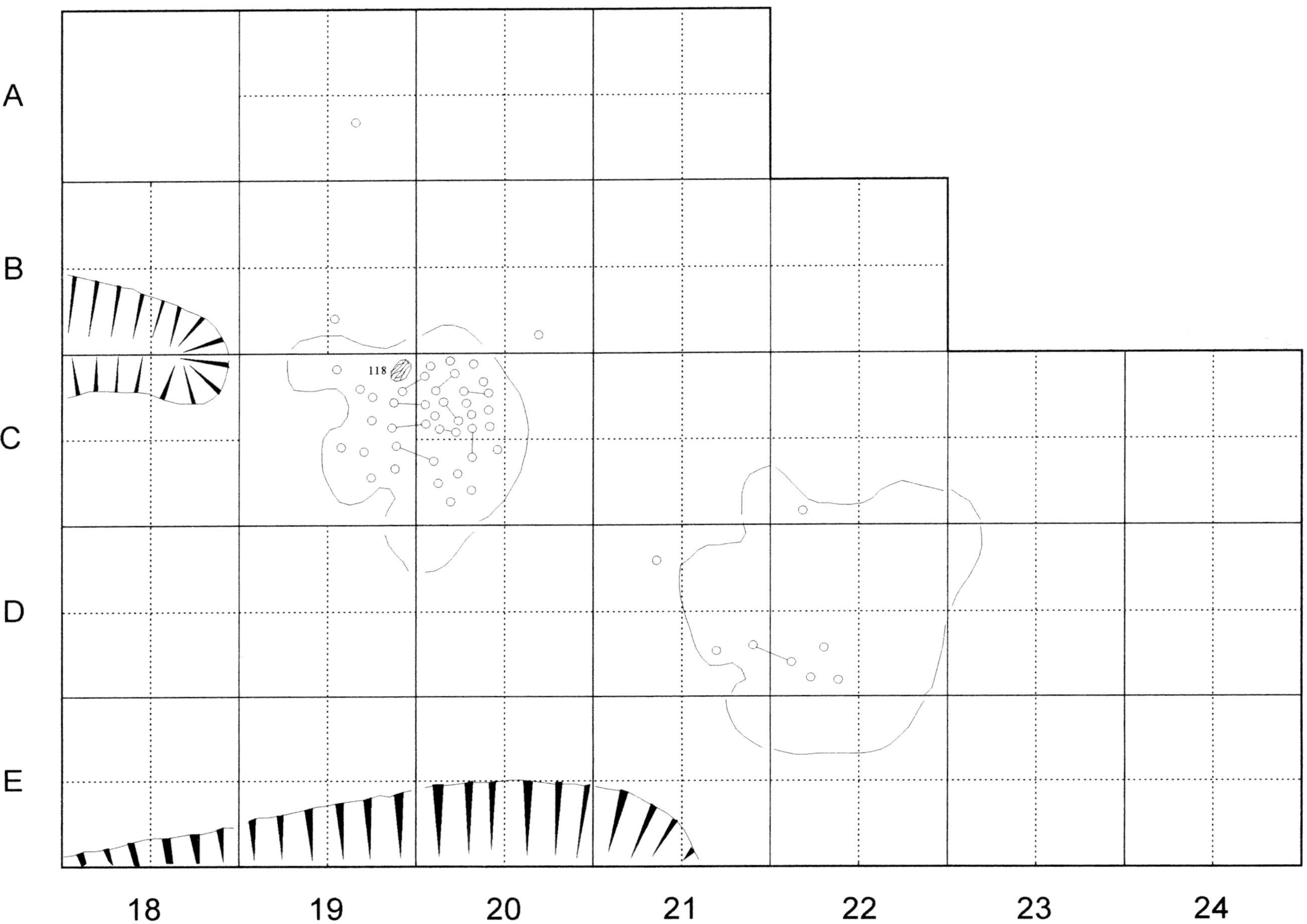

Figure 4.18 Avington VI: distribution of the refitted artefacts in group 118

Group 119

Despite the size of the original nodule, little of value seems to have been produced from this core. In addition to the core, there are 44 removals that have been refitted and less than six 'blades' appear to be missing as items that may have been removed for use elsewhere. The original nodule was some 270mm in length and approximately 100mm in diameter, it was somewhat irregular in shape being distinctly curved as in a banana and this probably caused the problems evident from the refitting of the main part of reduction sequence because the working face tended to develop excessive angularity between the two platforms which more than once required correction by alternate 'cross flaking.' The cortex is thin; internally the nature of the flint varied considerably and patination has emphasised this, viewed separately some removals would not be automatically associated with others although the refitting clearly demonstrates that they are so related. Fragmentation of the removals, especially those of a blade character, is marked; of the 44 removals recovered, 10 are fragmented, in some instances into three or more pieces. There is also clear evidence of several failures resulting from attempted blades terminating short.

The conjoined group (**Fig. 4.19**) shows that there are missing removals and that these were detached during an earlier stage of the reduction sequence; they include at least two large flakes, 100–120mm across, which are most definitely not in the assemblage. It is possible that at least some of the preparation of the crested blade also occurred at this stage but despite extensive searching no refits have been found to document this particular operation. However, the crested blade was detached at a surprisingly late stage in the overall reduction sequence. The earliest working for which evidence exists was the removal of a very large flake 120–140mm across, from the 'back' of the embryonic core (**Figs 4.19; 4.20**). This was found in transect C19 whereas the bulk of the refits were located in transects D21, 22. After this there was an attempt to strike blades from the upper platform; the first, of cortical character, has not been located but a blade intended to be of large or giant size terminated short and has been refitted (**Figs 4.19; 4.20**). At this point in the reduction sequence both ends of the core were extensively shaped and most of the shaping flakes have been refitted (**Fig. 4.19**). Two large flakes were also struck from the lower platform in order to form the lower part of the working face of the core (**Fig. 4.19**). At this stage the crested blade had still not been detached. Following the work just described, attempts were made to strike blades from the lower platform, apparently with some success since one or more of these removals have not been located (**Fig. 4.19**) but then an attempt to detach a large blade met with failure, as it terminated short (**Fig. 4.21: 1, 3**) but must nonetheless have been utilised as it exhibits bruising. In an effort to remedy the irregularity caused by this failure, some cresting occurred (**Figs 4.19; 4.21: 1**) and an attempt was then made to detach the crested blade; this was not immediately successful as the step fractures at the proximal end demonstrate (**Figs 4.19; 4.20**) and when it was finally detached it fragmented into three sections. Further cresting followed (**Fig. 4.21**) and then a series of blades were struck utilising both platforms. Two stages in this part of the sequence have been drawn (**Fig. 4.21**). The blades produced in this sequence are of varying quality and their size range is from 50–120mm in length. Two of these blades were located away from the main area from which this particular set of refits were recovered; one was found in transect D20SW but shows no obvious sign of use and this is also true of the second blade that was found in transect B19SE. The absence of any signs of use may indicate that rather than the blades having been removed the core was briefly worked in this area. At the end of this stage of the reduction sequence a blade from the lower platform, that was in all probability intended to run the full length of the core, terminated short (**Fig. 4.21: 2**) and together with other accumulated blemishes caused the working face of the core to be distorted. To correct this distortion a flake was struck across the middle of the face (**Fig. 4.21: 2** from the right-hand side as drawn); this last removal was found in concentration 2. However, a final attempt to work core 119 is indicated by the refitting of a small blade, 50mm in length and a further two hinge fractured pieces have been refitted, all of which were located in transect C20; the core itself was found in transect C19 and there is evidence of additional unsuccessful attempts to strike from it (**Fig. 4.21: 2**). Thus although the great majority of the refits are associated with concentration 2 centred on transects D21, 22 the first and last refits are associated with concentration 1 centred on transects C19, 20. As can be seen from the drawings, of the 19 removals of blade-like character that have been refitted, 10 were struck from the upper platform and the other nine from the lower platform (**Fig. 4.20**); it is possible to distinguish at least four stages prior to the final one with respect to the upper platform but with the lower platform there are possibly only two and these are much closer together.

Two of the refits exhibit bruising. One of the flakes detached in the main phase of shaping has three separate areas of damage, this flake and one section of the bruising may be seen in **Figure 4.19** on the upper right-hand side. The other piece referred to above appears in **Figure 4.21: 3**. The distribution of the refits described above is illustrated in **Figure 4.22**.

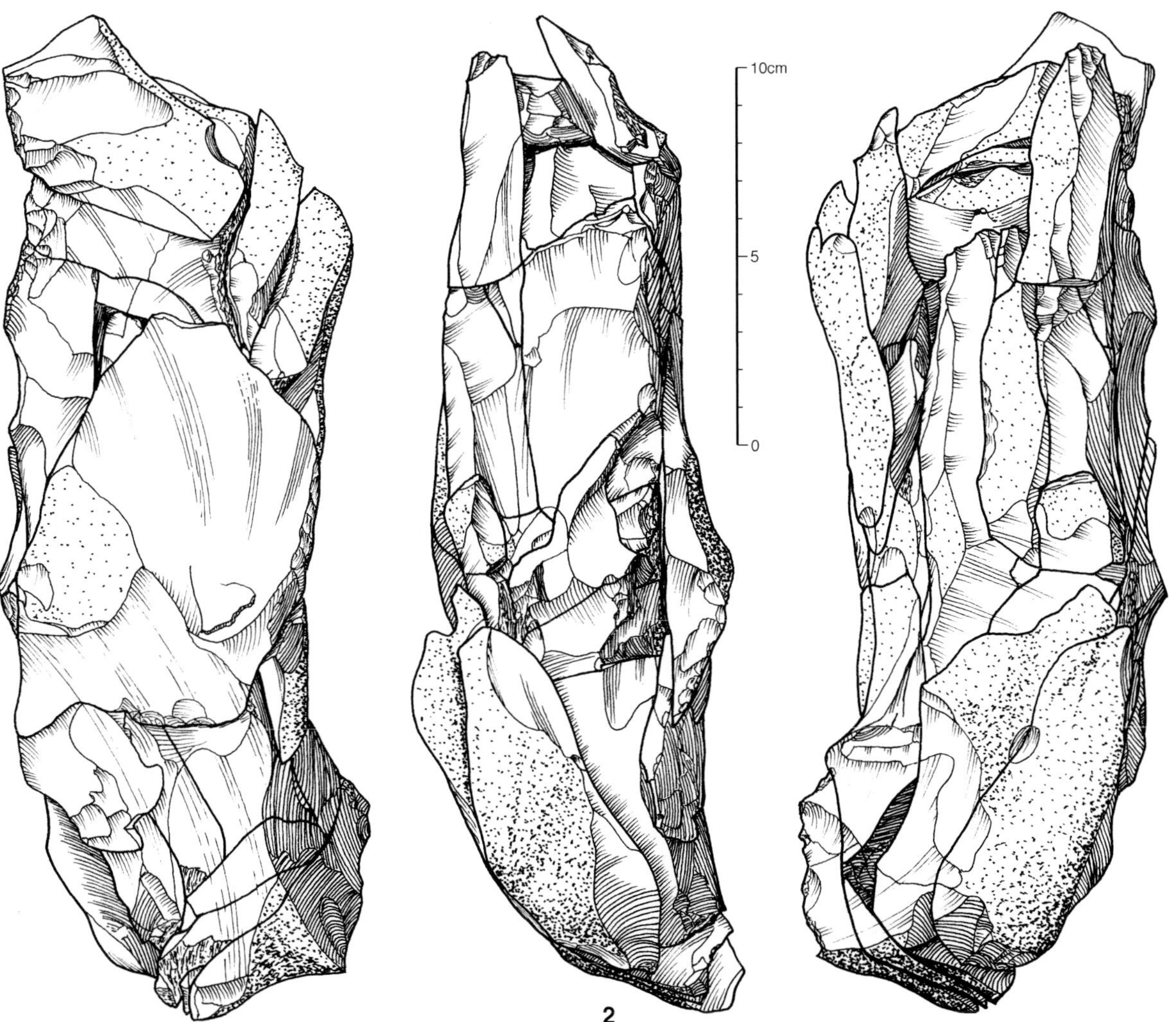

Figure 4.19 Avington VI: refitted group 119 showing an early stage in the reduction sequence

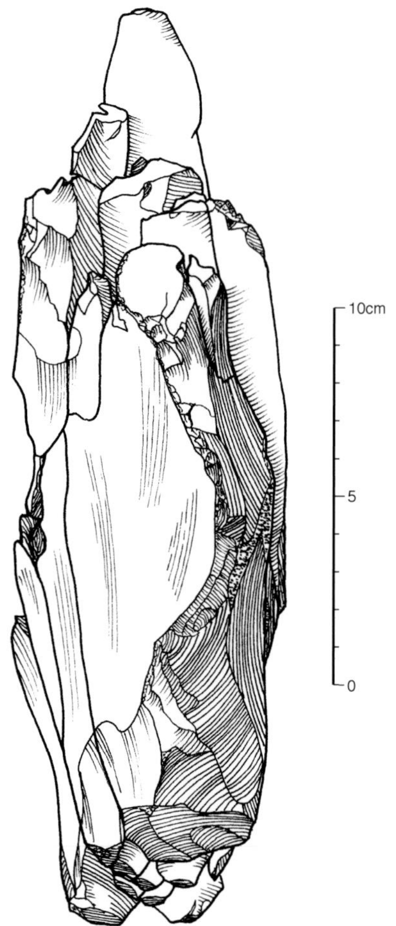

Figure 4.20 Avington VI: refitted group 119 at an intermediate stage in the reduction sequence

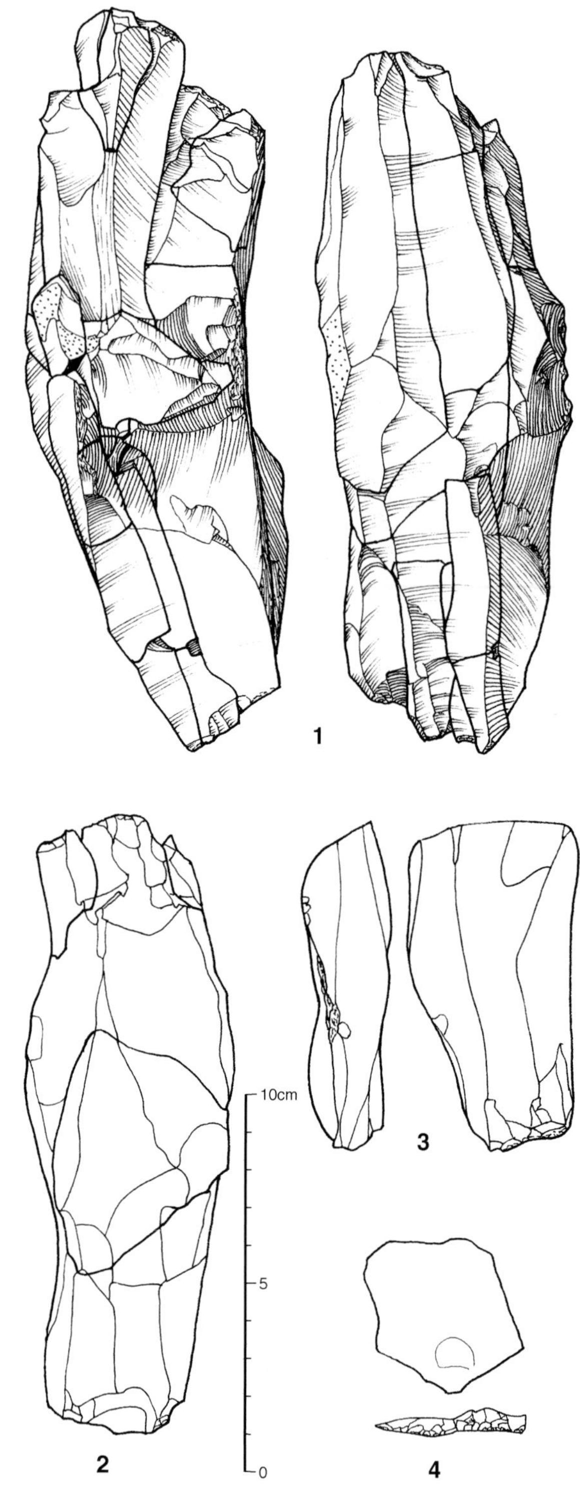

Figure 4.21 Avington VI: 1: refitted group 119 at a late and 2: later stage in the reduction sequence. 3: hinge terminated blade; 4: core rejuvenation flake

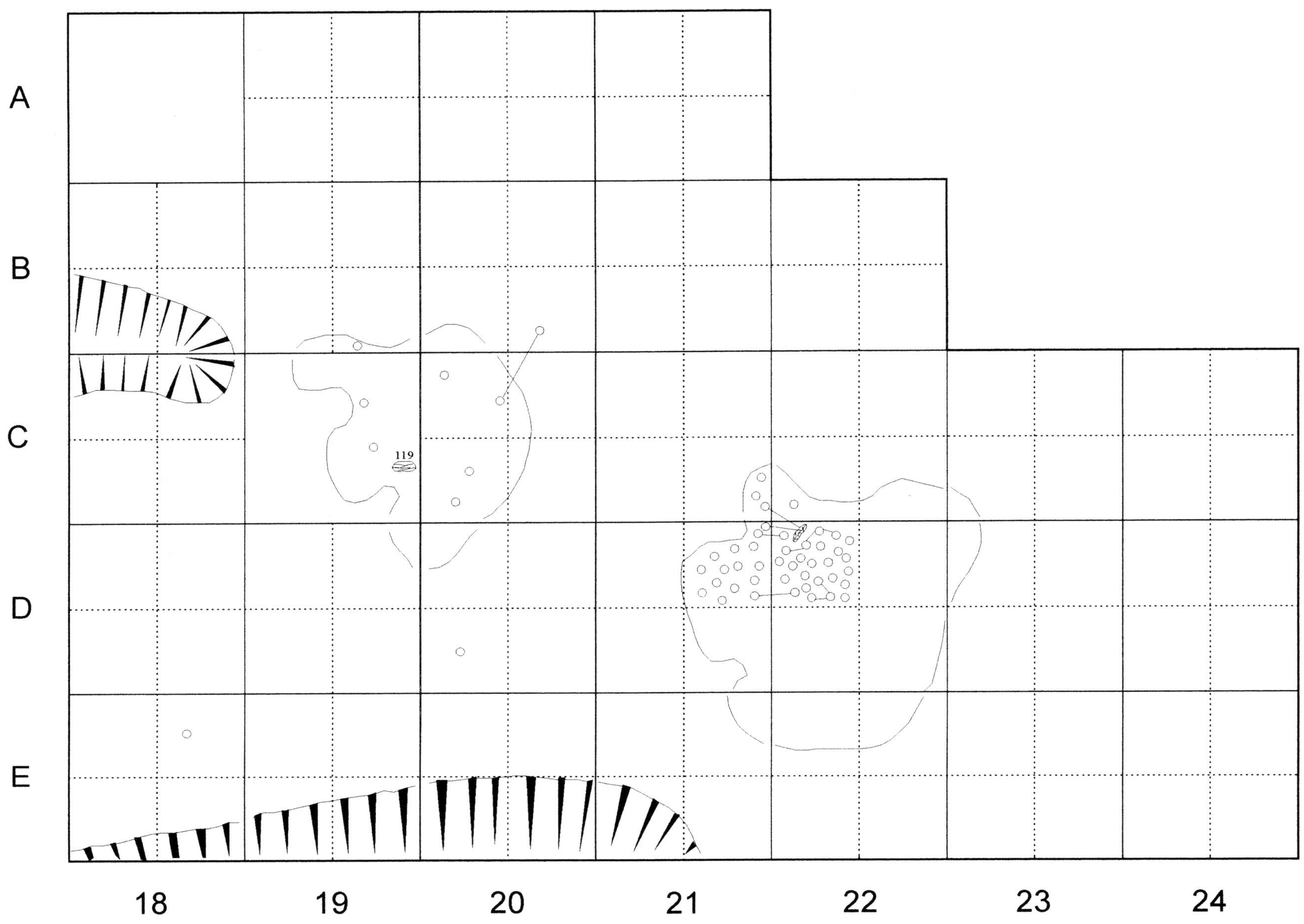

Figure 4.22 Avington VI: distribution of the refitted artefacts in group 119

Group 175

Although much of this group is missing, the reduction sequence can be ascertained with some confidence. There are 34 removals that have been refitted. The original flint nodule had a maximum dimension of at least 280mm, possibly as much as 300mm or even more; the other two dimensions were probably 50 and 120mm respectively. This compares with the core in its final form which measures 90 x 40 x 50mm, that is to say the core represents some 10% of the original nodule by volume. The raw material appears to have been a piece of tabular flint or at least a flat nodule; this was worked down an edge rather than across a face. The thin, pale sand coloured cortex has small surface irregularities which are unlikely to have survived significant abrasion such as entrainment in a body of gravel and suggests a probable source in the clay-with-flints. This suggestion is further strengthened by the occurrence of occasional ancient fracture surfaces. It is interesting to note that the flint knapper was prepared to use such a comparatively thin nodule.

The reduction sequence was divided between the two major concentrations; it began in the area of transect C22 and ended in the area of transect C20 (**Fig. 4.23**). The initial preparation of the crests would appear to have taken place outside the excavated area since no flakes have been found to refit either of the crested blades. This could equally be attributed to the fact that some of these flakes must have been small and consequently difficult to find among the mass of debitage but this is not an entirely satisfactory explanation as some were obviously much larger and would have been much easier to identify (**Fig. 4.24: 3, 4**). It is also worth noting that a short series of small flakes removed later in the sequence have been located and refitted, (**Fig. 4.25**). Initial preparation outside the area is thus the preferred explanation for the absence of these first removals.

The first flakes to have been detached during the reduction sequence that have been refitted were struck from the upper part of the core prior to the removal of the upper crested blade, (**Fig. 4.24**). This was followed by the removal of the upper crested blade. Before the second lower crested blade was struck, this time from the lower platform, there was some trimming of the crest (**Fig. 4.24**). The exact reduction sequence at this stage is, in fine detail, somewhat problematic but it is likely that the two crested blades and the concomitant blades proceeded broadly simultaneously with striking from both platforms, perhaps the upper leading. It cannot be stated with any certainty how many blades were produced during this initial exploitation of the nodule. Although the conjoin of the two crested blades is extensive, and the sequence relating the upper crested blade ultimately to the core is beyond doubt, the precise orientation of the two crested blades to the core is subject to some error because there is a gap between the crested blades and the underlying refits (**Fig. 4.24**). However, the extent of this gap and what it represents in terms of missing blades is open to question. Presumably the blades were satisfactory and were removed for use elsewhere. This part of the reduction sequence was ended by the production of two blades, one from each platform, both of which broke as they detached (**Figs 4.24; 4.25**). Thereafter, problems appear to have become more prevalent; probably because of an inherent fault in the flint the removals either broke or terminated short but the missing removals presumably equate with usable products. **Figures 4.24–4.25** illustrate this first stage of the reduction sequence, all the removals were found in the area of transect C22, concentration 2.

At this point, the core appears to have been moved to the area of transect C20. In this second phase, the initial action appears to have been the removal of a large part of the upper end of the core, perhaps in an attempt to remove the flawed flint that was causing the problems to which reference has already been made (**Fig. 4.25: 4**). Following this, after quite extensive preparation of the upper part of the working face during which several, perhaps many, spalls and bladelets up to 30mm in length were removed (**Fig. 4.25: 4**), three blades were produced which have been refitted. There then followed further reshaping of the upper platform and an attempt to strike from the new platform, however, this was unsuccessful and a series of flakes was detached to correct this problem (**Fig. 4.25**). After what was probably a final attempt to make use of the core, in which most or all of the intended removals either terminated short or failed to separate from the core, the lower end of the core was detached, again significantly shortening the length of core. Abandonment followed immediately or very soon after this point. It is interesting to note that whereas the core itself and most of the removals from this later stage of reduction were found in transect C20, a number of removals came from transect D20 (**Fig. 4.23**), so it is possible that the final stage embodies more than one attempt to utilise the core.

Of the 34 removals refitted, 7 or about 20%, appear to have broken during detachment. However, if allowance is made for those removals which have not been recovered then the percentage would be smaller, possibly some 12–15%, which would make it one of the more successful cores. Both of the crested blades exhibit heavy bruising, each crested blade having an extensive length of such bruising along each of its two edges. One crested blade had fractured into two and the nature of this fracture is suggestive of breakage caused by it being used to deliver a blow to a hard object (**Fig. 4.23: 3**).The other crested blade was found in three pieces; again, at least one of the fractures is consistent with its use as a hammer. No other removals from this core exhibited bruising.

Details of the distribution of this series are shown in **Figure 4.23**. The great majority were recovered from the Long Blade horizon or immediately below it, one removal and two fragments came from just above but the conjoins to these two fragments also came from the Long Blade horizon; the outstanding exception was a large fragment of a large blade which was found whilst stripping the overburden from above the Mesolithic layer (1979), that is at a depth range of 400–700mm, despite the large vertical displacement it was still within 1–2m of its likely original deposition point. The condition of this blade fragment suggests that it had been displaced for some considerable time. As previously noted, the binary horizontal distribution is consistent with the core being first worked in the vicinity of transect C22 and then subsequently transferred to transect C20, the latter phase possibly incorporating some working in transect D20.

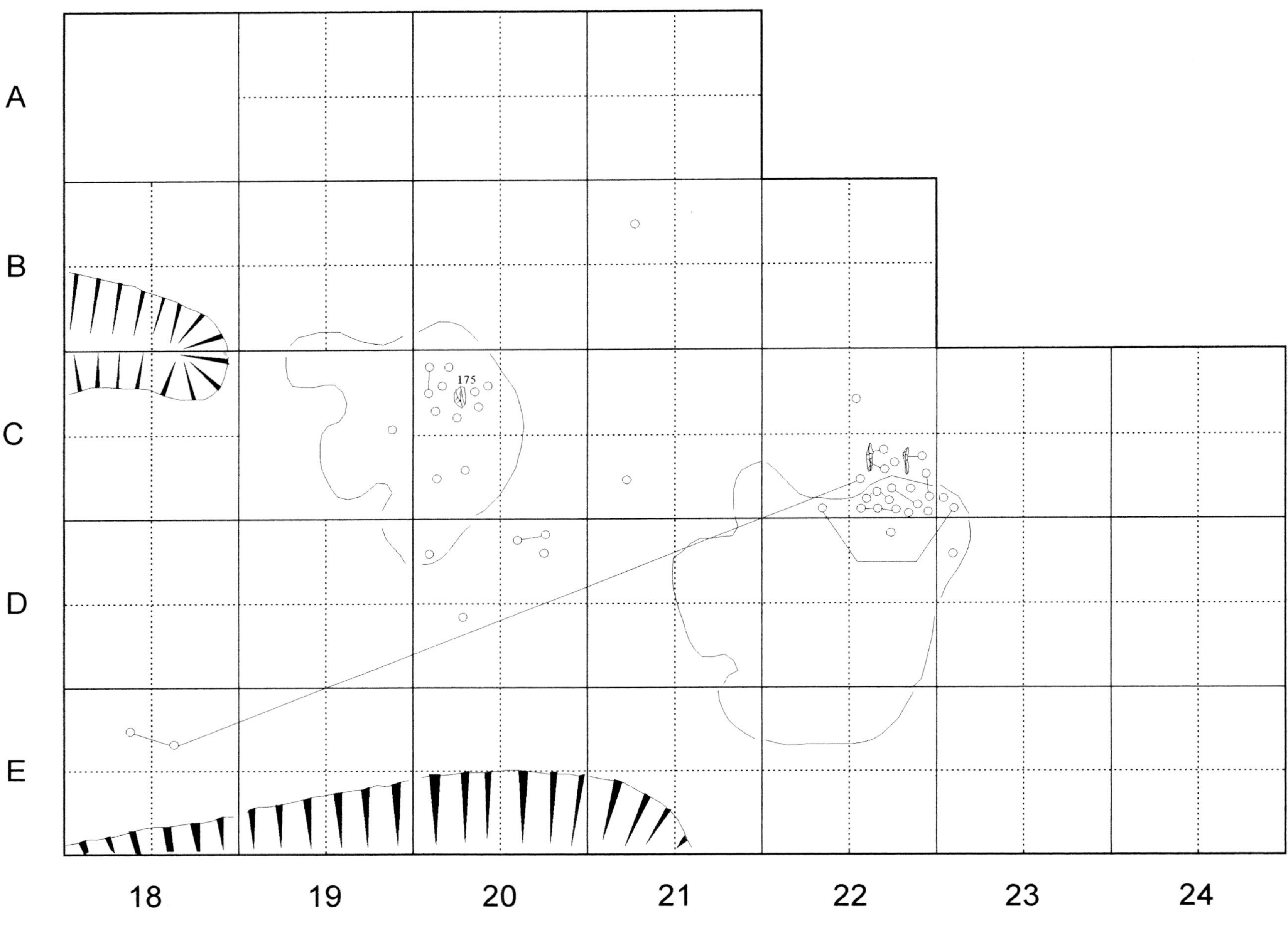

Figure 4.23 Avington VI: distribution of the refitted artefacts in group 175

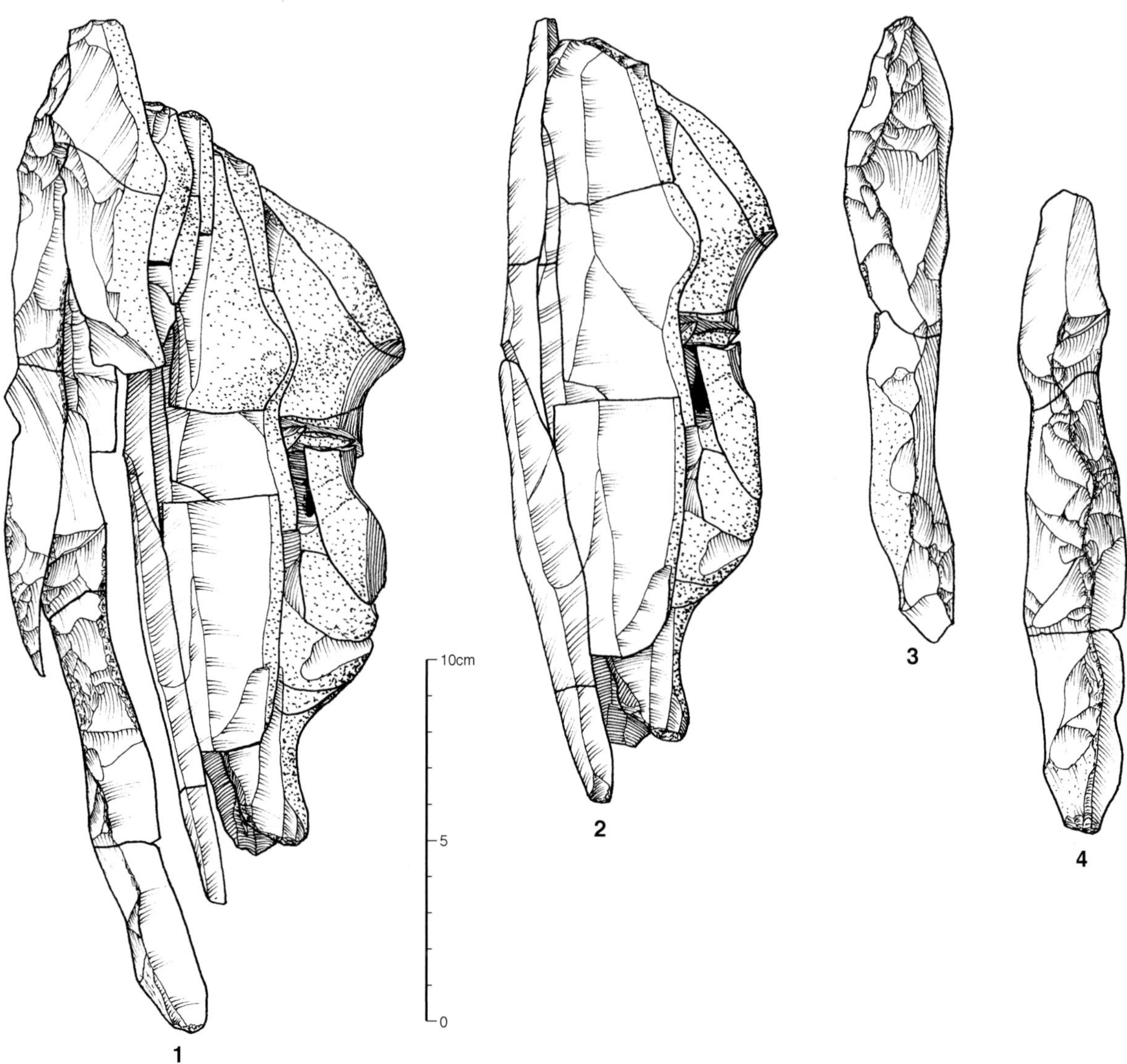

Figure 4.24 Avington VI: refitted group 175 at an early stage in the reduction sequence showing two crested blades

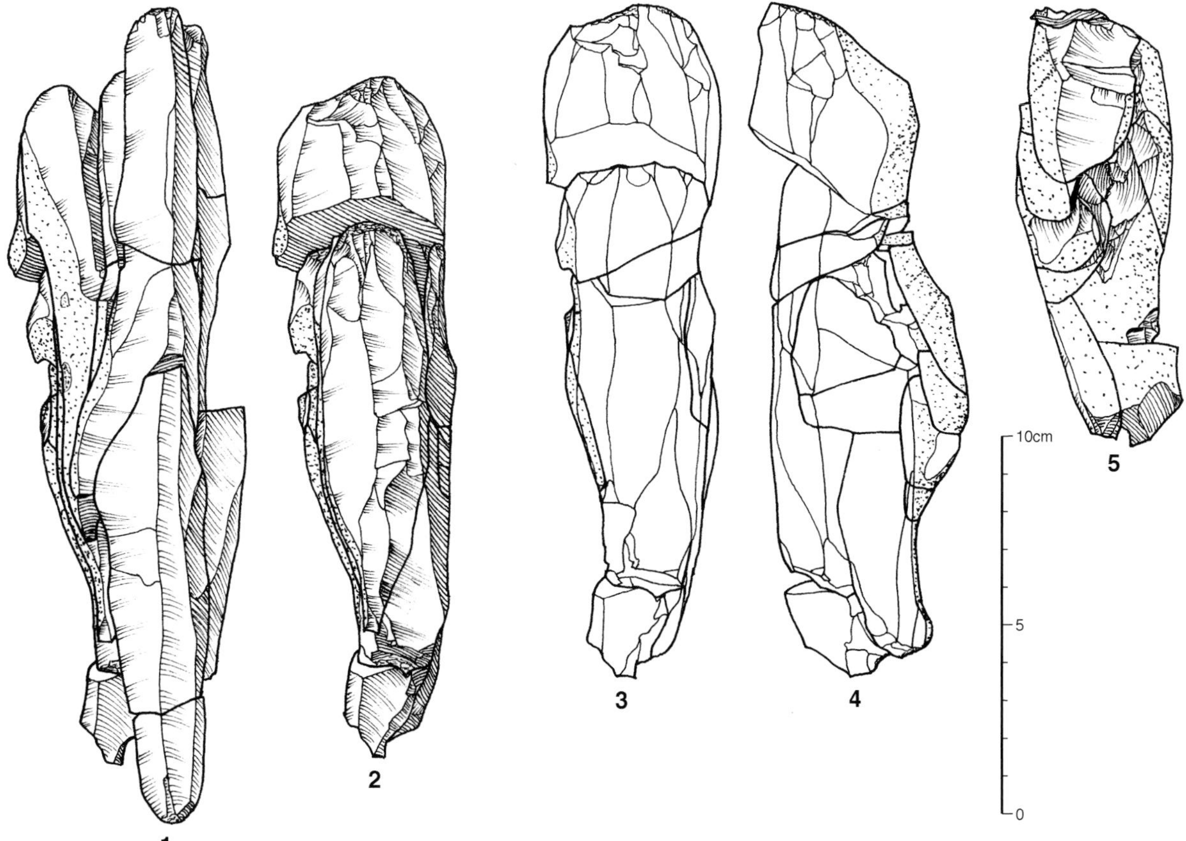

Figure 4.25 Avington VI: refitted group 175; 1: at an intermediate stage and 2: at a later stage in the reduction sequence; 3-4: crested blades

Group 204

As with most of these series, there are substantial gaps in this group (**Fig. 4.26**) and this could be taken as indicative of phases of working beyond the excavated area. However, it takes only one missing item to break a particular sequence and leave other items 'floating' and this series illustrates this particular aspect of refitting well. It occurs in a conjoined sequence in which the crested blade and four Long Blades, each in part cortical, conjoin to a core on which the cortex is contiguous with the refitted blades. It might be presumed that these partially cortical blades were just left behind as waste products but varyingly bruised edges indicate that they were used. However, this part of the sequence floats because the removals from the other side of the crested blade have not been refitted and this area of the nodule's cortex is not represented. Two conjoining Long Blades which retain substantial amounts of similar cortex and apparently identical flint were recognised but could not be added to the series as a whole. Such 'broken' sequences suggest that artefacts were removed for use elsewhere.

Although incompletely refitted the original nodule is likely to have been approximately 220 x 70 x 120mm and was somewhat flattened in shape with an irregular outline. There is some fine surface detail to the cortex which is thin, about 0.1mm, and rather nondescript in colour. Internally, the nodule was variable; in part the fracture surfaces have a matt appearance and a slightly abrasive feel which could be due to a rougher microcrystalline texture than is normal but the rest of the nodule has the more usual glassy character. Overall, the quality appears to have been satisfactory as comparatively few of the removals fragmented during knapping.

As in the case of group 118 there seems to have been an initial phase of working on the 'back' of the nodule (**Fig. 4.27, top row centre**) but the removals are missing. Despite careful searching, no refits could be found for the preparation of the crested blade; even the larger removals could not be located. The first removal identified is the crested blade itself, which apparently shattered into four segments, three of which have been found. This fragmentation must have occurred when the crested blade was struck as unlike the succeeding blades, it shows no sign of bruising. The two succeeding Long Blades were detached from either side of the crested blade; both were found broken in two and three fragments respectively, but both exhibit heavy bruising and the fracture pattern is consistent with them having broken when in use as hammers. The Long Blade formed by the removal of these three initial blades and subsequently detached has not been found presumably because it was a successful product removed for use. A significant volume of flint is missing and must represent several, perhaps many, removals; one non-cortical blade, 100mm long has been refitted, as well as a short series of semi-cortical blades linking the crested blade to the core. There are also some comparatively short removals struck from the lower platform which interleave with the longer removals from the upper platform (**Fig. 4.26**). The missing blades are assumed to be successful products removed for use. Up to this point, of the 11 refits identified, 7 had been struck from the upper platform and range in length from 100–190mm, the other 4 came from the lower platform and had a maximum length of 80mm. Just how many blades are missing must be a matter for speculation but a reasonable estimate would be 5–10 in total, struck from both platforms (**Fig. 4.26**).

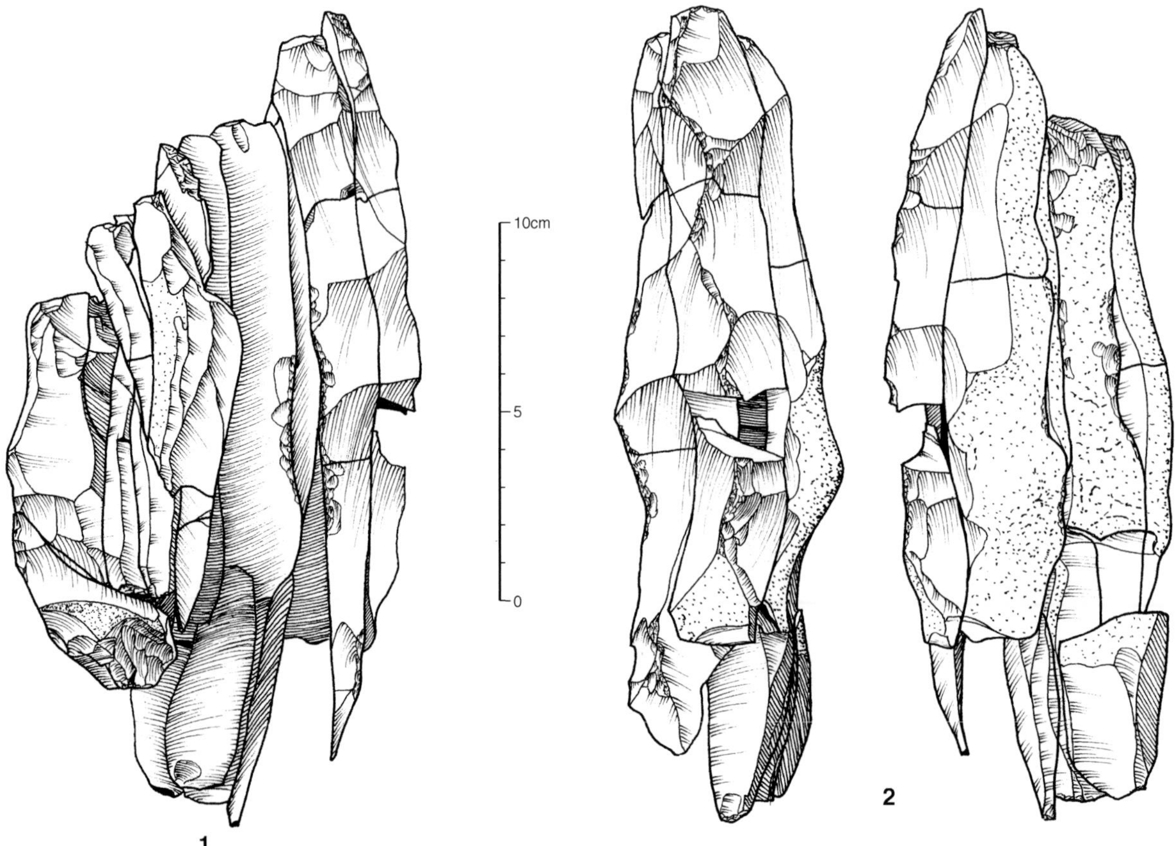

Figure 4.26 Avington VI: maximum extent of refitting on group 204

All of the refits discussed so far came from an area centred on transect D22NE, at about this point in the reduction sequence the core was transferred to concentration 1, transects C19, 20; at this stage the appearance of the core was as in **Figures 4.26: 1**. Either at the end of the preceding stage or at the start of this second stage blades began to terminate short; one such failure was recovered from transect C19 (**Fig. 4.27 right**) and some alternate flaking (**Fig. 4.27**) was used in an effort to resolve this problem. At about the same time the 'lower' platform was subjected to reshaping, possibly changing its orientation and at least 8 flakes were removed; 6 of these have been refitted (**Fig. 4.27**). After this, a series of removals involving both platforms was detached; 14 have been refitted of which eight came from the 'upper' platform and six from the 'lower'. In this part of the sequence nothing from the 'lower' platform appears to have been retained for use, the six refits appear to be all that were produced; there are a few pieces struck from the 'upper' platform that are missing (**Fig. 4.27**). In addition to these removals there was some working of the side of the core but no refits have been found (**Fig. 4.26**). There is one final fragmented removal which conjoined and fitted directly and wholly on the core. This removal presumably fell apart when it was struck. It was found in transect D22NW and the core was found nearby. It shows signs of further unsuccessful attempts to strike removals from the other platform (**Fig. 4.27**) which probably represent the last efforts to get blanks off it.

As previously noted, three of the large blades struck early in the sequence exhibited extensive bruising, just how much of the blade was bashed away may be appreciated in **Fig. 4.26: 2**. A further blade in this sequence also exhibited signs of use and this too was broken, the fragment with the evidence of use was found with the main group in transect D22, concentration 2 but the other fragment, of comparable size, was found in transect A19. This is an unusual degree of separation; assuming the blade broke in use, it may well have been that on breaking the one fragment fell in the area of use whereas the other fragment, initially retained in the hand, was tossed to one side. Of the 34 removals in the sequence of refits, six may be identified as having broken during knapping and all but one of these failures occurred in the second main stage of the reduction sequence. By comparison with other groups such as 195 described above (p. 48), the incidence of breakage during knapping is relatively low.

The distribution of the artefacts in group 204 may be seen in **Fig. 4.28**. Most of the removals occur in two relatively closely knit groups with the core itself between the two. There is probably little significance to be attached to the few pieces which appear dispersed; the separation of the two fragments of an utilised blade was discussed above. However, a small blade found in transect B19 and a larger blade from transect E21 may represent items that became displaced through use although neither show obvious edge damage.

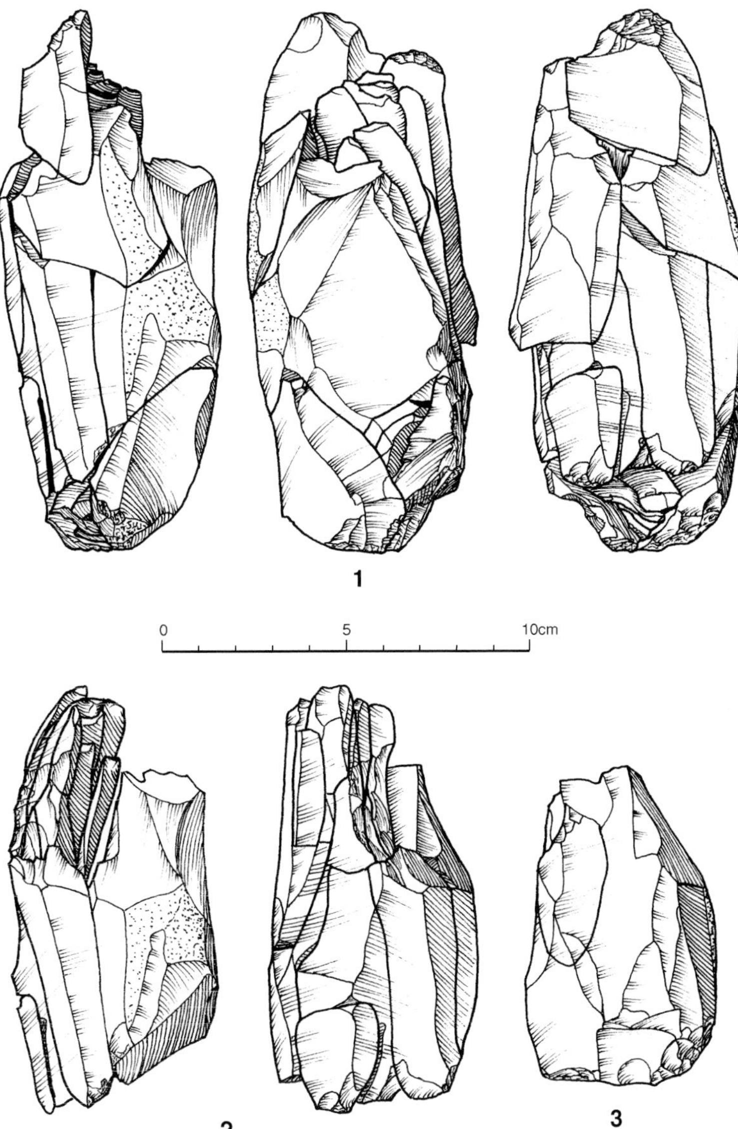

Figure 4.27 Avington VI: refitted group 204; 1: at an intermediate stage in the reduction sequence; 2: at a later stage; 3: last stage of core 204 with one refit

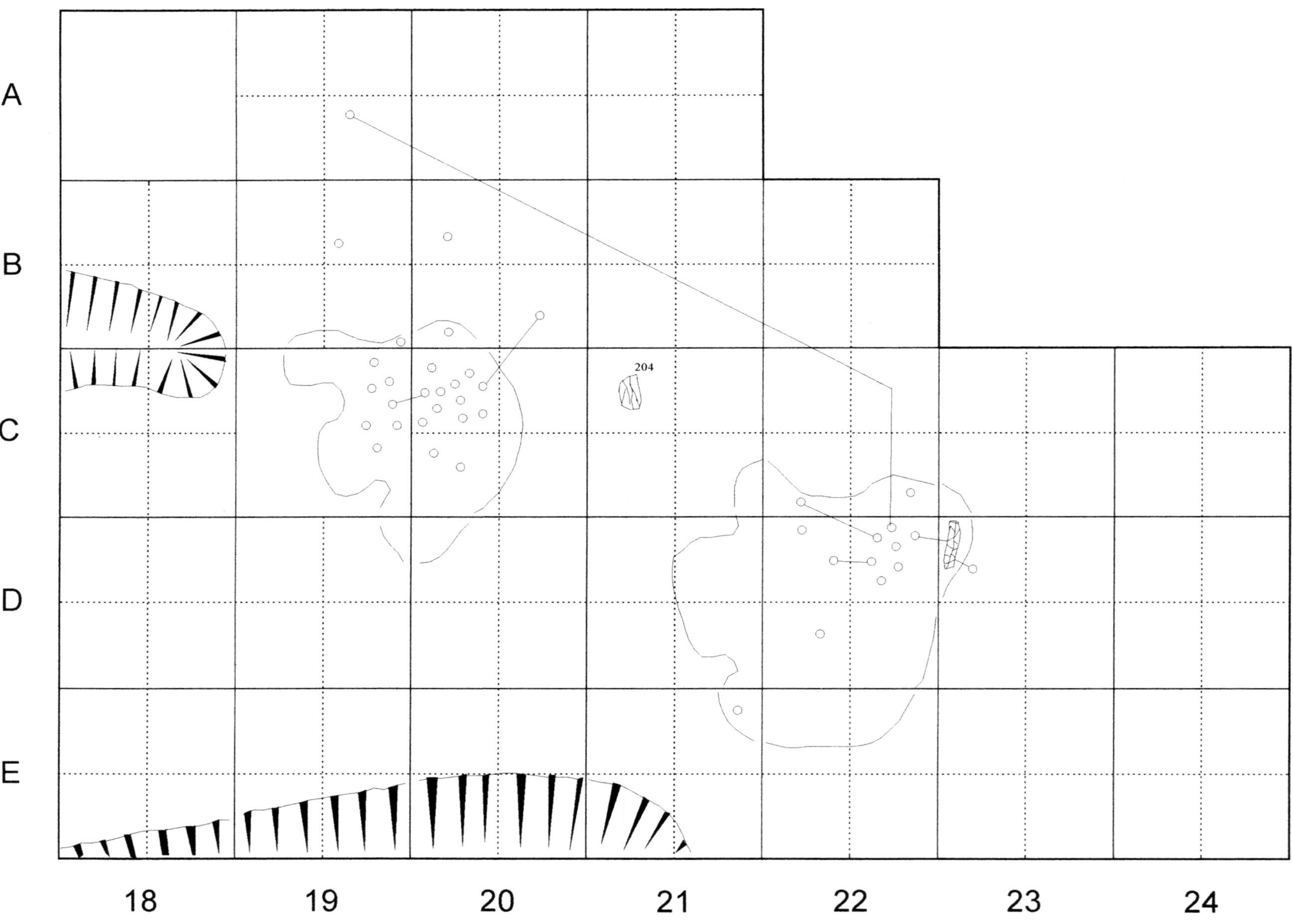

Figure 4.28 Avington VI: distribution of the refitted artefacts in group 204

Group 279

This is an unusually complete group despite the fact that there are some missing pieces. These have made the reconstruction of the original nodule difficult at a purely mechanical level because although the conjoins can be positively identified, only the use of a strong adhesive would have permitted secure assembly and this was felt to be unacceptable. Consequently, the drawings do not necessarily show all the refits appropriate to that stage of the reduction sequence and one or two refits may be a millimetre or so away from their true orientation.

There are 59 removals in this group; they include most of the cortical removals and, unusually, much of the preparation of the two crested blades. Despite the size of the original nodule, little of useful size or value appears to have been produced in the early stages of the reduction sequence. There are several missing blades and these are presumed to have been removed for use. The actual reduction sequence is detailed below. Originally, the flint nodule was at least 250mm in length with width and thickness of 120 and 70mm respectively. It was regular, rounded and flattened in shape. Although variable at between 2–4mm, the cortex was of above average thickness for the site; in part the sandy coloured outer surface was smooth but over much of the nodule it was deeply pock-marked. As a result of patination, the various removals generally took on a particularly characteristic appearance which greatly facilitated the refitting. Indeed, the distinctiveness of this flint could indicate a source not commonly exploited and, judging by the external appearance of the nodule, a clay-with-flint deposit would be the most-likely source.

It seems likely that the flint nodule was brought to the site with few or no previous removals and the conjoining artefacts interleave with each other in such a way that there is little if any doubt as to the outline of the reduction sequence. Two removals have been refitted to the upper platform which was created first; following this several, largely cortical, flakes of varying size were detached (**Fig. 4.29**). What would appear to have been a large flake struck from the nodule adjacent to those just described has not been found for refitting despite extensive searching of the assemblage. Such missing removals may indicate that strategically positioned flakes were struck at the source of the nodule, in part to test its quality. The scar left by the missing large flake was subsequently used as the platform from which the preparatory flakes of the first crested blade were struck. This latter process occurred in two stages. Firstly, a few small cortical flakes were detached and then a large non-cortical flake was struck using the first platform, this flake broke and at least two fragments are missing from it (**Fig. 4.29**). After this the major part of the cresting was completed (**Fig. 4.29: 1–3**). All of the removals identified so far form a close-knit group centred on transects C19–20, concentration 1.

At this point the embryonic core was remodelled by the removal of a substantial part of the upper section, replacing the first platform by another sloping in a different direction (compare **Figures 4.29: 3 and 4**). Why this remodelling took place is not obvious although the ventral surfaces of the larger flakes exhibit a degree of irregularity and possibly the quality of the flint in this zone of the nodule was regarded as substandard. The heavy flake detached in this reshaping was recovered from transect E19; there is evidence that it had been used as a hammerstone and this may account for its greater dispersal.

Quite what happened after the forming of the crested blade and the reshaping of the platform is a matter for conjecture. What is certain is that the crested blade and subsequent removals were found in an area centred on transect D22 in concentration 2. Thus there is a clearly documented case of a crested blade that was prepared in one area and, in all probability, struck from the core in a different area. It has already been noted that in the refitted groups including crested blades described above, there have been no examples where preparatory flakes have been refitted to the crested blades, despite diligent searching. The presence of some small cresting beyond the point at which the crested blade terminated suggests that it failed to reach the full length intended (**Fig. 4.30: 1**). It also fragmented into two or possibly three sections as it detached. The positioning of the crested blade on the flint nodule appears to correspond with a natural ridge.

Immediately following this first crested blade, work began on the second crested blade; this was diametrically opposed to the first and was struck from a platform formed at the lower end of the nodule as figured (**Fig. 4.29 lower left**). Like the first example, it too fragmented but only the distal section has been recovered (**Fig. 4.30: 5**). As with the first example, a large flake was detached and the scar formed used as a platform for the striking of several flakes, most of which have been refitted (**Fig. 4.29: 2**). It is interesting to note that this basic procedure of removing a large flake to enable a series of smaller flakes to be struck, resulting in an essentially one-sided crested blade, has been previously described in group 150. The large flake detached as the first stage in the formation of the second crested blade has not been found in contrast to the smaller flakes which were recovered; neither have the flakes which generated the initial lower striking platform (**Figs 4.29: 4; 4.30**). It is always possible that there were uses for larger flakes and as such they could have been removed but again it is suggested that there may have been preparatory work on this lower end of the nodule at the raw material source site.

After the second crested blade had been detached, the zone of cortex between the two crested blades was removed by flakes struck from the lower platform (**Fig. 4.30: 1**). This was followed by some detachments from the upper platform where three removals have been refitted: these include a pointed blade which was found further away in the area of transects A–B 21 where it may have been used although there are no obvious signs of use damage; a squat blade that probably represents an intended long blade which terminated short and thirdly a typical piece of blade production debris. At this point the lower platform was reworked and this was followed by a lengthy series of removals struck mostly from the new platform; of the nine removals struck from the lower platform and refitted, three are broken. One blade was found in transect A19, although not exhibiting obvious signs of use it was 90mm in length and originally possessed fine sharp edges ideal for cutting softer materials. When refitted, the removals from the lower platform indicate the existence of a further two or three significant removals that have not been recovered. In contrast the single large removal struck from the upper platform clearly indicates that several others were struck from this platform at about this stage and these were presumably removed for use elsewhere (**Fig. 4.40: 2**). This stage of the reduction sequence was brought to an end by the removal of a rejuvenating flake from the lower platform.

By now, the core had been reduced in length from an initial 240mm to one of 105mm. During this time there is evidence of attempts to produce blades which would have been about 150mm long but there is little or no evidence that such blades were successfully produced. Indeed, up to this point comparatively few useful products appear to have been struck. In the final phase a flake was struck across the face of the core (**Fig. 4.30: 3** lower middle left-hand side) and this was followed by several removals struck from the lower platform, of which six have been refitted. One of these six is a pointed blade, 80mm long, found in transect D20; as with the previous examples it would have served well for the cutting of softer materials. Three refits also indicate that use was also made of the upper platform during the final phase of reduction (**Fig. 4.30: 3**). However, the refitting shows clearly that this final phase yielded more than those pieces refitted and again these missing pieces are assumed to represent successful products. The core came to the end of its productive life when an attempt to detach a blade from the upper platform resulted in a plunging removal that virtually bisected the core (**Fig. 4.30: 4**). None of the removals in this group could be classed as a bruised edge flake or blade although, as noted above, one piece shows battering which suggests its use as a hammerstone.

The artefacts in this group were distributed in two essentially separate groups with the odd piece more widely dispersed (**Fig. 4.31**). Comment has already been made regarding the more dispersed pieces; they may well represent blanks that were utilised. The general distribution pattern overwhelmingly suggests that the nodule was first exploited in concentration 1 and was subsequently transferred to the area centred on D22 in concentration 2. This contrasts with several other nodules such as groups 118, 150, 175 and 204 which appear to have been worked first in the area of transect D22 and then moved to the area of transects C19–20. With respect to the vertical distribution, four pieces are recorded as coming from just above but close to the Long Blade horizon whereas seven pieces were found just below it.

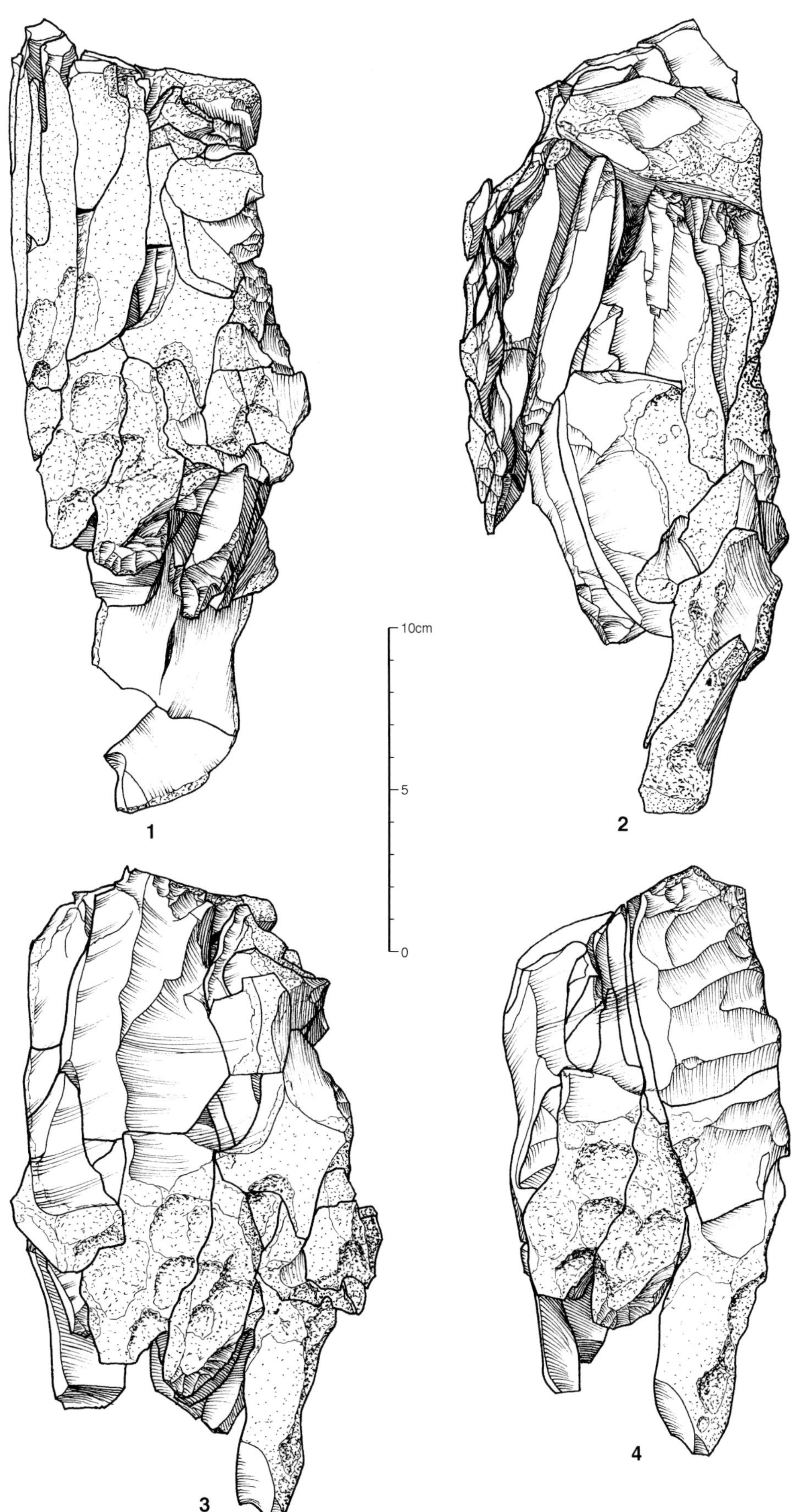

Figure 4.29 Avington VI: 1-2: maximum extent of refitting on group 279; 3: some cortical flakes removed; 4: crested blade evident after removal of more cortical flakes

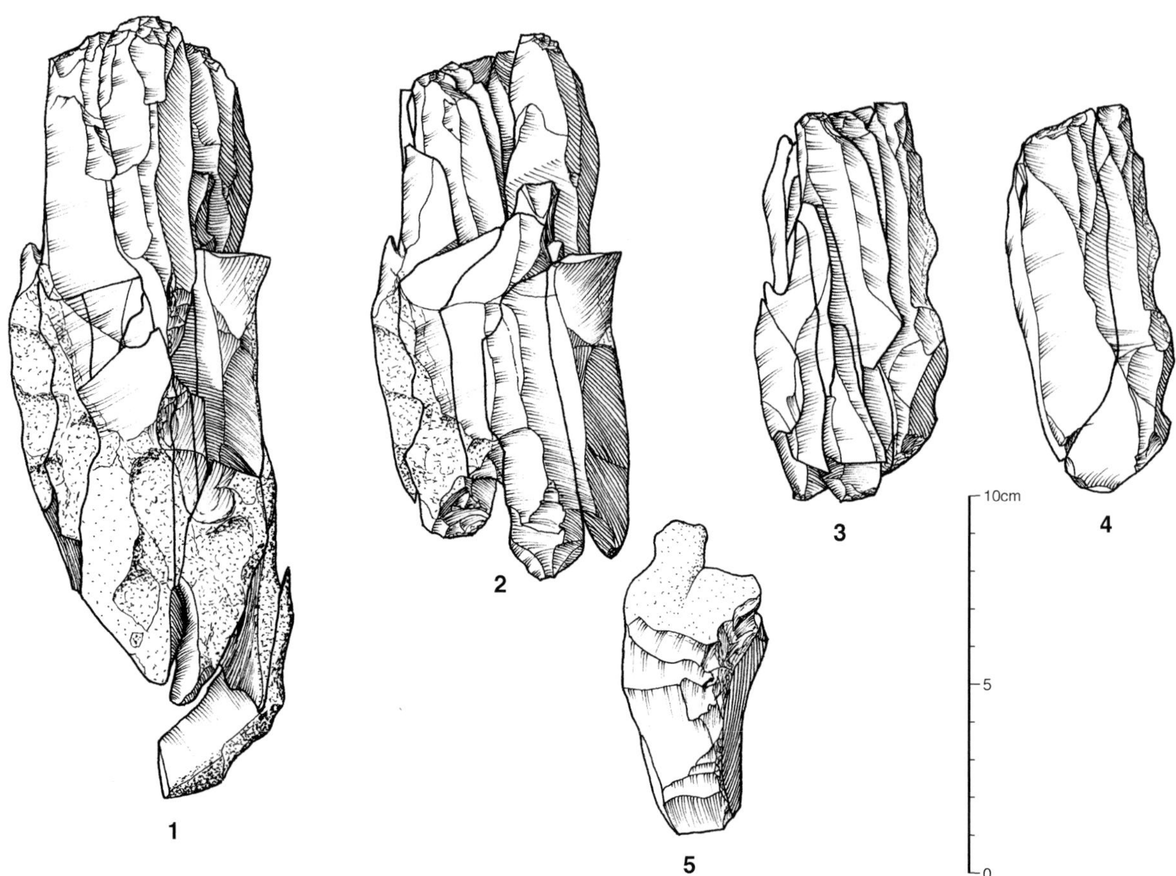

Figure 4.30 Avington VI: 1-2: refitted group 279 at an intermediate stage in the reduction sequence showing a fragment of a second crested blade; 3: dorsal view of crested fragment; 4: later stage of reduction; 5: core fragment refitted to plunged blade

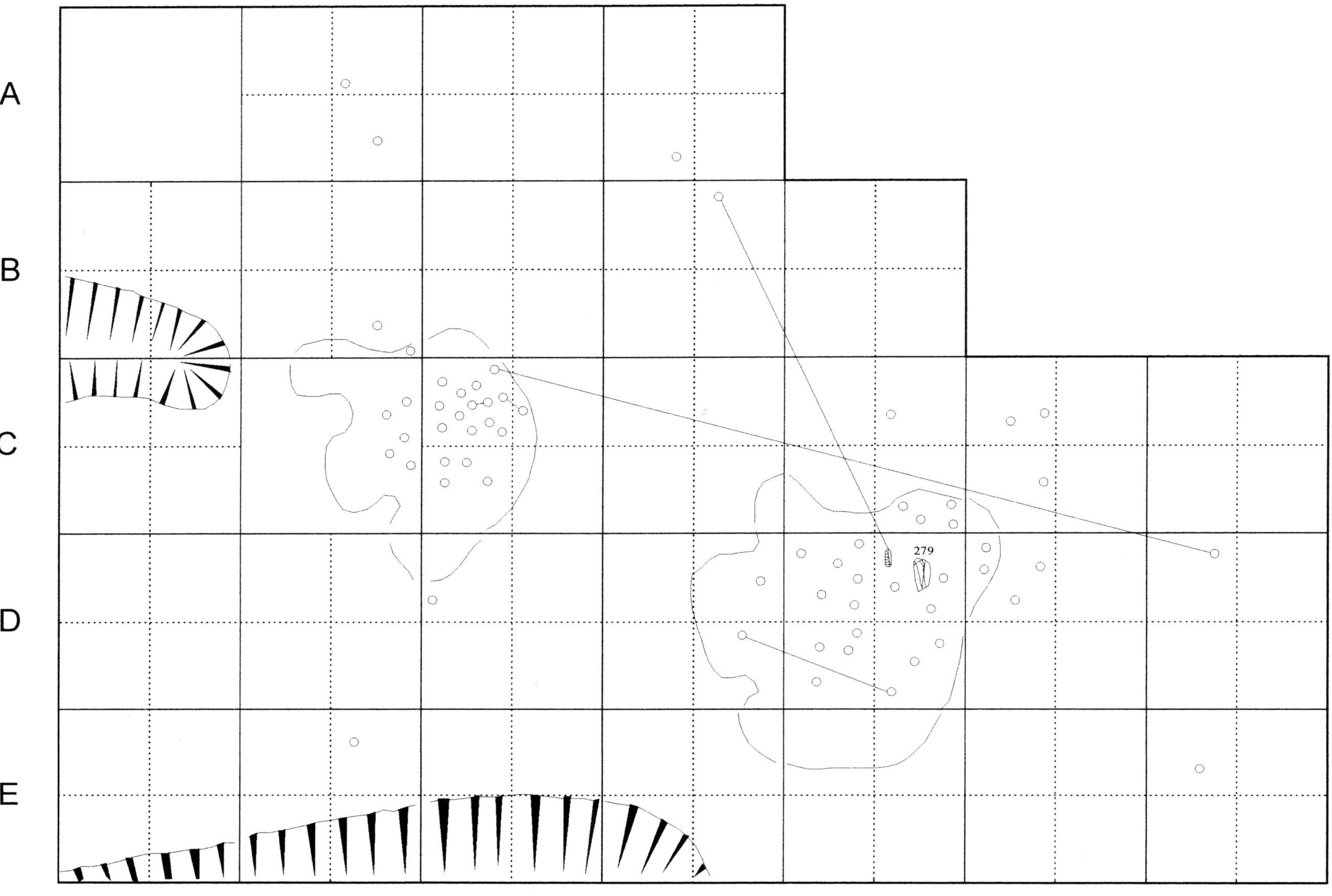

Figure 4.31 Avington VI: distribution of the refitted artefacts in group 279 showing conjoins within and outside concentrations 1 and 2

Group 211

As with so many of the previous series, the initial stages in the reduction of this core have not been refitted. Nonetheless, the dimensions of the original nodule may be estimated with some confidence: the minimum length would have been 160mm and the width and thickness 60–70mm, making it one of the smaller nodules. In shape it was somewhat irregular with hollows and protuberances, in cross-section rather rectangular. The cortex is thin, rarely exceeding 1mm and commonly less than 0.2mm in thickness; it exhibits fine surface detail that would presumably have been quickly erased in any abrasive situation; it is sandy in colour. On the evidence of refitting, the nodule was of variable knapping quality; as drawn, the lower part tended to fracture in an irregular manner and few, if any, successful removals were obtained; by contrast, the upper section appears to have been of better quality and several removals from this part have not been recovered. This dichotomy is reflected to some extent by the patination of the various refits. Despite being recovered from the same small area, the refits from the lower part of the core exhibit a different patination when compared to those from the upper section; the core itself exhibits a parallel differentiation. It may well be that at least in this instance the patination is reflecting differences in the physico-chemical constitution within the original flint nodule. Some confirmation that this might be the case is provided by experiments carried out by the writer in the early 1970s in which flint flakes, from the same nodule, were subjected to the action of alkaline solutions which caused a degree of differential reaction reflected by variation in the patina.

In its fully refitted condition, the nodule is far from complete, both the upper and lower striking platforms are present and much of the cortex is missing although what was to become the working face of the core is still largely cortical (**Fig. 4.32**). It may be estimated with some confidence that at least six–seven flakes had been previously struck including flakes 50–80mm in size. This initial flaking had revealed a small cavity lined with quartz crystals and some irregularity of fracture (**Fig. 4.32: 2**). Subsequently, a large blade/flake, approximately 120mm in length, was struck from an early lower platform but only a small distal fragment of this has been found (**Fig. 4.32: 3**). Following this several blanks were detached, mostly from the upper platform, removing much of the remaining cortex (**Fig. 4.32: 3**). Of these seven removals, five appear to have fragmented as they were struck. During this early documented phase of the reduction sequence the upper platform was quite frequently rejuvenated although not all of the flakes have been recovered (**Fig. 4.32: 2**). It would appear that only one or two 'blades' were struck between these rejuvenations. It is likely that approximately 10 rejuvenation flakes of 20mm or greater were removed from the upper platform during the life of this core, seven have been recovered (**Fig. 4.32: 7**); retouch across the edge of the platform rather than down from the top of the working face is a common feature of this core.

At the end of this stage of the reduction sequence the lower platform was extensively reshaped (**Fig. 4.32: 5**). Not all of the removals have yet been located; it is estimated that three to five are missing from immediately under the early cortical series and these are therefore presumed to be successful products. There is no certain evidence that a crested blade was prepared and struck, certainly nothing resembling a crested blade has been refitted. The core continued in use, rather more removals being struck from the upper platform than from the lower; the upper refits tend to greater lengths, 50–95mm, as compared to those from the lower platform, 35–80mm, and the degree of irregularity and fracture is greater in those from the lower platform. There are eight refits struck from the upper platform, of which only one exhibits significant fracture; it is estimated that there are a further four removals that have not been found, the indications are that these were well formed blades. Of the seven refits struck from the lower platform, five are fragmentary and there appears to be little of consequence missing. Throughout this middle phase of the main part of the reduction sequence the upper platform continued to be rejuvenated, the lower platform was not rejuvenated at this stage. What may be regarded as the final phase of the reduction sequence involved three removals; one was a rejuvenating flake from the lower platform, the other two attempted blades, one from each platform. Prior to the attempt to strike from the upper platform, the platform was subject to retouch across its upper surface, such retouch has been observed to be more common on the larger cores. The removal from the lower platform so distorted the platform that no further attempts were made to strike from it and the core was abandoned (**Fig. 4.32: 6**).

None of the removals in this series exhibit bruised edges but this is not surprising since even the largest removals are small when compared to those used for most of the bruised edge blades. In view of the fact that the majority of the blades from this core are small, particular care was taken to check the microliths for possible conjoins but none refitted.

The distribution of this group of refits is notable in two respects. Firstly, the horizontal distribution is discrete (**Fig. 4.33**). All of the refits came from concentration 2: a few occurred in a small area of transect D22, the majority in the south-west quadrant of transect C22 and the remaining items were close to and presumably contiguous with and part of, this grouping. Secondly, the vertical dispersal is unusual as it is biased to the lower levels. As previously recorded, artefacts were separately recovered and recorded in a series of vertical units; after excavation of the Mesolithic Horizon, the bulk of the intervening layer was removed and this was followed by the preparation of the Long Blade horizon. After the clearance of the prepared and recorded Long Blade horizon, the zone immediately below it was excavated. Of the 35 removals in this series, not one was found above the prepared Long Blade horizon. However, 17 removals were recovered from below the main Long Blade horizon. Of the residual 18 removals, 15 came from the main Long Blade horizon and the other three are reconstructed removals which in all three cases result from fragments from both the main and lower levels being reunited and thus span the two divisions. This vertical distribution pattern could indicate that this core was one of the earlier cores at the site, assuming that the occupation sequence was not purely transitory. However, since the pieces are small, there is the possibility that they simply slipped down among the larger pieces. When this proposition is tested, there is no evidence that the larger items in this refitted sequence occur higher in the section than the smaller pieces: larger items were found below the main Long Blade horizon just as much as the smaller pieces. On balance therefore this sequence appears to be one of the earlier sequences at the site.

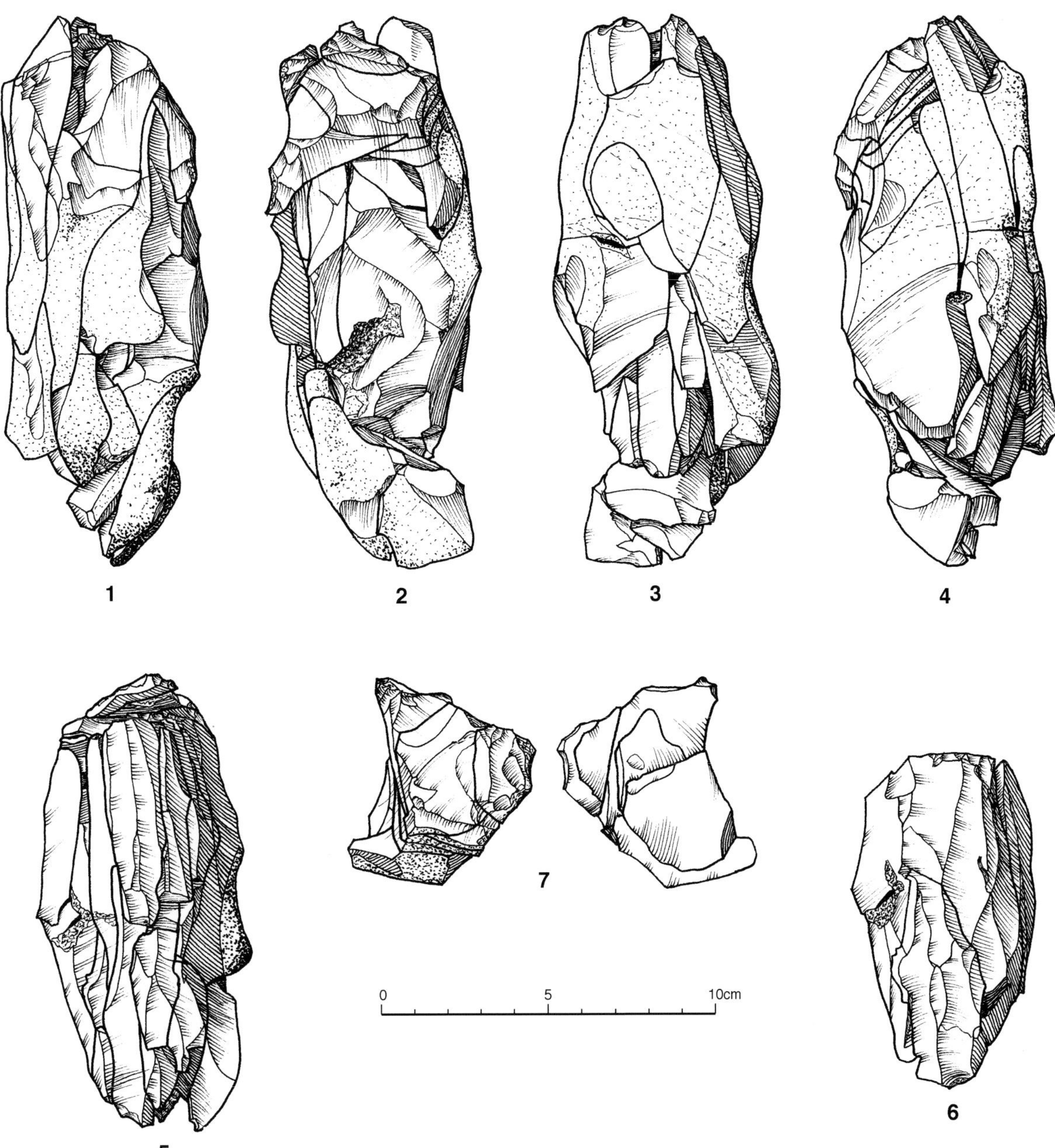

Figure 4.32 Avington VI: 1-4: maximum extent of refitting on group 211; 5-6: later stages in the reduction sequence; 7: seven conjoined core rejuvenation flakes

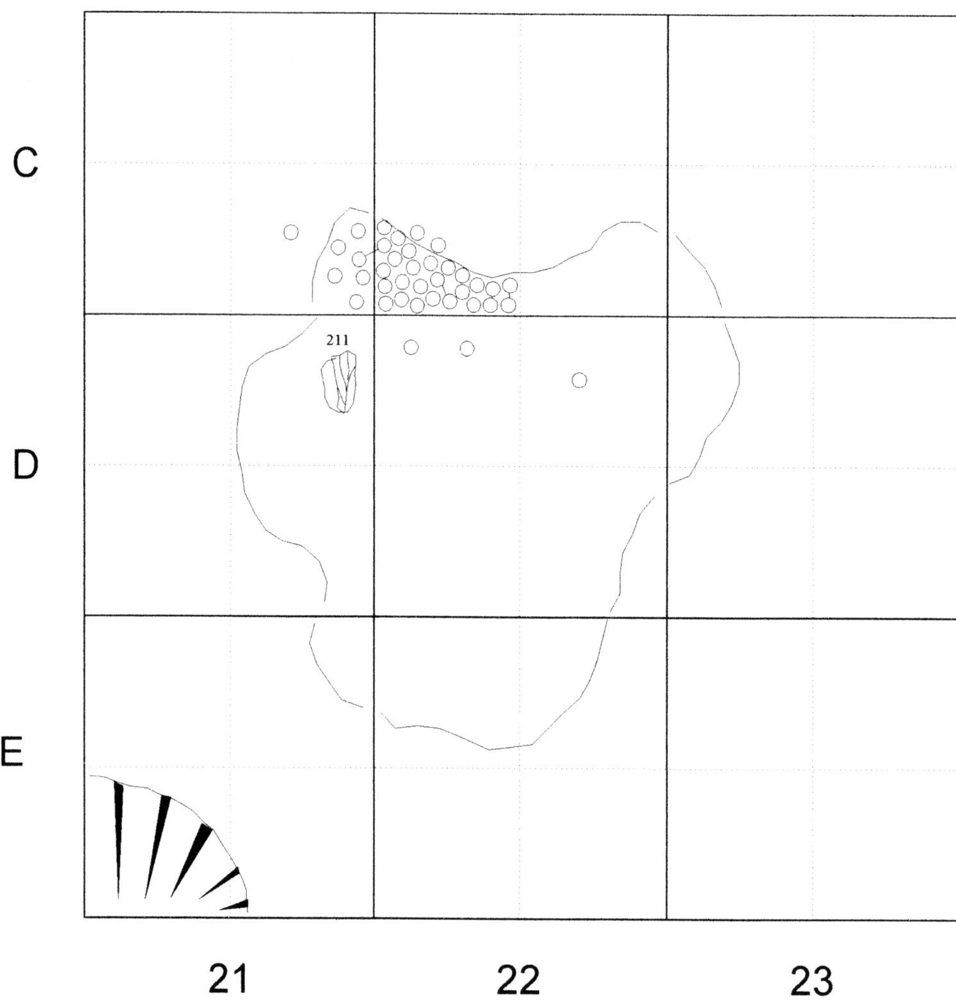

Figure 4.33 Avington VI: distribution of the refitted artefacts in group 211

Group 138

This group is another example from which the initial phase of working is missing; thereafter, the recovery is high and leaves the impression that little of value has been produced from this core. The exact size and shape of the original nodule must remain conjectural as little cortex was reconstituted when the group was put together. The minimum dimensions may be estimated at 170 x 100 x 70mm; it was probably rounded in shape. The cortex was thin, sandy coloured with greyish mottling; it also exhibited fine surface detail including faint raised lines. In these respects, group 138 closely resembles 211 as well as 204 and 195. The refitting shows that it was of poor knapping quality.

When all of the removals currently assigned to this group are refitted, they form a broadly wedge shape, as shown on the cross-section at the midpoint of the long axis (**Fig. 4.34: 6**). This shape appears to have been achieved by the removal of a few, perhaps only two, large flakes from the original nodule; the intersection of the two plane surfaces thus created was then refined to form the basis of the two crested blades (**Fig. 4.34: 1, 3**). During the initial working the two early platforms were also created. The first removal recovered and refitted is a crested blade struck from the lower platform; this was followed by a second crested blade struck from the upper platform, this latter removal displays the first signs of the material failure that was to be such a major feature of this group. The next removal was a rather irregular blade from under the second crested blade; this was found somewhat away from the main group of refits and may therefore have been used for some purpose. At this point the lower platform was brought back into use and a series of removals mostly 50–80mm in length, were detached; six of these have been refitted and one or two others are missing. A blade struck from the upper platform completes this first part of the reduction sequence, the crested blades and most of the immediately succeeding removals have been separately drawn (**Fig. 4.34: 2**). Even at this early stage, a major fault in the flint was manifesting itself, additionally, a large fossil, possibly an echinoderm, was revealed (**Fig. 4.34: 3**). Nevertheless knapping continued with removals from both platforms although not all have been refitted (**Fig. 4.34: 1, 3**). The major fault is clearly visible in figure **4.34: 2** running from centre-top and curving downwards to exit from the core lower left (as viewed). Further removals were detached and most of these have been refitted. They suggest that blades which in length would have been of the order of 100mm were the intended product but no such blade was produced; actual products include a blade ending prematurely in a hinge fracture (**Fig. 4.34: 9**) and an example that not only terminated short but which also fragmented in an extremely irregular manner, (**Fig. 4.34: 8**) other pieces are variously distorted due to the fault. The last removal from the core (**Fig. 4.34: 7**) does not have a simple ventral surface but exhibits two such surfaces intersecting at an included angle of 125–130°, the resulting scar rendered the core useless and it was abandoned (**Fig. 4.34: 5**).

The 28 removals refitted represent the greater part of those detached from the initial production of the crested blades to the abandonment of the core, they may be summarized in the following stages: one rejuvenating flake from the upper platform, there were others, possibly three or more, but all were small; three flakes struck to reshape the lower platform, where at least one additional flake is missing; 24 removals, all from the working face of the core, including 10 from the upper and 14 from the lower platform. There are only some four to six removals from this main part of the reduction sequence that remain unaccounted for. Of the 24 removals struck from the face of the core, 11 fragmented and several others were more or less severely distorted by the failure of the flint to knap truly. Retouch across the top of the platform is present in this sequence (**Fig. 4.34: 10**) and is shown by the four conjoined removals from the lower platform; a large removal (**Fig. 4.34: 7**) was detached from the upper platform. None of the removals in this sequence exhibit edge damage that may be described as bruising.

The core and nearly all of the refits were found in the minor concentration adjacent to concentration 1 in transects C19, 20 (**Fig. 4.35**). The group formed a scatter covering an area of approximately 1 x 0.5m, closely similar in dimensions to other such series. The two more dispersed pieces are a blade butt found in C20 and a 100mm blade found in C19. The former may have been deliberately broken in order to utilise the other section of the blade whereas the blank from C19 was that detached immediately after the crested blade and would certainly have had its uses. With regard to depth, the 28 removals are represented by 34 actual pieces of flint, as a result of breakage, 11 of the 34 are recorded as being recovered from below the prepared Long Blade horizon; none came from above.

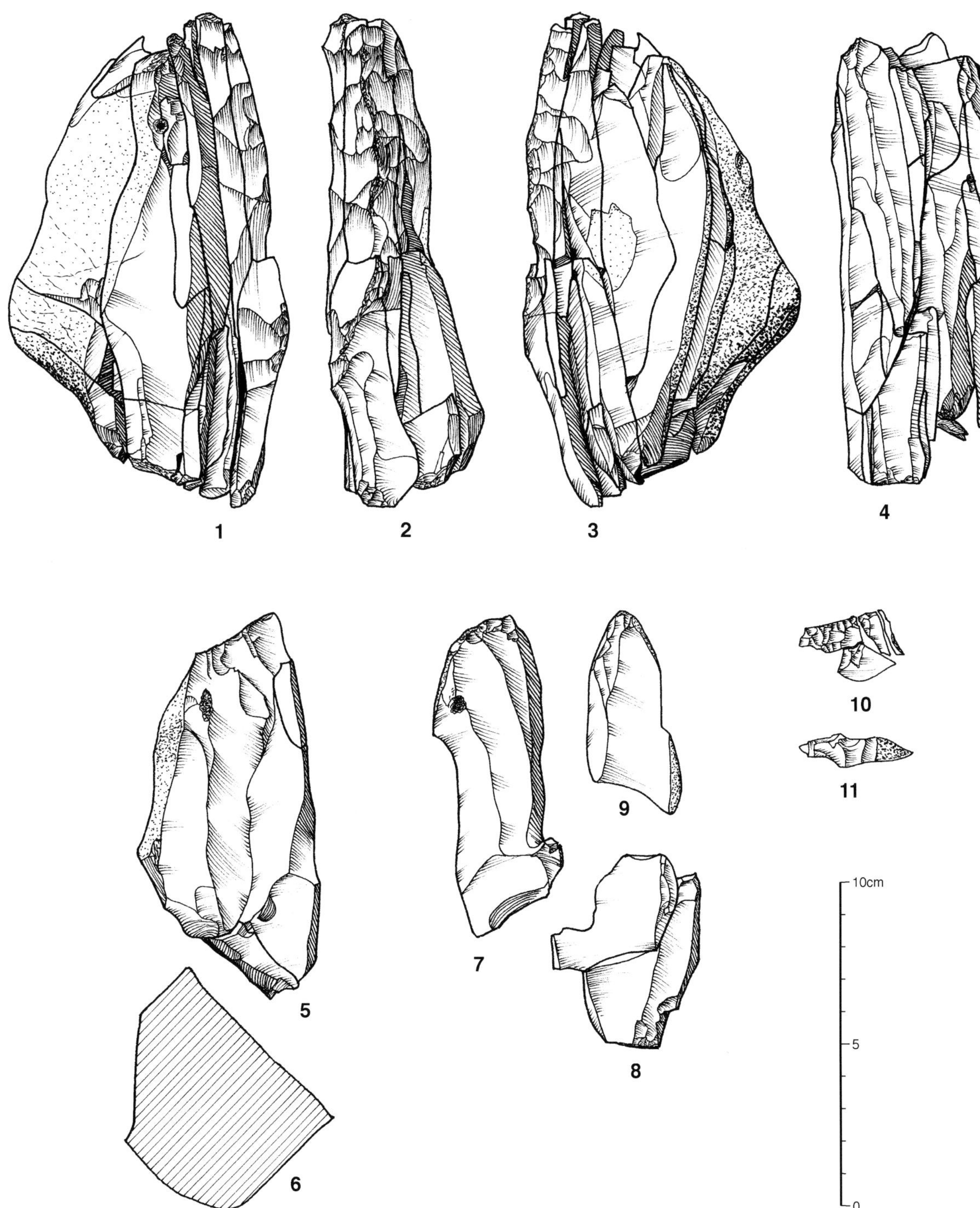

Figure 4.34 Avington VI: 1-4: maximum extent of refitting on group 138 showing crested blades and associated removals; 5-6: core 138; 7-8: hinge and step terminated blades (respectively); 9: fragmented blade; 10: view of facetted butts on four conjoined removals; 11: facetted butt of a large removal

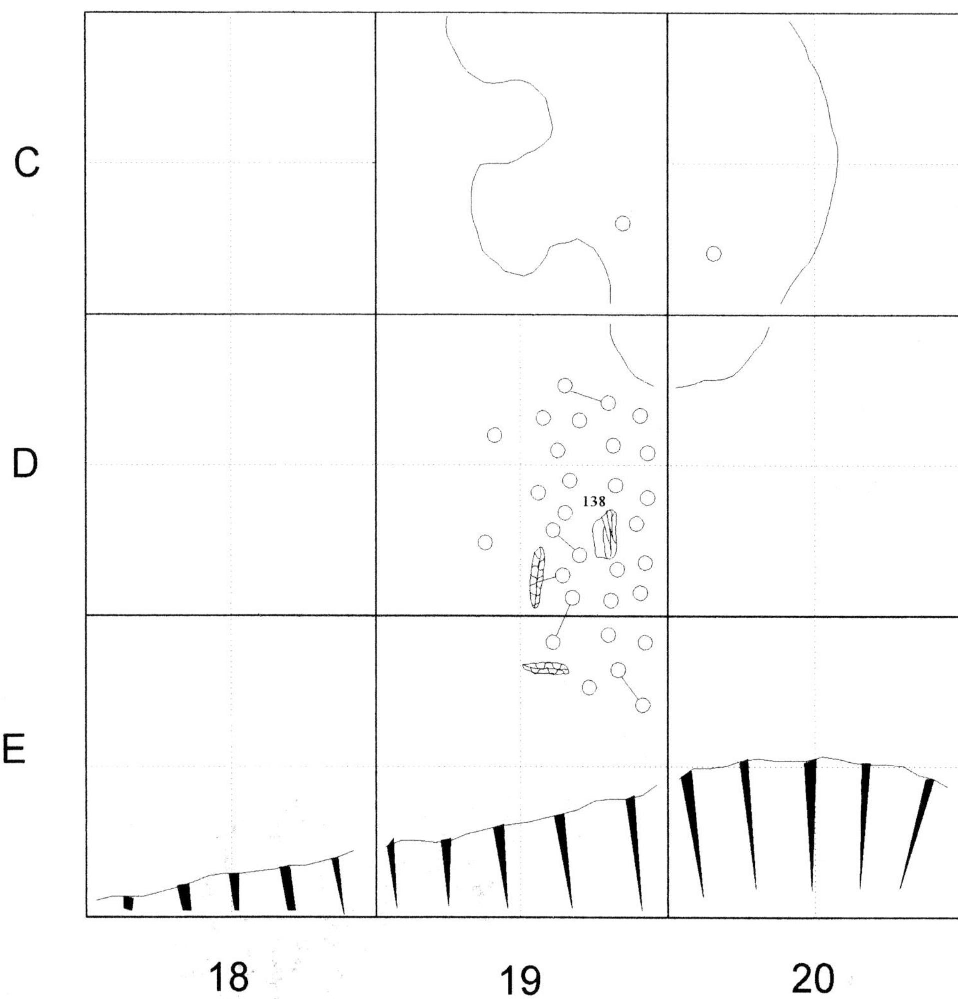

Figure 4.35 Avington VI: distribution of the refitted artefacts in group 138

Group 159

It is apparent from the refitting that the core in this group was part way through its blade producing life when it arrived in the area of transects C19–20. From this point on, the degree of recovery is generally high although there are some pieces that are unexpectedly missing. It is impossible to estimate accurately the size of the original flint nodule but it was at least 220mm in length, the width was probably of the order of 70mm and the depth, as rebuilt, is about 100mm but it was originally more, possibly as much as 120–140mm or greater. In shape it was flattened and decidedly irregular with protuberances and hollows. Where it remains, the cortex is thin and the colour varies from grey to sandy. The flint was not of good quality, it is not even clear exactly how many removals have been refitted, some items are obvious shatter pieces and two or more such pieces may have resulted from a single strike. A maximum of 21 removals have been refitted, of these at least 11 fragmented. In part this was caused by crystal lined cavities within the nodule. However, there are removals in the refitted reduction sequence that have not been recovered and some of these at least appear to have been well-controlled blades; these are therefore assumed to have been successful products removed for use elsewhere.

Viewed in its fully refitted state (**Fig. 4.36: 1–4**), the working face of the core is only approximately 40mm wide but in length was as much as 220mm (**Fig. 4.36: 3**). The scars of two large blades about 150mm long, and at least three smaller blades 50–80mm long, struck from the upper platform are visible. There is also some evidence that a crested blade was struck at the start of the main reduction sequence from the upper platform (**Fig. 4.36: 1**). Little can be written with respect to the lower platform, so much of this part of the core is missing; however, it can be stated with confidence that such a platform was present and several layers of removals were struck from it (**Fig. 4.36: 2, 3**). The reduction sequence carried out in the area of transects C19–20 involved both the upper and lower platforms, as may be seen from the overlapping conjoins (**Fig. 4.36: 1, 2**). Although the degree of fragmentation was high, not all the blades failed and not all have been refitted; at least three struck early in this phase are missing. An intermediate stage in the reduction sequence has been drawn (**Fig. 4.36: 5**). Reduction continued but increasingly the blades terminated short due to an accumulation of hinge fractures (**Fig. 4.36: 6**). Attempts at some point to reshape the lower end of the core appear to have failed but not all of the resulting flakes/shatter pieces have been found (**Fig. 4.36: 1–4**). There are further missing pieces, associated with the upper platform, from the final stages of the reduction sequence; some of these may represent pieces removed for use (**Fig. 4.36: 6**). What appears to have been the last removal from the core is a flake detached from what was left of the upper platform. This may have been intended to run the length of the core to remove the accumulated irregularities from the working face, but in the event it terminated short and the core was abandoned (**Fig. 4.36: 6**).

Although 159 was clearly a two platform core, little can be written about the second lower platform because the flakes and shatter pieces detached during the early stages have not been refitted. However, it is evident from the butt of one refitted blade that there was an attempt to reshape the lower end of the core which failed. Indeed, the lower end of the core is characterised by a dearth of refits, one rebuilt blade and major fragments of two other blades being the total achieved (**Fig. 4.36: 3, 4**), although there are a few other pieces which have been identified as belonging in all probability to this part. It may simply be that sufficient removals were taken away, to be used elsewhere, to render refitting impossible. However, it is hard to imagine that all of the various reshaping flakes and shatter pieces were of value and this poses the question of where they are. It is possible that the core was worked briefly outside of the excavated area and then returned to it. Virtually nothing remains of the upper platform with respect to the core itself; however, enough of the removals from it have been refitted to make it possible to identify a minimum of two successive platforms (**Fig. 4.36: 1**). Examination of the butts of the removals reveals that the upper platforms were primarily retouched across the top of the platform rather than down the working face. These upper platforms are associated with 14 refitted removals, not all complete and there is evidence of at least five further removals. The refits range in length from 70–150mm. None of the refits exhibit a bruised edge.

The distribution of this group falls within the general pattern; most are located in a small area with a few more widely dispersed (**Fig. 4.37**). Two blades occur further away; one found in C21NW was originally about 140mm long but now lacks its proximal end; the other originally about 90mm long but now missing its distal end was found in transect B22. Both had potential for use. A third item is a thick, rather irregular, flake from the lower end of the core that was found in transect E19; its character does not immediately suggest any application. Perhaps the most intriguing dispersal is that of an otherwise well formed blade, 137mm in length, that was rebuilt from three fragments; two of these, a distal segment 15mm long and medial piece 78mm long, were found in the main area in the northern part of transect C20, the third fragment, the proximal end 44mm long was found in transect E20; whether this latter fragment simply flew the 1.5–2m or was deliberately transported is a matter for speculation, although generally the fragments of broken blades were found close together. None of the three fragments exhibited signs of use.

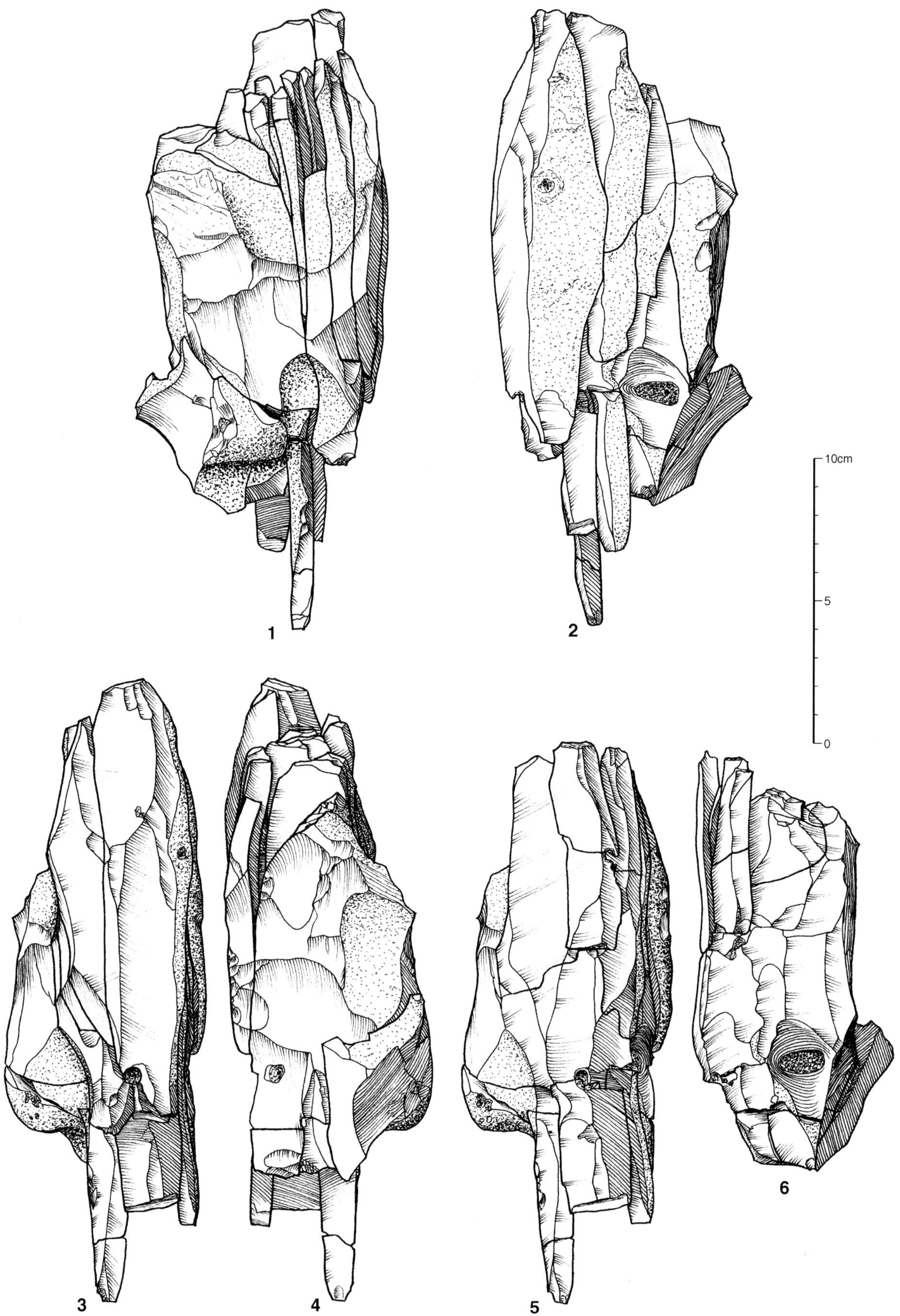

Figure 4.36 Avington VI: 1-4: maximum extent of refitting on group 159; 5-6: intermediate and late stages in the reduction sequence

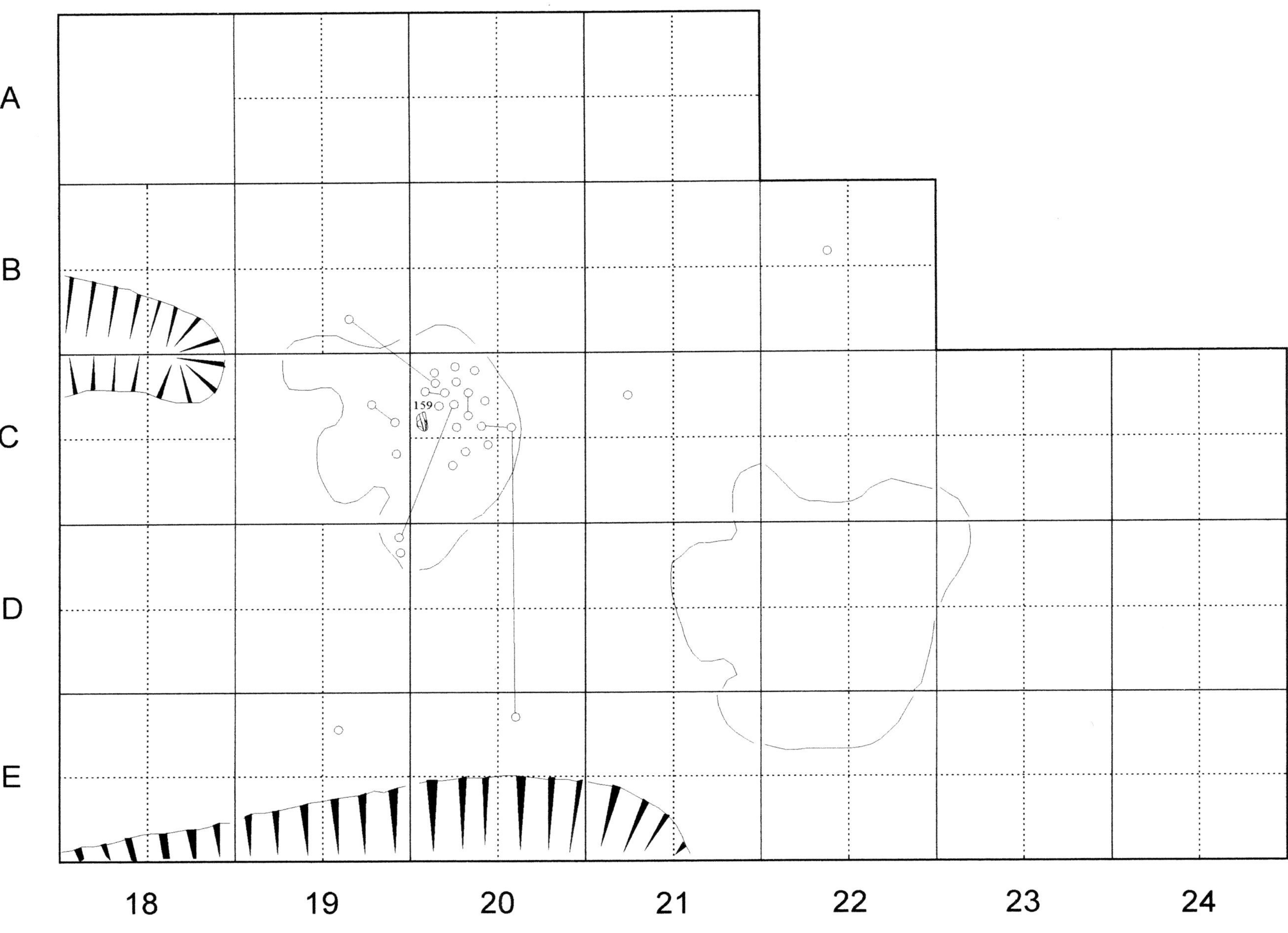

Figure 4.37. Avington VI: distribution of the refitted artefacts in group 159

'Giant' Blade group

This group does not have a number because it does not include a refitted core. It is probable that more flakes and blades of similar flint belong to it but cannot be conjoined. Such similar pieces may have originated from the same parent nodule as this group or they may belong to one or more other nodules, gathered perhaps from the same source. It is likely that this group represents a single comparatively short episode in a more extensive knapping sequence. The original flint nodule was at least 300mm in length and it is likely that it was between 80mm and 90mm in width, thus for its length it was relatively narrow allowing only three blades to be detached from the face, a characteristic also noted in groups 204 and 138 (**Figs 4.26; 4.27; 4.34**). The third dimension cannot be estimated; the nodule might have been cylindrical as in groups 119 and 154 or it might have been block-like as in group 158. The cortex is pale in colour, commonly smooth and, at 3–5mm unusually thick. In part the cortex divides into two zones, an inner smooth, apparently dense zone and a more general outer porous zone; a similar nodule of flint was noted in the field a few hundred metres to the south-west of the site, immediately to the south of the Hungerford Road (**Fig. 2.1**), where a thin layer of clay-with-flint capped the underlying chalk. As with so many of the rebuilt nodules, the removals were prone to break, a fault discussed further below.

Refitting this group showed that once again the initial phase or phases of working could only be surmised from the scars left by the earlier removals. None of the products of this work was present. Indeed, it is by no means certain whether the reduction sequence to be described represents an early working of the nodule or a later one. Examination of some cores, for example 118 and 154, has shown that nodules might be first worked on one side then turned and worked on the opposite side. What is clear in this series is that quite a lot of preparation was carried out before any attempt was made to strike blades. There is no evidence to suggest that a crested blade featured in this sequence. The early work included the production of several comparatively small removals of blade-like character from the face of the lower part of the core (**Fig. 4.38: 1**). There are also the scars of removals struck from 'front-to-back' and 'back-to-front' (**Fig. 4.39**); the scar of what may have been a large blade-like flake is also present (**Figs 4.38; 4.39**). The first removal

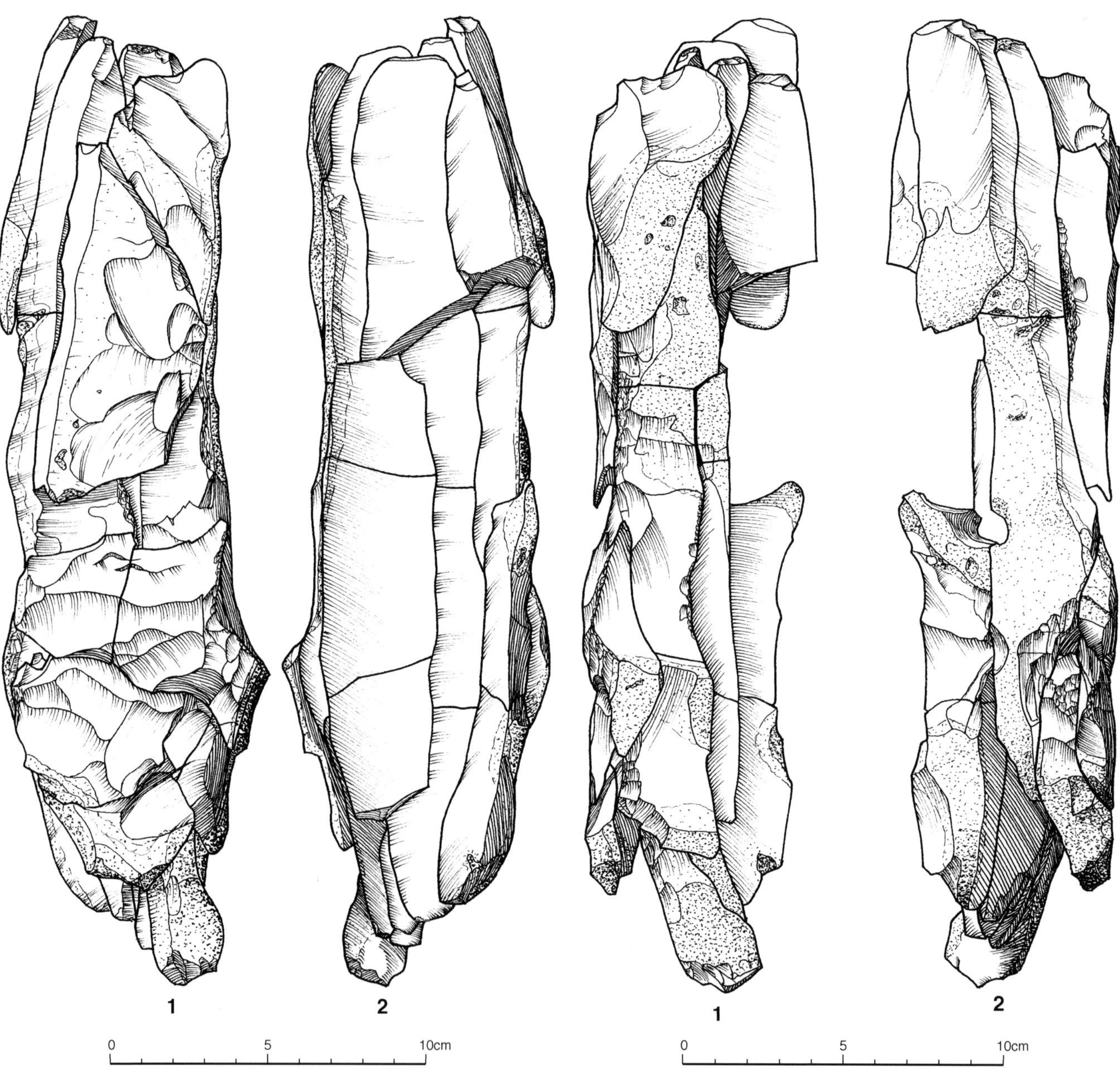

Figure 4.38 Avington VI: Giant Blade group

Figure 4.39 Avington VI: Giant Blade group

recovered is a flake struck somewhat obliquely from the upper part of the core; this was followed by a large blade-like flake. The latter was recovered but it fragmented although in part this may have resulted from use; three flakes, approximately 50–80mm in size, were then detached from the lower face of the core, striking took place from both sides and one of the flakes fractured (**Figs 4.38; 4.39**). There was also flaking from 'front-to-back', but only one piece has been refitted, however, several of the removals were less than 30mm and small.

At this point in the sequence two large blades, 232 and 235mm long respectively, were struck from the upper platform. Although both are broken (**Fig. 4.40: 1, 2**), it is certain that one broke as a result of use because the fracture is clearly associated with marked edge damage characteristic of bruising (**Fig. 4.40: 2**); in the case of the second, it is less clear but the fracture may well have resulted from use, its exact position being determined more by an inherent weakness in the flint than by the point at which the destructive force was applied (**Fig. 4.40: 1**). Following on from these two exceptionally large blades, a series of comparatively small blades, 60–85mm in length, including pieces which retain some cortex, were struck from the lower platform. The majority of these have been refitted (**Figs 4.38; 4.39**). Thereafter, attempts to strike large blades from both the upper and lower platforms appear to have failed at least initially. From the upper platform there are the butts of two potentially Long Blades, viewed in isolation, these could be taken to be the proximal fragments from fragmented Long Blades, in fact no other parts ever existed. These two butt ends interlock with blades struck from the lower platform, the junction marking a plane of destructive fracture or stress in the flint (**Fig. 4.38: 2**). Three blades, one retaining some cortex, struck from the lower platform also fragmented, breaking into two, three and at least four sections respectively (**Fig. 4.38: 2 bottom**). What happened after this point in the reduction sequence is unknown, no more refits could be found although as previously noted there are pieces in the assemblage that could belong to this series.

Platform retouch is variable in this series, the larger flakes exhibit little or no such preparation and these flakes have the large well-developed bulbs of percussion usually ascribed to hard hammer technique. However, some of these flakes do exhibit small retouch, although it seems that it played no part in their removal as may be seen in **Fig. 4.38**. The blades proper demonstrate a variety of retouch; the smaller blades retain little of the striking platform but some retouch down the face of the core can be observed, the larger blades show some faceting across the platform whilst the extreme proximal ends of the largest blades appear to have been battered to a smooth rounded outline.

Each of the first three blades struck, all of which are 'giants', exhibit bruised edges. The first blade shows a single zone of heavy bruising along an extended length, which suggests that it was used on a number of occasions as a bar-hammer. Each time that it was picked up it must have been held in a slightly different manner, thus the centre of percussion fell in a slightly different position along the edge of the blade producing an extended zone of wear (**Figs 4.39: 2 top; 4.38: 1, top**). In this particular example, the zone of battering occurs midway along the edge, however, if allowance is made for the missing butt fragment then it would occur at the theoretical centre of percussion. Thus it may well be that it fractured when in use as a bar-hammer and the butt, retained in the knapper's hand, was tossed or thrown to one side and thus beyond the limits of the excavation. The second blade (**Fig. 4.40: 1**) also exhibits a single length of bruising but in this case it is more restricted and may indicate only one or two applications, however, the use appears to have been quite intense to judge from the amount of the blade that has been worn away. The fracture corresponds to a point identified as a point where fracture tended to occur in other removals, whether the blade fractured when struck or when in use cannot be determined; if the blade was complete when brought into use as a hammer, the bruising is at the appropriate point given that the blade was held at the proximal end; if on the other hand it was already fragmented, then the bruising occurs where it would be expected if this major fragment had been held at the distal end. The third blade (**Fig. 4.40: 2**) shows the greatest use; both of the edges are bruised, one in particular is extensively bruised and it is suggested that this blade was repeatedly used as a bar-hammer before it finally broke. The positions of the separate zones of bruising along one edge indicate that in this instance the blade was held on some occasions at the proximal and on others at the distal end, each time that it was picked up it was held in a slightly different way and thus the slightly differing centres of percussion resulted in extended lengths of bruising.

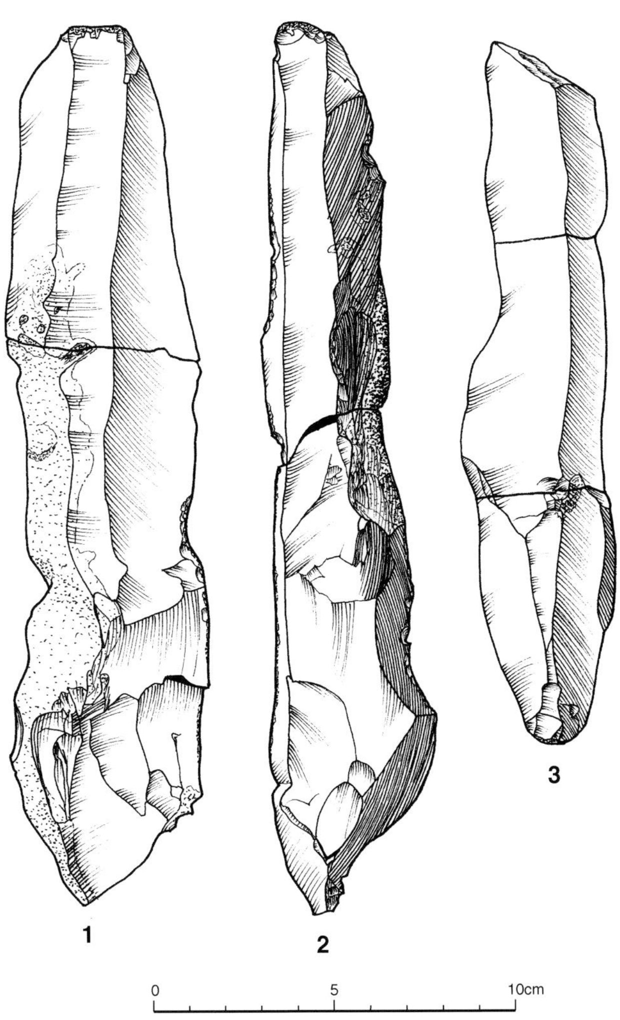

Figure 4.40 Avington VI: 1-3: Giant Blades fragmented during knapping. Proximal ends shown uppermost except in 3. Note bruising on 1

There are 18 removals rebuilt from 27 pieces in this partial sequence. The distribution of these pieces is such that nearly all are associated with the eastern half of transect D21; the other four pieces do not extend the distribution pattern by much (**Fig. 4.41**). One piece found outside D21 in transect E21 is the larger of the middle sections of the long blade that fragmented into four or more sections (**Fig. 4.38: 2**, bottom). It does not appear to have been subjected to use and its position does not significantly extend the distribution pattern. This group is another which like 119 and 211 occupies a discrete area of major concentration.

'Pock-marked cortex' series

Like the previous group this has no number because the core is missing. However, the recovery of the refits is high and this raises questions about the whereabouts of the absent artefacts. Enough cortical removals are present to allow a reasonable estimate of the size and shape of the original flint nodule; the length is likely to have been approximately 250mm and the width was 50–60mm, the third dimension is more problematical but a likely value would have been approximately 120mm. The relative narrowness is again noteworthy. In outline the nodule was rounded, somewhat pointed at least at one end and elliptical in cross-section. The cortex has a sandy colour and is comparatively thick, commonly 2–4mm, but its principal characteristic is that it is generally rough with frequent depressions some 5–15mm across giving it an easily recognisable appearance. However, the nodule was not unique to the site, there were at least one or two other similar nodules and, additionally, it shares some characteristics with the nodule used to produce group 279.

When reassembled, much cortex is visible but it is equally apparent that the earliest removals are missing (**Fig. 4.42: 3**); the scars of at least two large removals struck from the lower platform are obvious but, despite intensive searching, these could not be located in the assemblage. In this context it is relevant to observe that three of the scrapers (**Fig. 3.4**) have similar or identical cortex and, although none could be refitted into this series, this illustrates that flakes such as these could well have been taken away as blanks for retouched tools. Alternatively, these removals could have been part of an initial knapping sequence conducted elsewhere.

Less easily explained are the missing flakes from the series produced during the preparation of a crested blade subsequently struck from the upper platform. Although some of this work could have been executed elsewhere, simple superimposition indicates that some of the removals were struck after those that have been refitted. The absence of these later removals is hard to explain, they should have been easily identifiable and are therefore unlikely to remain concealed in the assemblage, on the other hand it is difficult to visualise them as having been used for any purpose and thus removed from the excavated area.

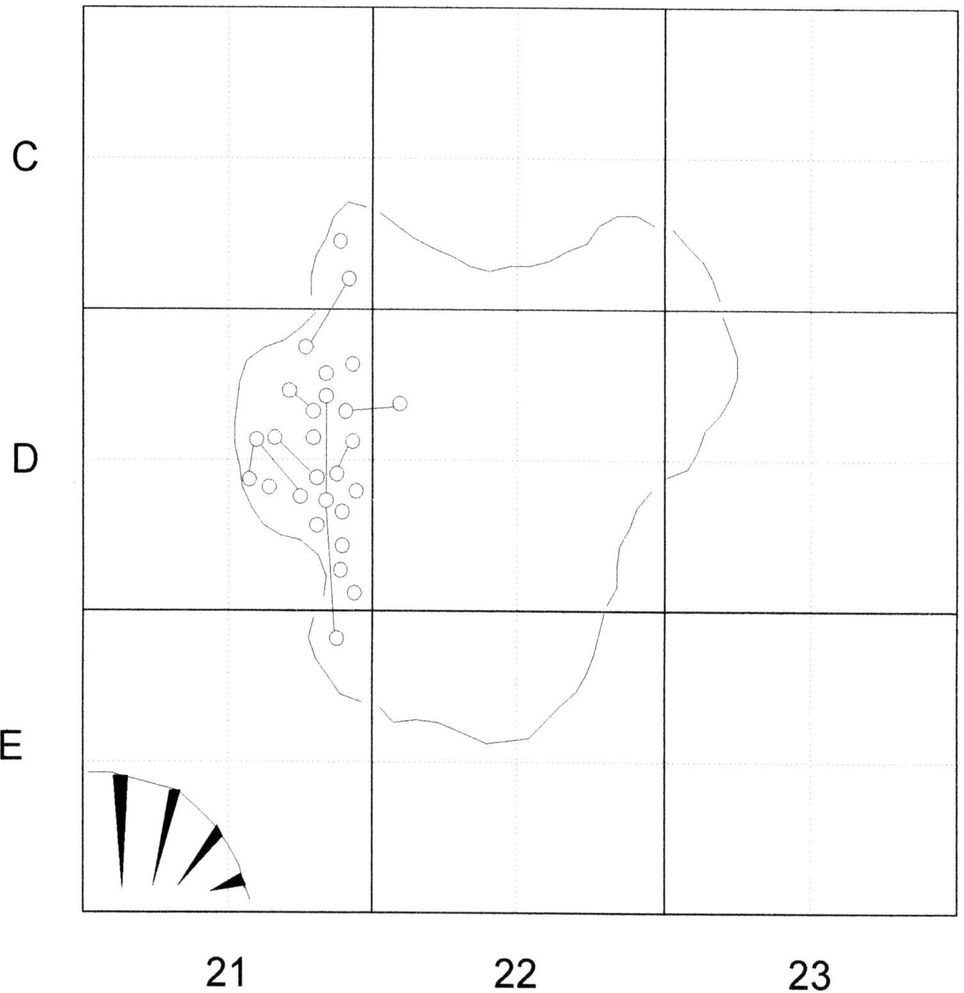

Figure 4.41 Avington VI: distribution of the refitted artefacts in Giant Blade group

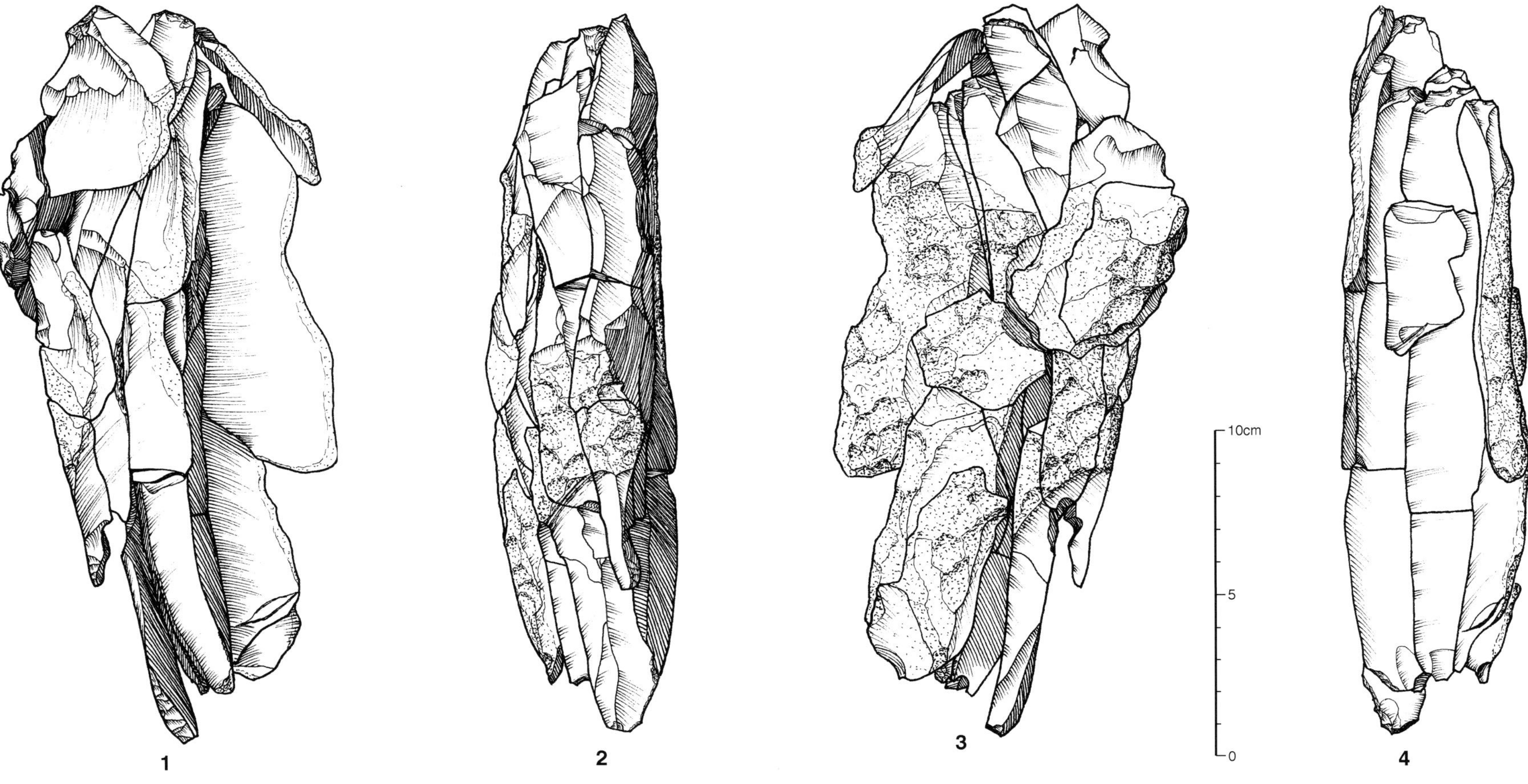

Figure 4.42 Avington VI: 1-4: maximum extent of refitting on 'Pock-marked' group

The first work involving this nodule for which there is certain evidence on the site was the preparation of the crested blade struck from the upper platform (**Fig. 4.42: 1, 3**). As noted, not all of the removals have been refitted and this includes the crested blade. A second crested blade struck from the lower platform may be represented by a conjoined distal end fragment (**Fig. 4.42**) but it is equivocal whether this fragment is from a crested blade. These blades refit in an overlapping series having been struck from both platforms (**Fig. 4.42**); of the nine refitted blades, seven are fragmented, two into three sections each. Inspection of the reassembled group suggests that some four or more additional blades were struck, divided more or less equally between the two platforms but these have not been found and may therefore represent successful products removed for use. During this sequence one flake was detached from the side of the core (**Fig. 4.42: 3**).

An interesting feature of this group is that it demonstrates the willingness of the knapper to exploit a nodule which, because it was narrow, resulted in a working face that was scarcely more than one or two blades wide. This inevitably meant producing blades which retained a significant amount of cortex (**Fig. 4.42: 2, 4**). At the end of the sequence described, the core was still some 170mm in length although possibly rather slender, nonetheless it presumably retained some potential and was consequently removed for use elsewhere. It is clear that during the reduction sequence represented by this group of refits both platforms were rejuvenated (**Fig. 4.42: 4**). Initially the upper platform was quite small and the flake which subsequently rejuvenated it is largely bordered by cortex (**Fig. 4.42: 2, 4**). One additional rejuvenation flake was found to refit to and below this early flake and to two of the blades; it has not been drawn, primarily because it was virtually impossible to support it in position. Where the blades retain a portion of the striking platform they clearly show platform preparation, mostly across rather than down the edge. The simple flakes, which have prominent bulbs of percussion, exhibit much less preparation.

One of the largest blades, 150 x 15 x 35mm, is extensively bruised on both edges. It was found in two pieces but, as in a previous example, the centre of percussion does not allow the question as to whether it fractured before or during use to be resolved. A second more slender blade, 144 x 11 x 23mm, this has a short zone of what appears to be typical light bruising bisected by a break which separated the blade into two sections, most unusually the bruising is along the dorsal ridge of the blade rather than on one of its edges and this could indicate its use as an anvil.

The distribution of this group is shown in **Figure 4.43**. The 23 removals are represented by a total of 29 pieces which are distributed almost throughout the major concentration centred on transect D22, one of the wider dispersals. Several pieces were found below the cleaned Long Blade horizon but the majority came from within it, two pieces were found in the slightly higher displaced group in the south east quadrant of transect D21. There appears to be no particular significance to be attached to a blade, 130 x 8 x 23mm, the two broadly equal fragments of which were found in transects B22 and D22.

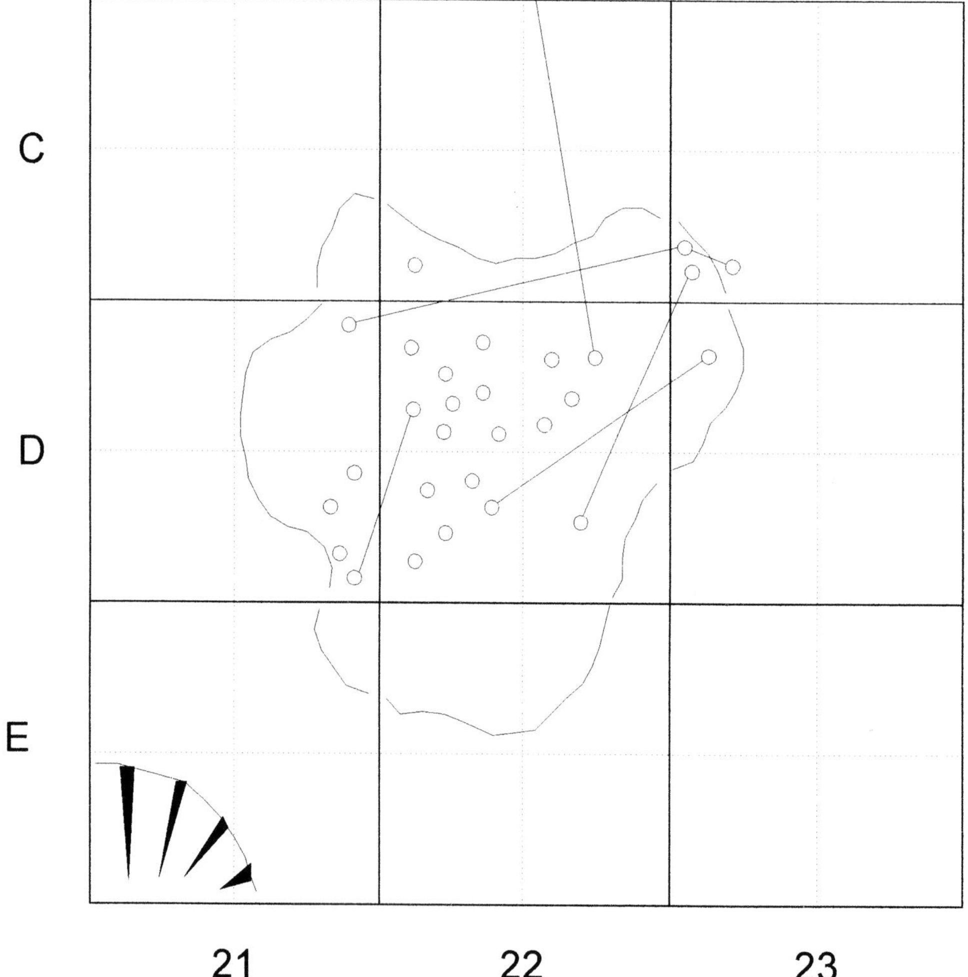

Figure 4.43 Avington VI: distribution of the refitted artefacts in 'Pock-marked' group

Group 141

By volume 80% or more of this nodule has been reassembled, the most noticeable missing pieces are associated with the formation and reshaping of the two platforms. The original nodule was approximately 150mm in length and 50–60mm in diameter. In shape it was broadly cylindrical; the cortex is of a sandy colour and exhibits much small slightly raised surface detail and occasional larger protuberances (**Fig. 4.44: 1–4**). This surface detail appears to reflect some intrinsic characteristic of the flint, which has a distinctive appearance when patinated: interrupted by a removal, a feature visible in the cortex can still be seen in the patination on the surface of the removal scar.

As the drawings show, no trace has been found of the flakes struck to form the initial upper or lower striking platform and there is no debitage relating to subsequent platform reshaping and rejuvenation. A single spall, 15 x 10mm, has been refitted to the lower platform. It is logical to assume that rejuvenation flakes struck during the production of the blades, as co-products, should have been amongst the numerous blades recovered and refitted. That they were not is something of a puzzle; this group has a parallel in group 132 described below where such a series was recovered. Also missing are a few early removals struck from various parts of the nodule (**Fig. 4.44: 1–4**). It is clear from the way the removals overlap that the reduction sequence utilised both platforms from the outset. The restricted nature of the distribution pattern (**Fig. 4.46**) suggests that all the refitted pieces belong to a single and quite brief knapping episode, quite possibly much less than an hour's work. There was one significant flaw in the nodule, the last trace of which can be seen in the drawing of the abandoned core curving down from the top and to the right-hand side (**Fig. 4.45: 13**); this flaw seriously distorted the removals from this part of the core and also caused some to break (**Fig. 4.45: 9** fails short; **4.45 :10–13** are distorted and fractured). However, the majority of the removals were more successful; most of a contiguous sequence of typical removals has been drawn (**Fig. 4.45: 1–8**). Once reassembled, it is possible to identify at least three blades and probably no more than five blades which have not been found and which were probably well formed, these are presumed to be the successful products. This compares to the 33 refitted 'blades', 20 from the upper platform and 13 from the lower, which are assumed to be discarded products. Given that there are a few missing pieces, probably in the small waste, the useful products would appear to represent only some 10% of the overall production excluding small spalls. At the end of the reduction sequence, attempts to strike from both platforms failed; the removals terminated short (**Fig. 4.45: 13**) and the core was abandoned. Both in terms of the circumference of the nodule and its volume approximately 75% of the nodule had been exploited. Platform retouch is present; early comparatively long removals occur across the top of the platform but generally the retouch occurs down the face of the core (**Fig. 4.45**).

The distribution of the refitted pieces is unremarkable except perhaps for being nicely discrete (**Fig. 4.46**) on which comment has already been made (above). A significant number of the pieces were found below the prepared Long Blade horizon but this may reflect the small size of many of the removals in this group because such small pieces can more easily filter down in the section.

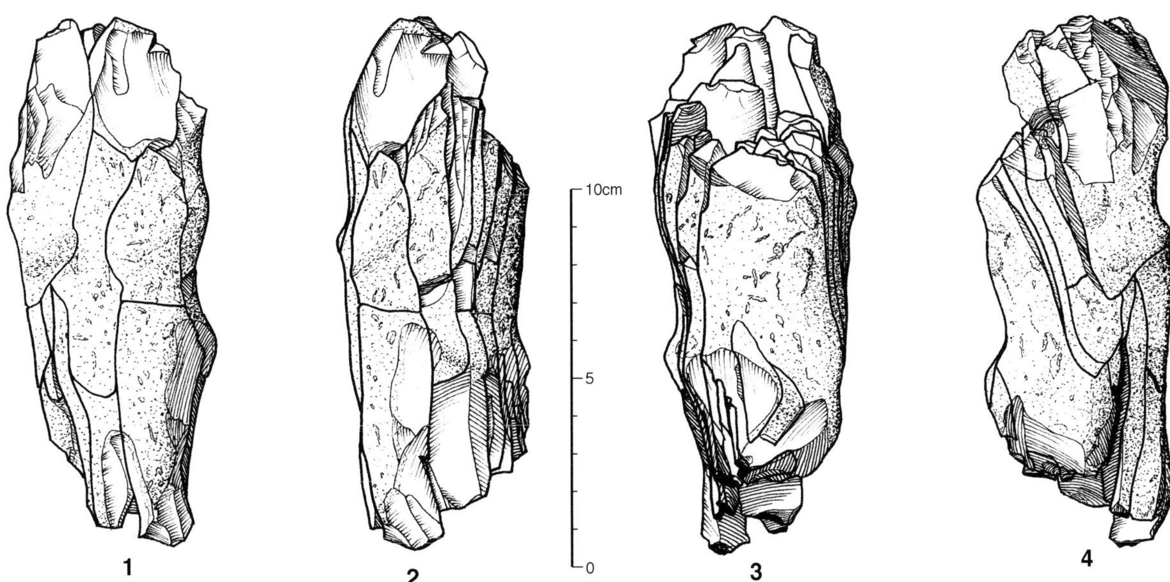

Figure 4.44 Avington VI: 1-4: maximum extent of refitting on group 141

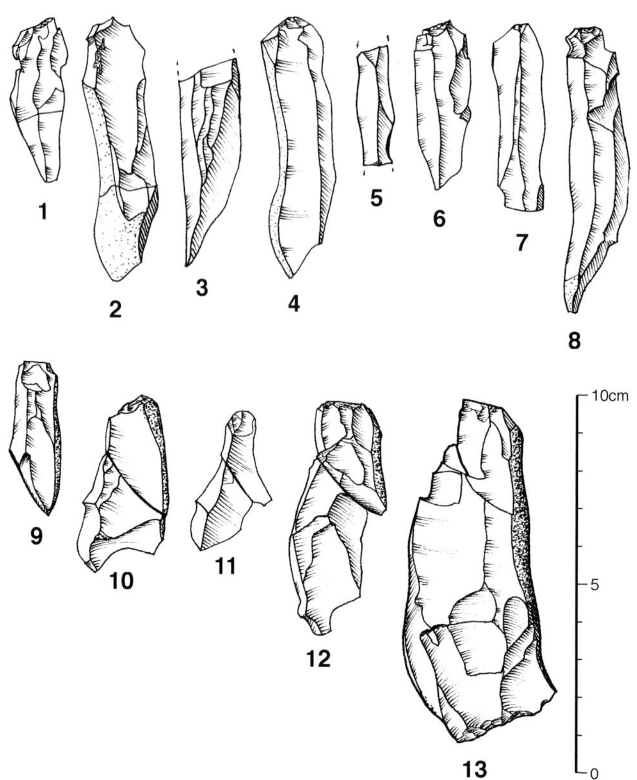

Figure 4.45 Avington VI: 1-8: removals from group 141 showing in 4.44: 3, 4; 9-13: successive removals which distorted due to a fault in the flint. Drawn with the proximal ends at the top

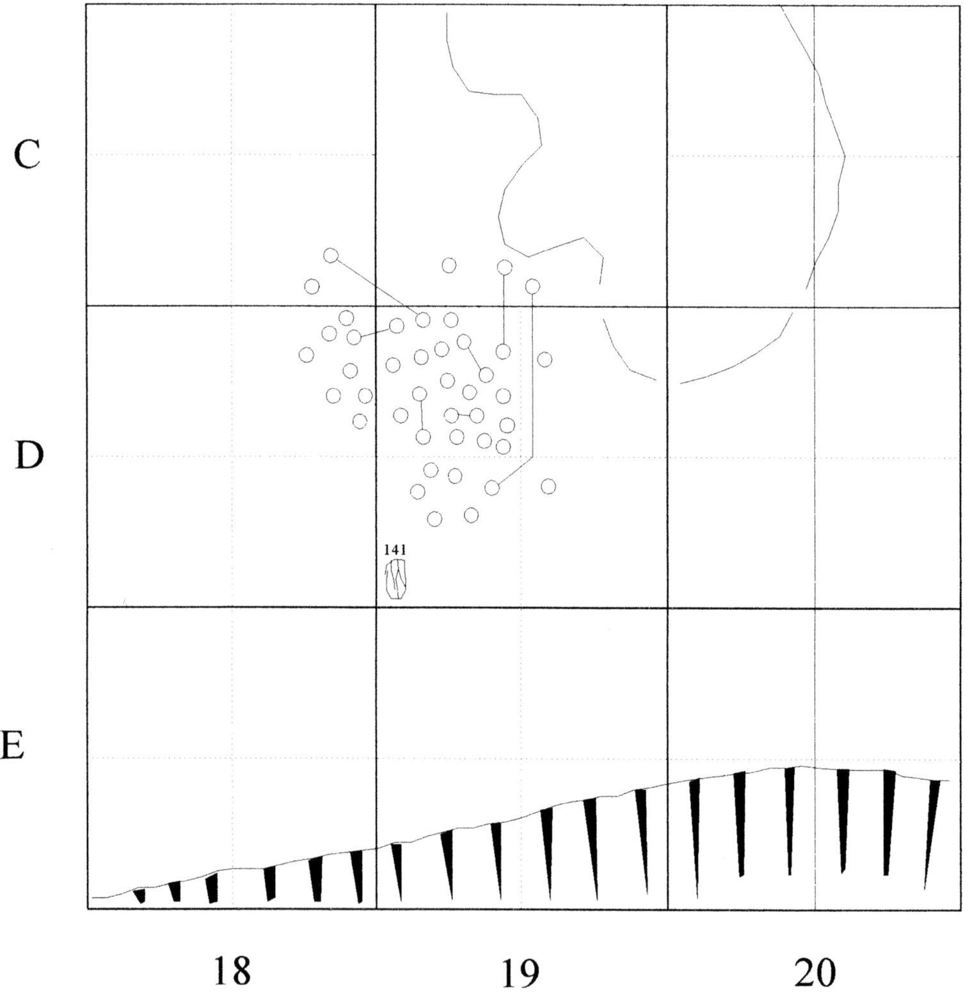

Figure 4.46 Avington VI: distribution of the refitted artefacts in group 141

Group 132

This group is similar to the previous group 141. Both utilised nodules with exactly the same type of cortex and the flint took on a similar appearances after patination. The reduction technique employed in the two cases is also similar. A further feature is that the two sets of refitted removals occupy virtually the same area. Consequently, it is tempting to ascribe the two groups to the same knapper working at one point in time.

As with group 141, the degree of recovery for this core is high and little of consequence is missing. The nodule of flint was originally approximately 120mm in length, mostly 40–50mm in diameter and, although rounded, somewhat irregular in shape. Subjectively, it is a little surprising that such a nodule was chosen.

It is possible that some earlier work was carried out elsewhere; the lower striking platform may have been formed by the removal of a single cortical flake. Judging by the pattern of the patination on the scar forming the platform this flake should be instantly recognisable but in the event it has not been located. The upper platform may have been formed by a series of small flakes, <20mm, which may have escaped detection. During the reduction sequence the upper platform was modified and six flakes of varying size have been refitted (**Fig. 4.47: 1, 3**). There are a few, mostly small, cortical removals missing. There is no reason to suppose that the main reduction sequence, as shown in the drawings, was anything other than a single brief knapping operation. From the outset both the platforms were utilised, the 20 refits to the working face of the core divide equally between the two platforms. Generally, other than spalls, the removals vary in length from 30–60mm; the largest is 80mm. Refitting suggests that few blades are missing, possibly no more than three at the most or again about 10% of the probable total yield of blade-like removals. From the outset, about 33% of the removals fragmented and towards the end of the sequence distortion is also apparent; two comparatively large thick removals failed to remove the problem and the core was abandoned. The writer has observed on many other occasions that the worst quality flint is often to be found towards the centre of the nodule. When it was abandoned, approximately 50% of the circumference of the original nodule had been exploited representing an equal proportion of the volume. When abandoned, the two cores, 132 and 141, were similar in size despite having originated from rather different raw nodules. Retouch was applied to the platforms, as is usually the case with the smaller cores; it occurs down the face of the core, not across the platform.

The distribution has been set out in **Figure 4.48** and can be seen to correlate with the distribution for group 141. This also applies to the vertical distribution in which approximately 33% of the pieces came from below the exposed Long Blade horizon. Two pieces are outside the main distribution and although neither exhibit obvious signs of use both have edges which could be visualised as having uses: one is a small blade, 60 x 20mm, found in transect E20, the other a bladelet, 30 x 10mm, from the south-west quadrant of transect C18.

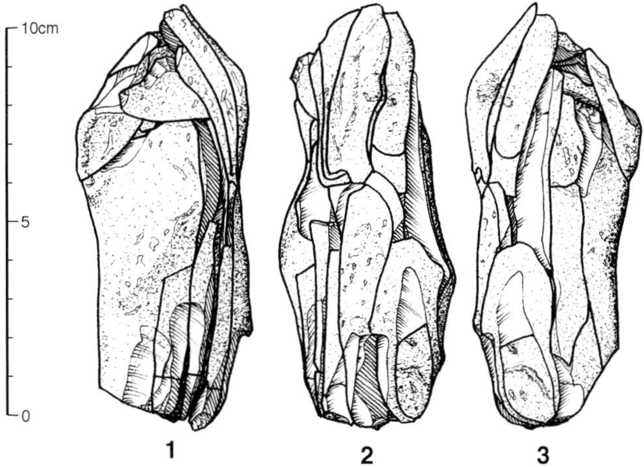

Figure 4.47 Avington VI: maximum extent of refitting on group 132

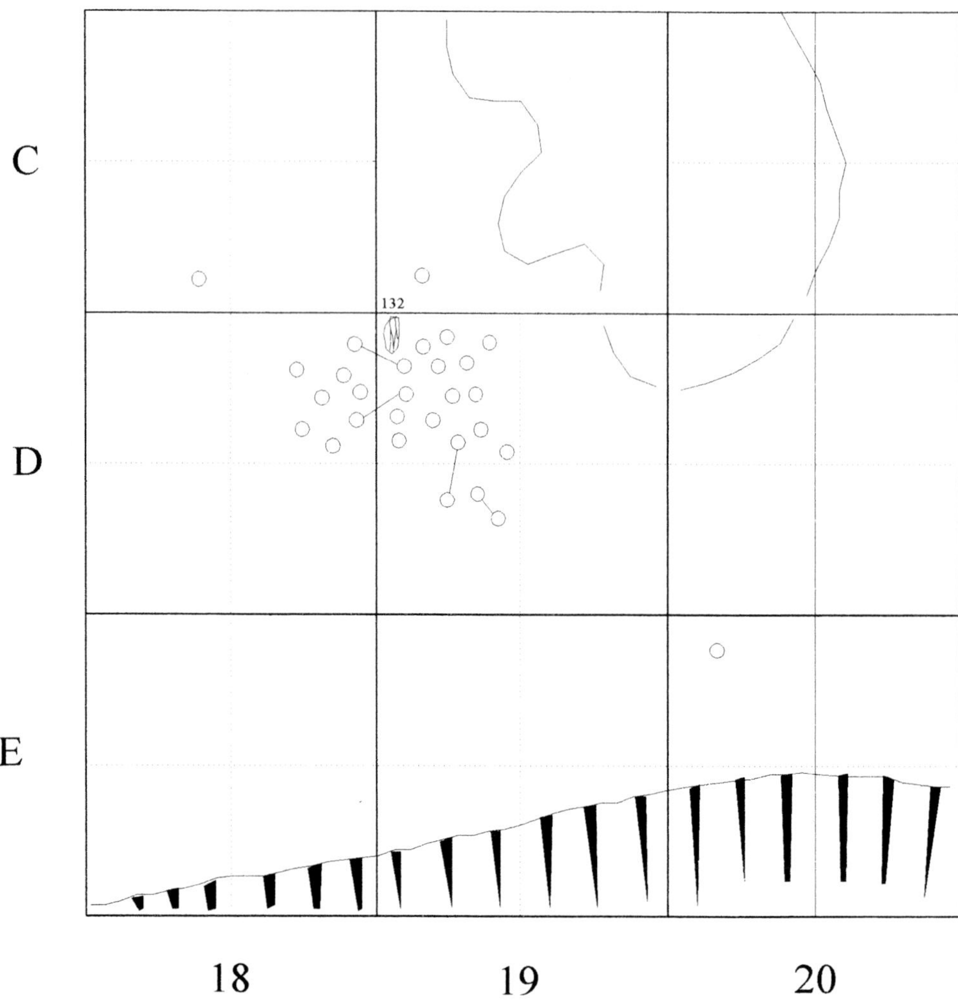

Figure 4.48 Avington VI: distribution of the refitted artefacts in group 132

Short series

There are many short series of refits. These mainly consist of three to five pieces but there are also longer sequences. However, these do not in general extend the range of observations presented above. It is possible that with further effort at least some of these short series could be built into more extensive series but it is doubtful whether this would reveal anything further about either the knapping methods and techniques or the significance of the groups.

Reduction sequences and *chaîne opératoire*

The detailed description of the 18 major refitted groups at Avington VI allows some general comments to be made about the Long Blade technology practised there. The method applied to all of the nodules indicates that the knappers intended to produce the longest possible blades from the raw material available. Sometimes these blades are as long as or longer than 150mm but often they are less than 100mm. These smaller blades are sometimes missing as in the case of group 264 in which a sequence of blades only 30–60mm long struck from a relatively small nodule are absent. This suggests that small regular blades were also regarded as useful products taken from the site for use elsewhere. They may have been used to produce the small retouched pieces noted on this and other Kennet Valley Long Blade sites and for the production of microlith segments as indicated by the occasional presence of microburins. The production of small retouched pieces in this way is quite different from the deliberate bladelet production technology used in the Early Mesolithic and will be discussed further in chapter 9.

The production of Long Blades required a great deal of preparation and in examples such as group 279 much of the volume of the nodule is wasted in the process. In this respect the technique might be described as heavy on its resources or 'expensive' and this may be the reason for its occurrence where flint is abundant. The preparation is also interesting in other respects. The Avington VI knappers seem to have been willing to work with any shape of nodule, such as the pear-shape of 195, tabular 175, cylindrical 141, banana-shaped 119, narrow Giant Blade group and irregular 159, regardless of the amount of preparation it required to obtain just a few regular blades. This apparent carelessness in selection is particularly reflected in refitted groups such as 158, 264, 137 and 150 which are almost complete as they had failed to produce much before they were abandoned. At various stages in the sequences the knappers can also be found adapting their technique to overcome faults caused by inclusions or natural fractures in the flint some of which would have been visible at an early stage but did not deter the use of the nodule.

The absence of primary decortication or *entame* flakes or nodule protrusions suggests that the earliest stages of most of the sequences took place elsewhere, probably at the flint source. In most cases it is cresting that is the first process to take place on the site as in the case of groups 175, 204 and the 'pock-marked' group. The cresting may be struck off as one blade or in two sections from opposed platforms depending on whether the crested edge is relatively straight or more convex respectively. Some groups show more than one crested refit sometimes, as in group 150, this may provide a new start after an initial failure or an additional crested piece occurs later in the sequence and is used to rejuvenate the blade producing capacity of the core as in group 119. The high incidence of crested pieces at Avington VI may be accounted for in this way but is discussed further in relation to other sites in chapter 9.

Crested pieces and the large thick removals that follow them are often heavily edge damaged or bruised suggesting their use as soft hammers. The characteristics of the ventral surfaces suggest the direct use of 'soft' flint hammers throughout the reduction. Whether this reflects a lack of both other lithic and organic alternatives or a preference cannot be determined.

On some cores preparation is followed by the alternate removal of blades from two opposed platforms. This can be clearly observed in groups 175, 204, 279, 138 and 159, as well as the Giant Blade group. Turning the core to detach removals from each end helped to keep the working face reasonably flat and regular; this prevented blades detaching short with hinge and step terminations and allowed the removal of good regular blades running the full length of the face. Such blades are generally missing from the groups presumably because they were the desired products which were taken away for use elsewhere. However, several groups include refitted blade fragments which broke as they were struck and represent failed attempts to remove well-shaped thin sectioned blanks. In addition to these failures, there are examples of hinge and step fractures which sometimes precede platform rejuvenation or the adjustment of the working face at the platform edge to correct subsequent removals; such adjustment is visible on many of the refitted proximal dorsal surfaces.

The knapping technique used at Avington VI may thus be described as using two opposed platforms from which blades could be simultaneously and alternately detached after preparation. To achieve this direct percussion was applied using a soft stone hammer. Sometimes the core is turned between each removal but in some examples a short sequence may be removed from one end before the core is turned. Sometimes the quality of the flint was not ideal for this purpose and the groups show that the knappers were constantly making decisions and adapting their technique to allow for flaws and inclusions in the flint. These decisions may not all have been made within a single phase of knapping as in some cases parts of the refitting groups have been found separated in different scatters suggesting the possibility of discard and subsequent opportunistic recovery. The same technique may be seen in use at other Long Blade sites in the Kennet Valley and more widely. The purpose for which the blades were required is unknown as they were for the most part removed from the site. The concentrations of debitage which remain incorporate discrete scatters which show little disturbance and the overall impression is one of a factory site ideally placed for the exploitation of local materials and perhaps other domestic activities.

The same knapping technique may be seen in use at other Long Blade sites in the Kennet Valley and more widely. These are compared and discussed further in the following chapters.

Chapter 5

Avington VI Long Blade Site: an Overview

The Avington VI Long Blade site is defined entirely in terms of its flint assemblage. No organic materials survived and no features indicative of a camp site, such as hearths or pits, were found around between or amongst the knapping debris. Indeed, on the evidence available, the site can only confidently be said to have been used to exploit flint and little else. A review of the assemblage and of other local resources offers some insights into this and other possibilities.

The lithic assemblage

The evidence of the typology and technology of the lithic assemblage is equivocal when it comes to deciding whether Avington VI was simply an industrial site or whether other living activities took place there. Tools are relatively rare; there are a modest number of scrapers, some carefully made and others less so, but burins and piercers are few in number. In addition, there is a small yet significant number of microliths including several damaged examples. If it is correct to identify the bruised edge blades as hammers used in flint working then at first sight the tool kit is both small in extent and limited in variety. However, most of the blades and many of the flakes could have been used for some purposes without any retouch. Hunting together with the associated tasks of butchery and skin preparation and concomitant maintenance and refurbishment of the hunting kit would account for at least most if not all of the assemblage. In this case the discrete scatters and dense concentrations of artefacts may offer a skewed picture of the knapping areas of a site that may simply have consisted of spots of activity over a wide area where the palimpsest of those that did not involve knapping may be barely detectable. As the review of the location and ecology of the site will show, Avington VI may well have been a good place to make camp. Equally, a case could be made for it being a factory where good cores, blanks for tools and a few finished tools were produced for use elsewhere. The refitting offers some support for this.

On the basis of the refitting it seems that cores are probably under represented in the assemblage. In the Long Blade horizon as a whole, some 4,500 waste flakes, blades, spalls and chunks are present. Refitting has shown that 50 such pieces refitting to a core is probably above average. Such an average would imply the existence of at least 90 cores whereas only 50 or so cores have been identified and many of these clearly produced less than 50 removals, markedly so in some cases. There may have been a net export of cores from the site to sites where a wider range of activities took place or, to sites in areas where flint was less available or of lower quality. Such an export might well tend to be of cores of above average quality.

A similar disparity may well exist with regard to the microliths. It appears likely that many of these artefacts were destined to be used as tips or barbs in arrowheads or other types of projectiles. The effort involved in making microliths is comparatively small compared to the total effort expended in the manufacture of the projectile as a whole; therefore it is reasonable to suppose that a damaged microlith would be removed and replaced rather than the whole weapon being discarded. Use of damaged microliths has been noted in the assemblage (p. 40) and would imply that such repairs may have been carried out there whereas the complete microliths may have been discarded unused, for whatever reason, or simply have been lost accidentally. However, it seems reasonable to suppose that most microliths manufactured at the site would be lost in the chase away from the site and this would account for the fact that so few have been found on site. The small amount of the kind of specialised debitage associated with microlith manufacture, such as microburins, does not necessarily contradict this as microliths can be prepared in other ways, as can be easily demonstrated by applying retouch to a small blade using any suitable object such as another blade. Microlith production does not automatically require the production of microburins. It is quite possible that microlith production was a major task at the site despite the relatively small number recovered.

The extended refitting programme indicated that generally the largest flint nodules had been subjected to some minor working outside the excavated area; it would seem intrinsically unlikely that this was in another part of the site and more probable thay they were tested for knapping quality at their source and, if judged suitable, would then have been brought to the site for exploitation, thus saving unnecessary expenditure of effort. In this context it is perhaps worth noting that on three occasions at least the writer has found in the Kintbury–Hungerford area groups of simple flakes, retaining variable amounts of cortex and with prominent bulbs of percussion. These occur on steeply sloping areas where the underlying chalk is still only covered with a thin layer of soil and would therefore have been a potential a source of flint. All three occurrences are on the side slope of the valley within 200m of the flood plain but the flakes could of course be of almost any period and are at best only suggestive of the process described above. Nevertheless a review of flint resources emphasises that Avington VI was the focus for several different flint extraction points.

Flint resources

It has already been noted that flint-bearing chalk, close to the surface, occurs within a few hundred metres of the site, to the east, south and west. Field walking a few hundred metres to the south of the site revealed large flint nodules in a thin soil capping the chalk; these nodules closely resembled some of those nodules which were rebuilt during the major refitting exercise described later in this volume. It is extremely likely that during the Zone III–IV transition, there would have been many exposures of flint gravel on the current flood plain. Gravel digging approximately 1km north-east of the site disclosed a 'head' deposit of weathered chalk rich in large nodules of good quality flint beneath the gravel and such weathered chalk has also been observed beneath the flood plain gravel. A further potential source of flint is the area of Tertiary deposits to the south of the site where the writer has observed a large nodule of flint, c. 30cm in length, in the bed of one of the small streams that drain these deposits; one such stream forms the eastern boundary of the Avington VI site. Large flint nodules are also known to occur at the junction of the chalk and the Tertiary strata above it. Given these local flint resources Avington VI can be said to have been well supplied with raw material for knapping and it is clear from the nature of the refitted nodules that a variety of these sources were tapped. It is also evident that all stages of the knapping sequences took place on site but that relatively few retouched tools remained there and the bruised edge blades could have been used in knapping rather than working another material such as antler. This raises the possibility that the site was used purely for knapping and that other activities took place elsewhere. This is a possibility but it should be noted that the locality had plenty to offer in terms of other resources and that, if Avington was a factory site, the 'living' sites were probably not far away.

Other resources

West of Newbury, the Kennet Valley cuts through the chalk which is capped with large areas of clay-with-flints, particularly to the north of the valley. To the immediate south of the valley there is a considerable spread of Tertiary deposits, overlooked by the high chalk escarpment. Within a 10km radius of the site such a varied geology would have supported diverse habitats offering a wide variety of fauna and flora for exploitation.

The fauna and flora of the Late Last Glacial has been discussed by Campbell (1977). It is sufficient here to draw attention to a few principal points. The limited palaeobotanical evidence available suggests that at the time of the Long Blade occupation the area surrounding Avington VI would have been open with few, if any, trees. This would favour grazing animals such as wild horse and reindeer together with other smaller mammals. There would have been a variety of birds, especially wildfowl, including both resident species and seasonal migrants, some of which would have been big enough to be worth hunting. What is currently regarded as the flood plain would then have presented a very different aspect. At times during the latter part of the last glacial, the flow rate of the River Kennet would have been much greater than at any time in the last 12,000 years (Collins *et al.,* 1996). This would have required a channel or, more likely, a series of braided channels, too large for the subsequent flow. When the Long Blade horizon at Avington VI was occupied large areas of free-draining gravel would have been exposed with plant colonisation beginning to take place. It would be some centuries or even millennia before the channels became obstructed and silted up and the forerunner of the modern flood plain with its deposits of marl/tufa and peat began to form.

In Long Blade times the valley floor would have been quite an attractive area for people, offering freedom of movement and a variety of resources including flint, large mammals, wildfowl and fish. It should be remembered that the River Kennet is essentially a chalk stream, especially in its upper reaches. As such, it is less prone to flooding, its flow rate simply slowly increasing or decreasing with the season and the year. Another aspect of chalk streams is that they are recognized as biologically unusually productive although the climatic regime will have an effect on this aspect. Until historical times, the Thames system of rivers had a good population of salmon and the Upper Kennet would have presented ideal spawning grounds for salmon and sea trout. Rivers, which have a good run of migratory fish, which have done most of their feeding in the sea, are noted for producing large pike, a fish which is also susceptible to the hunter. Such rich pickings are good reasons for thinking that Avington VI would have been an attractive spot for Late Glacial people living at the end of Zone III – beginning of Zone IV and despite the absence of direct evidence it seems possible that the site could have been used for more than just flint knapping although there is a lack of direct evidence for any other activities and good indications of material being removed for use elsewhere.

Frequency and duration of activity

During the excavations the Long Blade horizon seemed to consist of a generally low density scatter of artefacts together with two closely spaced intense concentrations. This pattern suggested that the site had not been occupied intensively or for a long period as this would have caused more dispersal of the artefacts. Indeed, the quantity and organisation of the artefacts appeared to be consistent with brief visits to the site with perhaps flint knapping as the major, or even the only, objective. The absence of any evidence for a shelter or everyday domestic activities also seemed to confirm short visits perhaps of only a couple of hours to a flint knapping factory site. This impression suggested that the refitting would be straightforward and the only difficulty would the shear number of items to be refitted together: approximately 5,700 sizable pieces and a much greater number of smaller pieces. Nevertheless it was expected that a large part of the assemblage would conjoin to form just a few reduction sequences and this seemed to be confirmed as short series were fitted together during the excavation and post excavation processing. However, when the description of the assemblage had been completed and refitting began in earnest a more complex picture began to emerge.

The refitting actually suggests several, perhaps many, visits to the site rather than just a few. Judging from the spatial distribution of some of the refitted pieces most knapping operations may only have involved a few removals at a particular spot and the cores were in many cases then moved some distance before knapping resumed, perhaps on a different occasion. However, it is difficult if not impossible to distinguish between many short-duration visits and fewer but longer occupations as in both cases the debitage from the earlier knapping operations will tend to have become dispersed even if it were initially concentrated. The distribution of artefacts across the site shows that the knapping occurred in a relatively small area within which there were two intense concentrations but observations made during excavation and the refitting show clearly that actual knapping was not confined to the two major concentrations C19–20 and D21–22 (**Pls 1–4**). Examination of the catalogue indicates that in those transects close to the major concentrations, the frequency of artefacts recovered from below the Long Blade horizon is comparable to that recorded from the exposed surface; in contrast, in those transects away from the main concentrations, the number of artefacts from the surface is much larger than that for the artefacts from below. How so many artefacts came to be concentrated in the way that they were can only be a matter of speculation. There is no way of estimating either how many individual occupations there were at the site, their duration or the overall time span from the first to the last occupation. Neither can the size of the site, defined in terms of the distribution of the artefacts, be safely estimated; that so many artefacts have so far defied refitting may indicate that the site is actually larger than has been thought; any major extension of it would in all probability exist to the north, under the electricity substation.

Dating

Dating the Long Blade horizon at Avington VI is problematic. There are no organic remains so faunal comparisons and radiocarbon age estimates are not options but fortunately, the stratigraphy, the nature of the flint assemblage and the new technique of Optically Stimulated Luminescence (OSL) are consistently indicative of the age of the site.

The stratigraphy observed and described at Avington VI has also been documented elsewhere in this part of the Kennet Valley (Collins *et al.,* 1996) and is consistent with the transition from the Late Glacial to the early Holocene. Palaeobotanical studies by David Holyoak (1980) provide some supporting evidence to the geological interpretation. An attempt to provide further refinement and direct evidence for Avington VI was attempted by Barton *et al.* (1998); although the new samples added nothing to the picture, they did confirm that the Long Blade horizon is close to the junction of pollen zones III and IV which is usually estimated as about 10,000bp.

This estimate is in keeping with the general character of the flint industry. Assemblages which incorporate the production of large Long Blades from cores commonly, but not always, with two platforms and in which a proportion of the blades exhibit bruising, together with scrapers, burins and a variety of microlithic forms, are widely distributed throughout north-western Europe. A number of regional variants have been identified (Schild, 1996). These industries are usually assigned to a period of a few centuries either side of 10,000bp, often on the basis of radiocarbon age estimates. The Avington VI assemblage fits perfectly well into this general context.

Barton *et al.* (1998) also took samples and background measurements for an OSL age estimate. Inevitably with a relatively new technique there are uncertainties about the age obtained because assumptions have to be made with respect to the degree of saturation of the samples over the millennia (ibid). However, the age estimate of 10,250 + 250 bp (Oxford laboratory reference 1523b) is consistent with the results from the other relative dating methods set out above.

Chapter 6

Wawcott XII

Introduction

Wawcott XII (NGR: SU 408675) was discovered by the writer in 1964 (**Fig. 6.1**). It came to light as a result of systematic field walking in the Wawcott area which over several years led to the discovery and investigation of more than 30 sites each identified by a number expressed in Roman numerals. Most of these are Mesolithic sites, one of which, Wawcott III, has already been published (Froom, 1976) and the remainder of which are the subject of a further publication (Froom, in preparation). Wawcott XII is reported here because of the similarity of the artefacts with those from the Long Blade assemblage at Avington VI.

Location

The site is located on the southern side of the flood plain overlooked by the steep sided elevation known as Irish Hill, the top of which is some 35m above the level of the flood plain. Irish Hill was potentially a source of flint. A small stream joins the main river approximately 0.5km to the east; this stream has its origins in the Tertiary strata to the south. The artefacts discovered suggest that the site dates back at least to the early post-glacial so a greater thickness of deposits might have been expected across the site than the 150–200mm exposed by excavation. The most probable explanation for this is that considerable deposits, mostly peat, have been removed in historical times (Peake 1935). Currently, the site and this part of the flood plain are below the general level of the River Kennet, which often flows within what are obviously man-made banks; drainage of the local area is provided by a system of channels which probably owe their origin to the peat digging. Subsequent to the removal of the peat, some areas were left derelict; in such areas, the vegetation gradually recovered and tree cover established as in the Wilderness (NGR: SU 400676) whilst other places became rough grazing, as with this site.

Fieldwork, excavation and stratigraphy

The field in which Wawcott XII is located was cultivated in 1964 and cultivation continued into 1965. During this period several visits were made to collect surface finds. The finds looked promising and in the summer of 1965 several small trial trenches and a main trench 12ft (3.6m) by 12ft (13.4m^2) were excavated in the hope of finding an *in situ* site. A further collection of material was made in 1971 when once again the field came under cultivation.

Unfortunately, the excavations revealed that all stratification at the site had been destroyed by the agricultural operations. The sections showed that prior to the first ploughing which occurred in the mid-1940s, there had been approximately 15–20cm of peaty soil covering the site; at the base of this layer traces of a silt were observed, probably the relict of a once more extensive layer. The basal gravel had an uneven surface on which there were localised spreads of fine grained marl. The artefacts were recovered from across the surface of an area of approximately 15 x 20m but a large proportion of them occurred in a marked concentration associated with a patch of the marl located towards the centre of the spread.

The lithic assemblage

None of the artefacts from Wawcott XII can be regarded as stratified because of the disturbance caused by the peat digging and ploughing described above. However, the condition, typology and technological characteristics of the artefacts suggest that they are derived from a primary context site that was disturbed and do not represent a random mixture accumulated by natural processes. This is confirmed by the presence of refitting items. In this sense the Wawcott XII collection may be regarded as an assemblage although inevitably the inferences that may be drawn from the study of such an assemblage are limited.

Assemblage composition and condition

All of the Wawcott XII artefacts are made of flint. The composition of the assemblage is summarized in **Table 6.1**.

Table 6.1: Composition of the Wawcott XII assemblage

Microliths & microburins	5
Utilised pieces	2
Cores & core rejuvenation flakes	35
Blades	335
Flakes (sampled)	103
Miscellaneous debitage	520
Total	1,000

As can be seen from the figures, the assemblage is almost entirely made up of debitage. Although microliths, for example, are commonly under represented in surface collections for obvious reasons, there is every reason to expect larger forms such as endscrapers and burins to be recovered. The absence of such forms from this assemblage is therefore viewed as significant. Conversely, cores tend to be over-represented because they are bigger. In this assemblage, the core:blade ratio is much smaller than that for the excavated Long Blade assemblage from Avington VI. However, this result is probably due at least in part to cores, tending to be at least partially exposed during cultivation and thus easily recovered whereas blades, especially in the smaller sizes, are not exposed to the same extent and the recovery rate is correspondingly lower. The writer has also observed that different operations such as ploughing and harrowing may favour the recovery of different artefact types. Such considerations as these render detailed statistical comparisons invalid in many cases.

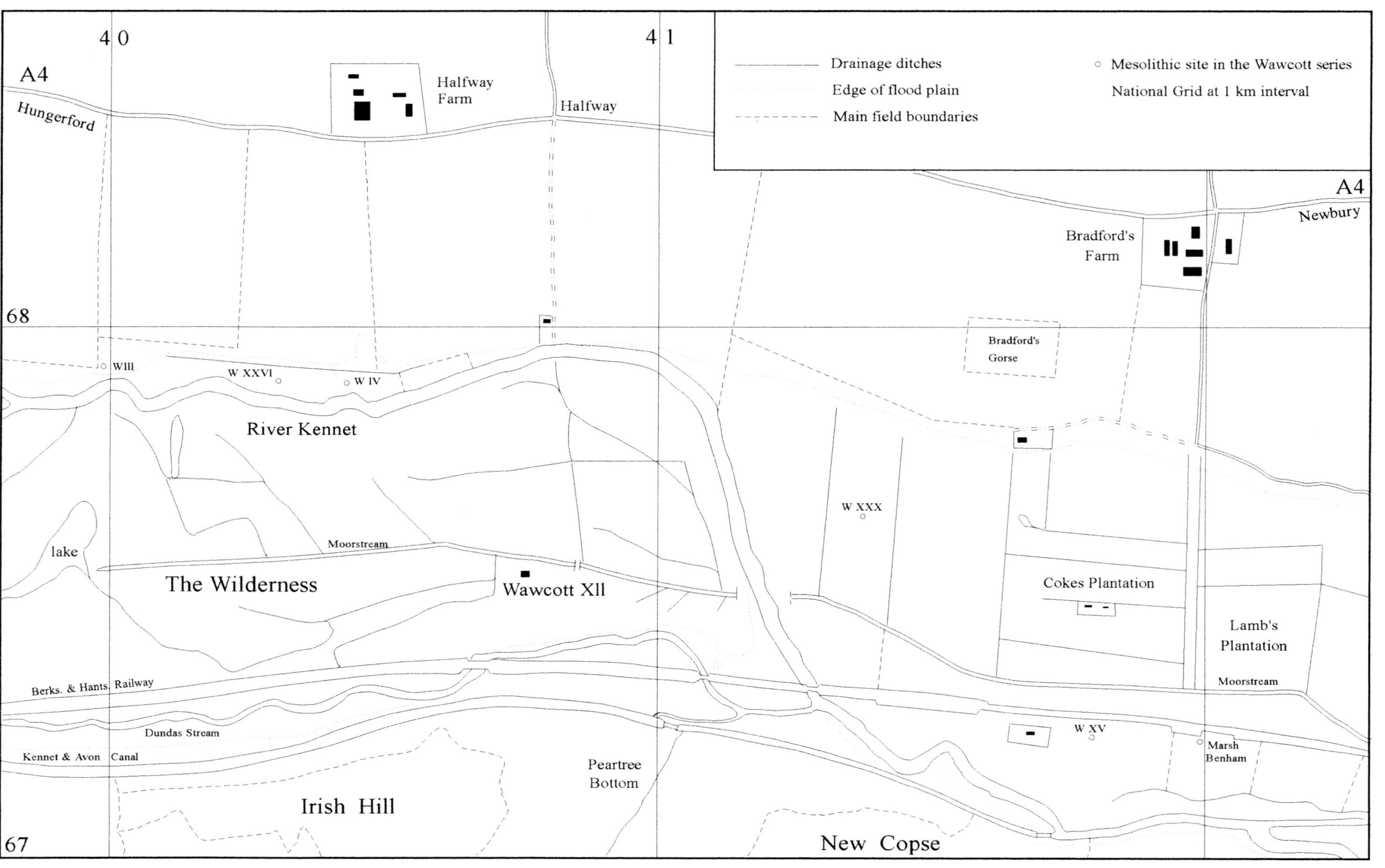

Figure 6.1 Wawcott XII: location

Further difficulties arise from the fact that the artefacts are often damaged as a result of the various agricultural operations. Damage caused by modern machinery is easily identified on a heavily patinated piece but the age of a break can be less obvious on an object that is not patinated. Furthermore, many artefacts, especially the larger ones, have been struck glancing blows which have detached spalls, sometimes along several centimetres of an edge. Unless there is a clear distinction between the freshness and patination of the 'retouch' scars produced in this manner and the original surface of the artefact the identification of utilised pieces, including bruised edge blades, may be problematic.

Most of the artefacts are not markedly patinated but a few have a blue-white patina such as is common in a calcareous environment. Some pieces are stained by iron compounds and their colour may vary from ochreous yellow through browns to distinctly violet hues, all in the space of a few centimetres; the stained artefacts also occasionally show traces of blue-white patination as well.

Tools

As is evident from Table 6.1, few tools were recovered from Wawcott XII. There are two microliths complete enough for identification and the proximal fragment of a third. One of the microliths is a Type A obliquely blunted point (**Fig. 6.2: 2**). It may have been discarded unfinished, it retains traces of a microburin scar and this is at an angle to the line of blunting which may indicate that its separation from the microburin was not entirely successful, so the point may not be as long as intended. The trapezeform microlith illustrated in **Figure 6.2**: 1 was found on the surface of the patch of marl towards the centre of the site during the excavations of 1965. It is broken and burnt but appears to be made from a dark flint. The microlith fragment (**Fig. 6.2: 3**) has fine inverse retouch on the side opposed to the main blunting but whether or not this is original is questionable; this piece was also recovered during the 1965 excavations.

The low frequency of microliths at Wawcott XII is probably not a collecting bias; the same paucity is reflected in the debitage. Only two completely typical microburins are present in the assemblage, one from a microlith blunted on the right side and another blunted on the left side (**Fig. 6.2: 4, 5**); these were produced from blades made of a dark flint which is comparatively rare in the assemblage.

The microliths are the only certainly retouched forms. There are no large tools such as endscrapers or burins; the absence of endscrapers is particularly noteworthy as they are normally such a common element and unlikely to be the result of collecting bias. Although the artefacts tended to be concentrated in a small area, when the field was under cultivation a much larger area was searched so the sample collected is almost certainly representative of the assemblage which may consequently be said to include few tools or utilised pieces. Only two possible examples of the latter were found. One of these is the proximal fragment of a large blade (**Fig. 6.2: 6**) which has some evidence of use on the surface and both edges of what appears from the patina to be an ancient break; the nature of the use is inevitably indeterminate. The identification of the second utilised piece is less secure; it is a blade (75 x 6.5 x 21mm) which, although lacking a burin facet indicative of deliberate burin manufacture, does have a natural burin aspect. Abrasion on this area might result from its adventitious use as a burin but may equally be modern in origin.

Cores

The cores from Wawcott XII resemble the Long Blade cores from Avington VI with one notable difference: the Wawcott XII cores tend to be distinctly smaller. Although the different sediments at these sites have resulted in the two sets of cores exhibiting markedly different superficial appearances, the flint raw material types appear to be similar with the exception of a dark coloured flint often with pale flecks at Wawcott XII which was not observed at Avington VI. Overall, the cores from Wawcott XII have a neat appearance and suggest the production of blades mainly in the length range of 60–100mm although the range includes shorter lengths with blades of 30mm or even less appearing to have been deliberately produced. The neatness of appearance may in part be attributed to the quality of the flint worked; the flint selected by the Wawcott XII knappers is less flawed by frost damage and inclusions than that used at Avington VI so the step fractures and shattering caused by such faults are absent.

There are 24 cores in the main assemblage; only three are single platform cores, these include two large examples with lengths of 185mm and 160mm. Limited refitting suggests that these were abandoned early in the reduction process as was, in all probability, the smaller third example. As reduction ended prematurely, it is possible that all three single platform cores might have been intended as two platform cores. The smallest core was subsequently used as a hammerstone.

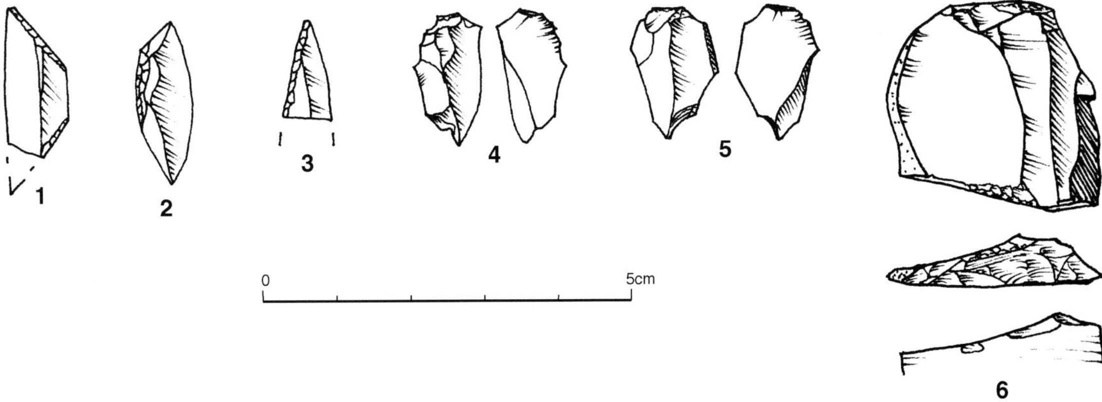

Figure 6.2 Wawcott XII: retouched pieces. 1-3: microliths; 4-5: microburins; utilised blade fragment

The majority of the cores from Wawcott XII have two platforms and share the same pattern as those from Avington VI. The one significant difference between the two sites is that the Wawcott XII cores are smaller as shown in **Table 6.2**

Table 6.2: Comparison of core lengths at Wawcott XII and Avington VI

Length (mm)	<70	70–100	>100	Sample size
Wawcott XII	33%	29%	38%	21
Avington VI	6.5%	37%	57%	46

Taking into account the sample size, the Wawcott XII cores divide equally between the three size ranges whereas more than half of the cores from Avington VI are longer than 100mm and few are less than 70mm. As at Avington VI, the striking platforms vary; both simple platforms resulting from a single removal and platforms formed by several removals are present. The alignment of the platforms with respect to each other also varies as at Avington VI; some are directly opposed and roughly parallel with one another (**Figs 6.3; 6.4: 4, 5, 7**) others have two platforms which are inclined in opposite directions where the core has been rotated about the long axis by as much as 90° (**Fig. 6.4: 2, 3, 6**). A rather different type of asymmetry is demonstrated by a core (**Fig. 6.4: 1**) on which one platform is square to the major axis and has been struck for most of its circumference whereas the second platform at the opposite end is at a distinctly acute angle to the major axis. In most of the two platform cores the two platforms are symmetrically disposed to each other with respect to the long axis. Several of the cores exhibit marked indentations around the periphery of the platform suggestive of the follow through of some form of punch and further evidence of indirect percussion has been noted on the blade butts described below (p. 105).

As in the description of the Avington VI cores the two platform cores have been divided into two types depending respectively on whether or not they show preparatory removals additional and unrelated to those forming the platforms and working faces. The distinction between these two types is not absolute, typological differentiation never is, but most were found to be clearly one type or the other; 10 are Type 1, lacking additional flaking and 11 are Type 2 with additional removals. Type 1 cores are proportionally more prevalent at Wawcott XII than at Avington VI, and it is noticeable that the cores that have additional flaking are larger but, as the refitting of the Avington VI material has shown, the size of a core as found is not necessarily a guide to its original size and character prior to or during reduction. Typical examples of Type 1 cores have been drawn (**Fig. 6.4: 4, 5, 7** and refitting **Fig. 6.7: 1**) and include a particularly elegant example (**Fig. 6.4: 3**), in this latter case the two platforms are inclined in opposite directions because the core has been rotated about the long axis. One unusually large example of a Type 2 core was found broken into two pieces; the fracture appears to be ancient and the pieces refit to form a core 250mm in length (**Fig. 6.5**; Froom 1972a, 18, fig. 4.1). The working face of this core appears to have failed because of a fault which caused an irregular fracture; similar problems appear to be associated with the lower platform. It is would appear likely that an attempt was made to exploit the back of the core, as at Avington VI where the refitting demonstrates that cores such as 118 (**Figs 4.15–4.16**) and 154 (**Figs 4.10–4.12**) could be rotated 180° during reduction. In this Wawcott example a large flake has been detached perhaps as a first step in the formation of a crest. However, either this or a subsequent blow caused the core to break and it was abandoned. This core also demonstrates that although the Wawcott XII cores are generally smaller, large nodules were also occasionally exploited. Indeed, some of the group 2 cores have little or no cortex and from their general character could well represent cores which had been extensively reduced as in the example shown in **Figure 6.4: 2** which also has a refitted rejuvenation flake. The overall shape of the group 2 cores exhibits the same variation as noted on the Avington VI cores. One core is markedly rectangular with a distinctive flat back (**Fig. 6.3**); another (not drawn) exhibits a crest although it is not truly triangular in cross-section.

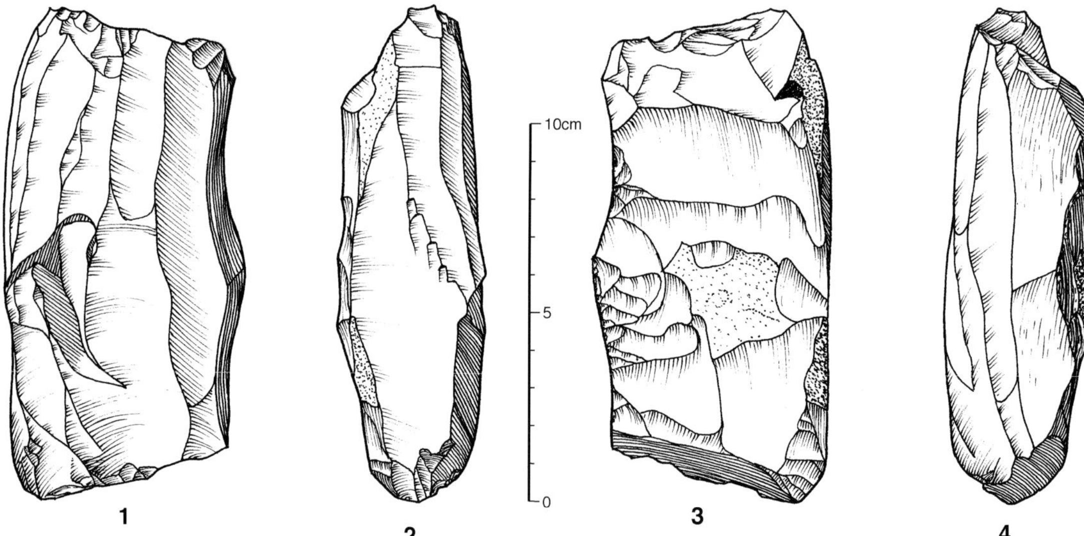

Figure 6.3 Wawcott XII: bipolar core with opposed removals on one working face and lateral removals on the flat back

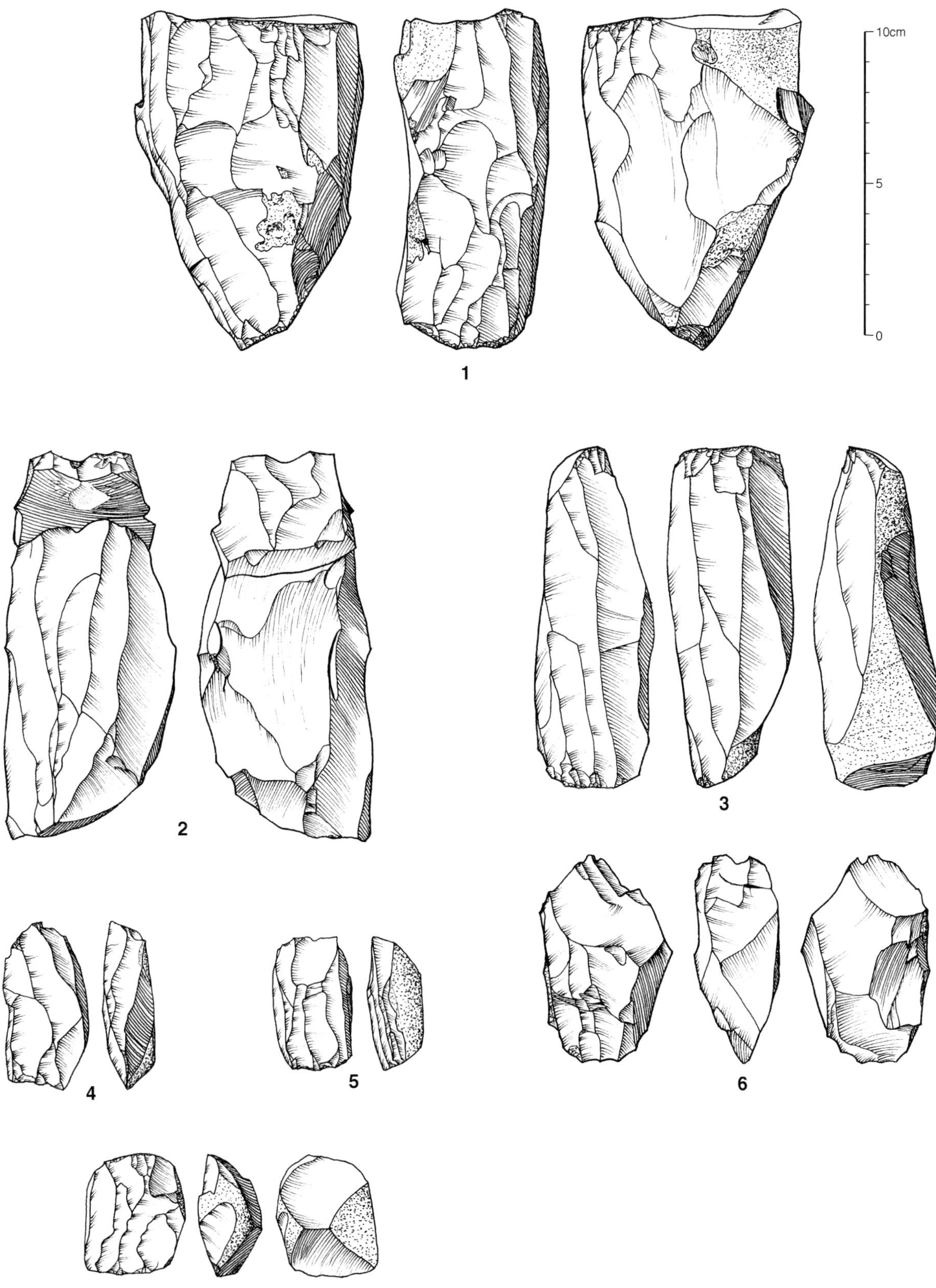

Figure 6.4 Wawcott XII: bipolar cores

The cores show that flint from various sources was utilised although patination made identification difficult or even impossible in some cases. In most of the cores the cortex is thin (<0.5mm) and closely resembles that noted at Avington VI; this also applies to the less common thicker cortex (1–2mm or occasionally thicker) which sometimes has pock-marks 1cm or so across. The flint beneath tends to be dark, translucent and often has frequent inclusions; in thinner sections it can appear brown. The source of most of the flint used on the site was local; only one type has not been observed by the author during a life time of field walking in the Kennet Valley although this is not to say that it does not occur locally. This flint is black rather than dark and is inclined to a matt rather than gloss appearance; it often has numerous small pale inclusions. It is relatively rarely used but two of the small cores, as well as the two microburins and possibly the trapezeform microlith (**Fig. 6.2: 1**) are made from this type of flint. Four small-medium sized cores are made on a similarly dark flint which incorporates little pale flecks rather than the inclusions observed in the more common type. A few of the cores exhibited areas of bright gloss with a varnish like appearance which the writer has only previously encountered on artefacts from the Lower Palaeolithic site at Knowle Farm, Savernake,Wiltshire.

Core rejuvenation flakes

The Long Blade assemblage from Avington VI indicates that the rejuvenation of core platforms could involve the removal of flakes and spalls as small as 15mm or less. Inspection of the Wawcott XII cores and rejuvenation flakes indicates that although most of the platforms have been formed by a single removal, multifaceted platforms which involved the removal of several flakes are present. This would suggest that core rejuvenation flakes are under represented as might be expected with small items in what is essentially a surface collection. It is also possible that some examples have simply not been recognized as a result of damage caused by agricultural machinery.

There are 11 rejuvenation flakes that have the characteristics of core tablets (**Fig. 6.6**). In shape their widths are similar to their lengths, which range from 90mm–35mm; in size these flakes correlate with the cores previously described. The flakes appear to have been struck from cores at various stages in the reduction sequence. This aspect of core technology appears to be identical with that at Avington VI. The one observable difference, the relative frequency of rejuvenation flakes to cores, cannot be relied upon because of the differential recovery that exists between excavation and surface recovery. However, the difference is also consistent with a reduction in the size of the industry: smaller cores are likely to produce relatively fewer rejuvenation flakes.

Hammerstones

Two items have been recognised as hammerstones by virtue of localised battering and incipient cones of percussion. One is a single platform core weighing 255gm from which only a few removals had been deliberately detached and which was otherwise largely cortical; it shows a single area of quite intense battering. The second item is a major fragment of a large rejuvenation flake weighing 225gm; it may have broken when struck from the core or possibly while in use as a hammerstone a purpose for which it appears to have been heavily used.

Crested blades

Seventeen crested blades have been identified; 11 of these have removals along both sides of the crest (**Fig. 6.8: 1, 2, 4**), the other six crests have been achieved by removing flakes from one side only. In the latter case the other side of the crest is commonly the scar of a blade-like removal. Most of the examples do not retain any cortex and where cortex is present it covers only a small fraction of the upper surface. The ratio of lateral:unilateral cresting is 1.8:1, exactly as in the Long Blade assemblage at Avington VI. The ratio of crested blades to ordinary blades cannot be estimated with any confidence because too many small blades are believed to be missing. Similarly, the ratio of crested blades to cores cannot be measured with any real accuracy since cores are probably over-represented but there is a suggestion that at Wawcott XII crested blades were produced less frequently than at Avington VI.

In general terms, the crested blades from Wawcott XII are shorter than those from Avington VI. There is only one long example of a crested blade from Wawcott XII the length of which is 183mm. Before it was detached from the core part of the cresting, this piece had already been removed by the detachment of blades; part of one such blade has been refitted (**Fig. 6.8: 1**). The remaining crested blades range from 126mm–50mm. One of the smaller examples has been refitted to a broken blade which also displays traces of cresting, the blade was struck after the crested blade and together they demonstrate the extensive nature of the cresting (**Fig. 6.8: 3**). At Avington VI there is a higher proportion of long crested blades with several examples in the range 160–220mm, as well as smaller examples. Dispersion diagrams for the crested blades show that, as at Avington VI, the average length:width ratio is 4:1 and the average width:thickness ratio is 2:1. The removals struck to form the initial crest were commonly 10–30mm in width with occasional larger removals up to 50 or 60mm in width. Of the 17 crested blades identified, 7 are incomplete but the extent to which this fragmentation is the result of modern agricultural activity is uncertain. Similarly, it is difficult to identify with any certainty those crested blades with a true bruised edge as opposed to those damaged in recent times; however, two examples appear to have genuine ancient bruised edges.

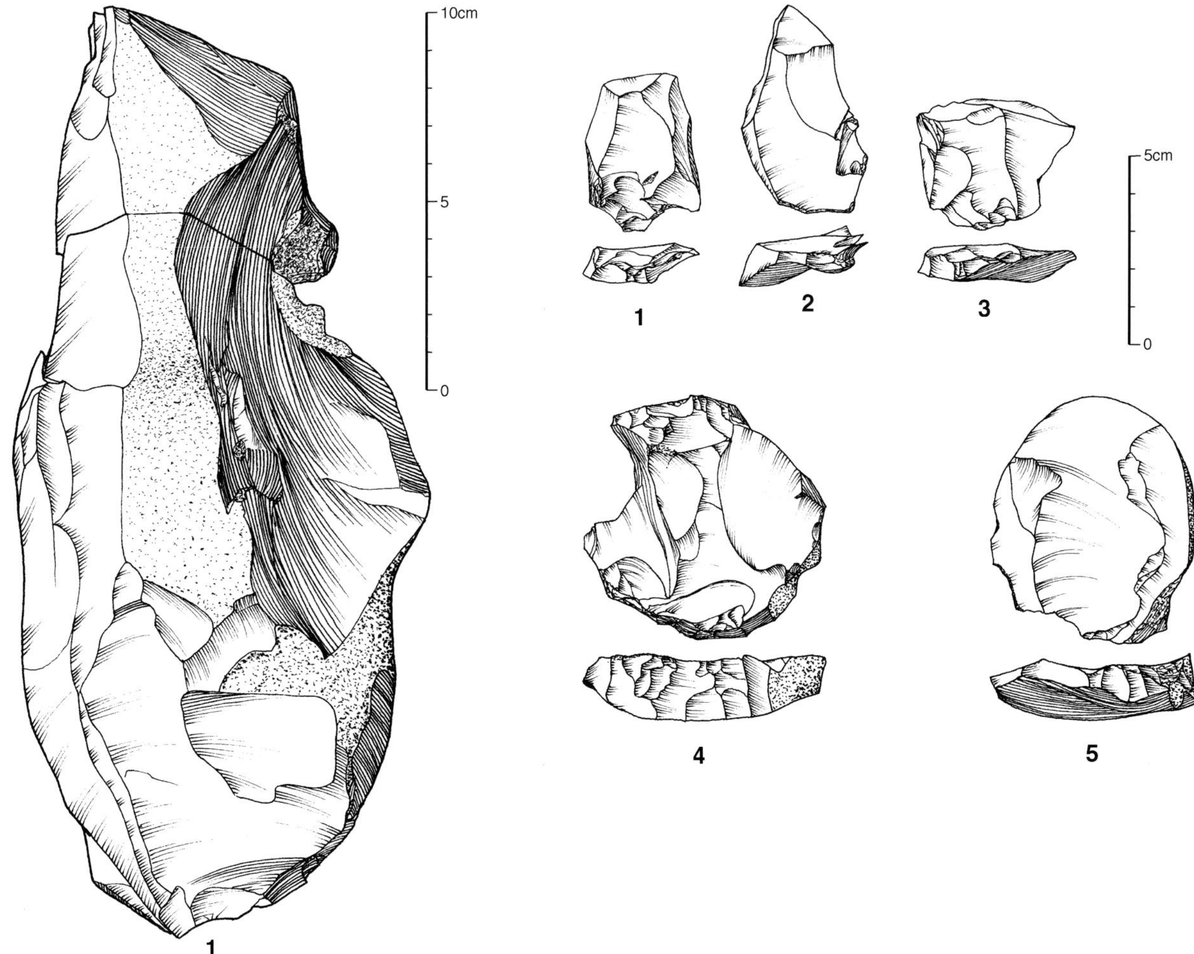

Figure 6.5 Wawcott XII: large bipolar core found in two pieces due to ancient break

Figure 6.6 Wawcott XII: core rejuvenation flakes

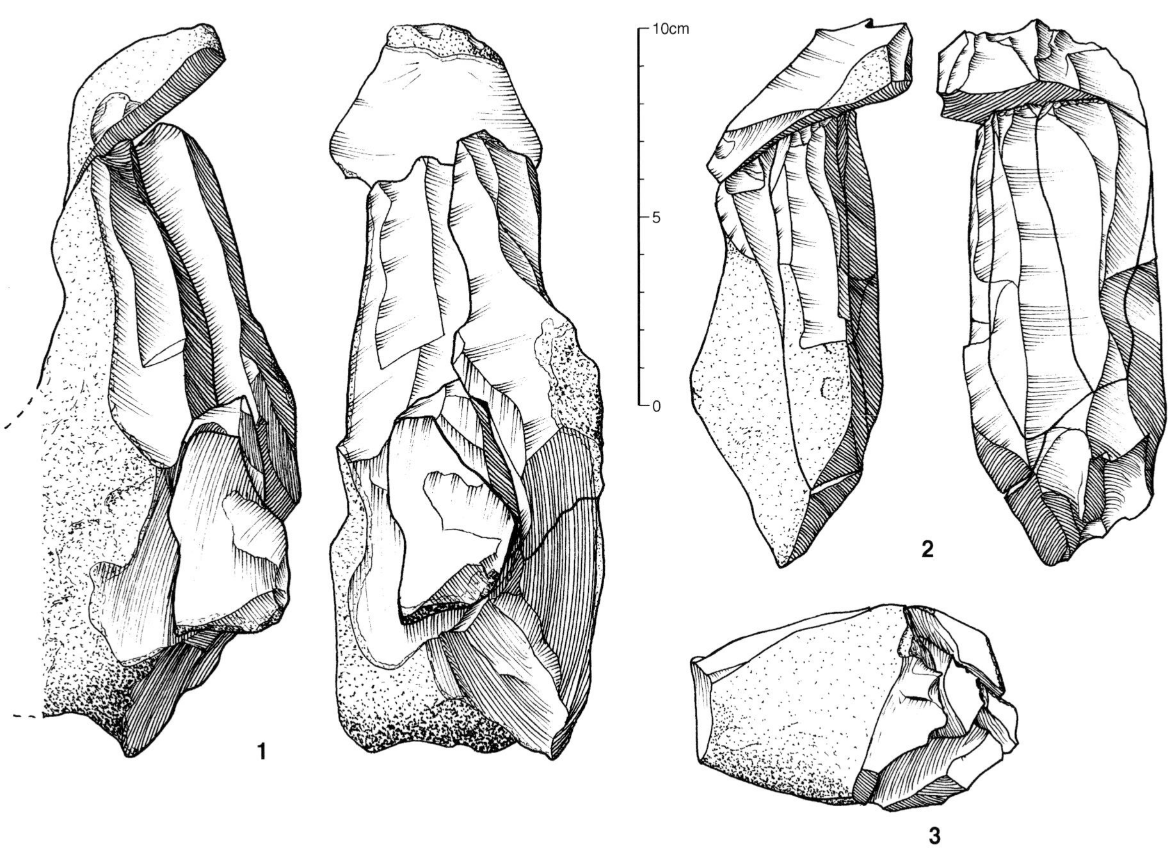

Figure 6.7. Wawcott XII: large bipolar core showing refitted platform preparation flake and conjoined removals from an early stage in the reduction sequence

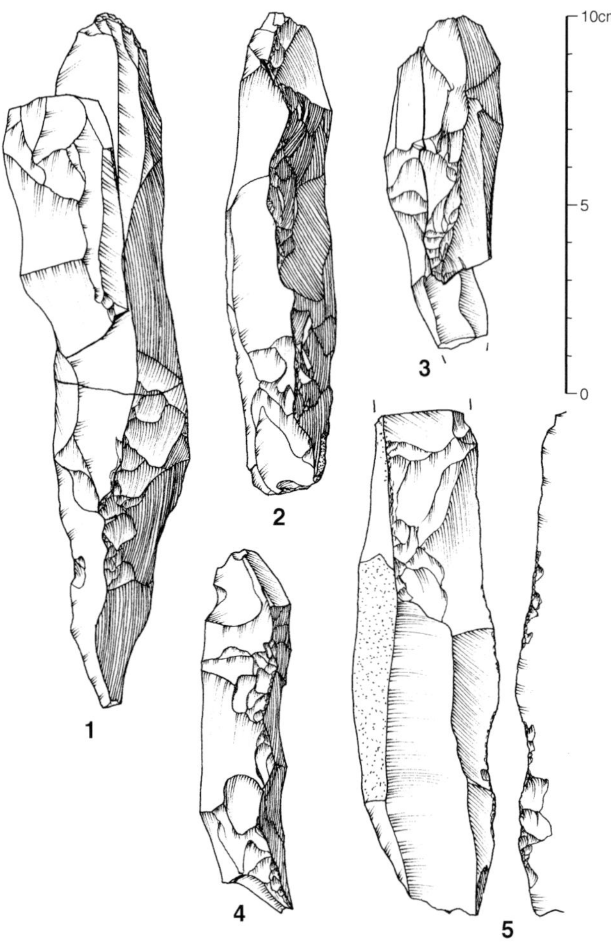

Figure 6.8 Wawcott XII: 1-4: crested blades; 5: bruised edge blade. Drawn with the proximal ends at the top

Blade fragments

Numerically blade fragments form a major group but it is evident that, in some examples at least, the breakage is relatively recent and probably results from damage by agricultural operations; in other examples it is equally obvious that the break surfaces are ancient whilst in some cases it cannot be decided either way with any confidence. The blade fragments total 182 items including 67 proximal fragments, 43 middle sections and 72 distal fragments. One crested blade and 8 plain blades have been reconstructed from fragments. The degree of fragmentation of blades cannot be estimated with any confidence in this assemblage because of the uncertainties expressed above but there are 128 complete blades and 67 proximal fragments giving a ratio of 1.9:1. This indicates that 33% of the blades are either failing to separate properly from the core or suffer subsequent breakage. Beyond this, study of the blade fragments does not significantly extend the range of observations that can be made from a study of the complete blades.

Complete blades

In addition to the 17 crested blades already described, there are 136 blades which are complete or only slightly damaged. This is a comparatively small sample and equates with approximately a single transect such as C19–C20 or D22 from one of the main concentrations at Avington VI. This in itself places constraints on any statistical analysis; however, a more serious constraint is that the Wawcott XII assemblage is essentially a surface collection and is not therefore a truly representative sample. Nonetheless, some useful comparisons can be made. The blades have been analysed using the same scheme as that used for the Avington VI Long Blade assemblage, dividing the blades into five groups. The distribution of the Wawcott XII blades between these five groups was numerically similar to that observed for the Avington VI blades. There are also similarities with respect to the general appearance of the blades: as at Avington VI the outline shape varies with parallel-sided and pointed forms both common, as well as occasional elliptical examples; the number of dorsal arêtes varies but most blades have two or three or occasionally more.

Metrical analysis also produced results comparable with those from Avington VI. A length:width dispersion diagram shows that virtually all of those items classified as 'blades' are enclosed by lines of gradient 1:2 and 1:5, a good median line being 1:3. In this respect the dispersion is indistinguishable from that for Avington VI. There are, however, two discernible differences. Firstly, the Wawcott XII blades rarely exceed 135mm in length whereas Avington VI has a significant number in the range 135–200mm with occasional examples as long as 200–250mm. Blades from both of the major concentrations at Avington VI exhibit a length distribution that was bimodal, there is no convincing evidence that such a bimodal pattern exists at Wawcott XII. These observations reinforce the comments made with regard to the size of the cores. Thus there is strong evidence that the blades at Wawcott XII are not as long as those in the Long Blade assemblage at Avington VI. The dispersion diagram reveals a relative scarcity of blades in the length range 20–60mm compared to Avington VI. However, this may be more apparent than real and could be attributed to bias inherent in surface collecting because small blades are intrinsically less likely to be exposed by cultivation; conversely this effect should cause large blades to be over-represented, thus emphasising the significance of the relative scarcity of the larger blades. However, although small blades were not recovered in any number, small blade cores are well represented. This suggests that the smaller size of the Wawcott blades is a real characteristic of the assemblage.

Table 6.3: Triangular coordinates for the Wawcott XII blades

Blades with >10% cortex	Regular blades with <10% cortex	Irregular blades with <10% cortex
(22 blades)	(63 blades)	(35 blades)
0.692	0.718	0.680
0.235	0.218	0.256

Calculation of triangular co-ordinates (**Table 6.3**) to describe the relative proportions of length, width and thickness of the blades, produced values which agree closely with those obtained for the blades from Avington VI, although there is a slight tendency for the Wawcott XII blades to be somewhat wider in proportion to their length (**Table 6.4**).

Table 6.4: Comparison of triangular coordinates for blades from Avington VI, Wawcott XII and Crown Acres

	Avington VI	Wawcott XII	Crown Acres
Cortical blades	0.719; 0.217	0.629; 0.235	0.708; 0.227
Non cortical, regular blades	0.736; 0.238	0.718; 0.218	0.726; 0.215
Weighted means	0.731; 0.232	0.711; 0.222	0.722; 0.280

Blade butts were also measured and the quantity previously defined as the Striking Platform Quotient calculated. In general terms, the result closely paralleled that obtained for Avington VI although there is a tendency for the Wawcott XII blades to register slightly smaller values (**Table 6.5**). This may only be a reflection of the absence of many or possibly most of blades smaller than 60mm from the sample, resulting from surface collection. It was observed that with the Avington VI blades the Striking Platform Quotient was somewhat length dependent, tending to smaller values as the length of the blade increased. However, a small number of blades produced exceptionally high values for this quantity because unusually large amounts of platform were retained on the blade butt (**Fig. 6.7: 3**) suggesting a different technique from that normally employed.

Table 6.5: Comparison of Striking Platform Quotients across sites

	Avington VI C19-20	Avington VI D21-22	Wawcott XII	Crown Acres
0-0.2	29%	36%	58%	74%
0-0.5	72%	74%	84%	97%

The majority of the blades, approximately 80%, have butts which indicate some retouching to adjust the striking platform prior to striking. However, retouch across the top of the platform is rare and retouch down the top of the working face was much the dominant type. This could well be a reflection of the shorter lengths of the blades struck at Wawcott XII; at Avington VI it was commonly the longer blades which exhibited retouch across the top of the platform.

None of the complete blades exhibits a bruised edge that can be assigned with any confidence to use in ancient times. However, a large fragment, 132 x 18 x 40mm, of a long thick blade (**Fig. 6.8: 5**) does appear to possess a true bruised edge as the patination of the damage scar surfaces is the same as that of the rest of the fragment surface. The low incidence of bruised edge blades at Wawcott XII may result from the production of smaller blades as at Avington VI such utilisation tends to be associated with the longer blades.

Flakes

As far as possible the Wawcott XII flakes have been analysed using the same variables and methods as used for those from the Avington VI Long Blade assemblage. Exact comparison is not possible since, as with the blades, it is virtually certain that many flakes, especially the smaller flakes, were not recovered. Analysis of the lengths of the flakes revealed that five are in the range 100–140mm whereas Avington VI produced only a single flake in this range; the numbers of flakes in the range 60–99mm appear to be proportionate at the two sites. A length:width dispersion diagram produced a scatter almost entirely enclosed by lines of gradient 2:1 and 1:2, exactly comparable with the corresponding diagram for Avington VI. Observation of the cortex shows that the Wawcott XII flakes retain more. This could be a reflection of a tendency towards the exploitation of smaller nodules of raw material because the surface area:volume ratio changes with the size of the nodule. This is consistent with other observations on the Wawcott XII material but an alternative explanation might be that surface collecting will tend to yield the larger primary flakes which are intrinsically more likely to have a high proportion of cortex. Several flakes were noted that appeared to be the ends of flint nodules that had been detached in order to create the initial striking platform of an embryonic core (**Fig. 6.7**).

The majority of the flakes exhibit prominent bulbs of percussion; approximately 20% of the flakes were detached by blows impacting on a cortical area whereas the remainder were struck from a prepared surface. A minority of the flakes show just a point of percussion and retain little or no trace of the striking platform on the butt. On these pieces the bulbs of percussion are also more dispersed and may suggest the use of an indirect percussion technique using a punch to produce blades. Only 10% of the flakes have faceted butts although this may be subject to error due to the amount of cultivation damage present.

One patinated flake has heavy bruising on part of one edge; it is 100 x 52mm and similar to examples of bruised edge flakes in the Avington VI Long Blade assemblage.

Refitting

While work on the assemblage was in progress the possibility of refits was kept under constant review. However, given the disturbance of the assemblage, it is not surprising that comparatively few actual refits were found although close matches for flint type and patination were relatively common. Both of the large single platform cores were found to have refits, two and five respectively, the nature of which encouraged the belief that both of these cores had been abandoned early in the reduction sequence. The more extensively refitted core (**Fig. 6.7**) was made from a rather irregularly shaped nodule, one end expands into a considerable protuberance (not fully shown in the drawing) reminiscent of core 264 from Avington VI (**Fig. 4.3**). As can be seen in **Figure 6.7** the first step in the reduction process was the removal of the end of the nodule to form a striking platform. This was followed by several lateral removals, some as large as 90mm, which may have formed a crest. However, the early longitudinal removals appear to have been more or less unsatisfactory, the flint in the lower central zone of the core exhibits irregular fracture, at least one blade-like removal fragmented and only the distal section has been refitted. A third core was refitted to a core rejuvenation flake which indicated that the core had subsequently been extensively reduced, with removals having been detached to a depth of up to 30mm (**Fig. 6.4: 2**). Another core was refitted to a rejuvenation flake and four blade-like removals (**Fig. 6.7: 1**); these latter removals are notable for their large butts (**Fig. 6.7: 3**), the values for the Striking Platform Quotient for these removals being 0.24, 0.38, 1.3, and 1.4. One other core was refitted to a removal that terminated in a hinge fracture. A number of conjoins were also located among the blades and flakes. Two of the smaller crested blades were found to refit (**Fig. 6.8: 3**), one on top of the other; the largest crested blade was refitted to a fragment of a blade-like removal (**Fig. 6.8: 1**); two large blades, struck from opposing platforms, conjoined and the major fragment of a third blade was added to them. Finally, two simple flakes were refitted to each other; they appear to represent the end of a flint nodule detached in the initial stage of core formation.

Summary

Wawcott XII clearly fits into the general context of Long Blade sites. Unfortunately, as with Avington VI, there are no organic remains that can be reliably associated with the site although in the case of Wawcott XII a few such items were recovered including some unidentifiable bone fragments and the remains of the left upper molar of a horse identified as *Equus caballus* at Reading Museum. However, surface finds of bones and teeth are quite common in the peaty deposits of the flood plain in the area and little significance can normally be attached to them. Taking into account the absence of proper stratification at the site, dating remains somewhat speculative and is inevitably unsatisfactorily based on parallels for the lithic assemblage.

Microlith production was at least a minor activity at Wawcott XII but there are too few microliths to permit sensible discussion; the trapezeform (**Fig. 6.2: 1**) is rare in the writer's experience, although an example is known from the neighbouring site of Wawcott XXX (Froom, 1994; in preparation) which is regarded as an Early Mesolithic site and other examples have occasionally been found in the assemblages from other local Early Mesolithic sites. Indeed, further work on the Wawcott XXX assemblage (Froom, in preparation) shows that at that site trapezeform microliths are associated with a small group of artefacts which belong to the closing phase of the occupation. This suggests that although they are Early Mesolithic they are not contemporary with the earliest use of Wawcott XXX. This probably indicates that at Wawcott XII the trapezeform microlith, the two microburins and a small number of cores and blades should be regarded as evidence of a later use of the site that is not related to the Long Blade assemblage. By contrast, truncated blades are known to occur with Long/Bruised edge Blade assemblages in both the Somme Valley (Fagnart, 1989; 1991) and the Paris Basin (Hinout, 1997) and are clearly associated with the large cores and blades.

In general terms, the debitage from Wawcott XII compares closely with that from Avington VI. There are, however, differences in detail. The cores and blades tend to be smaller at Wawcott XII although the very large two platform core indicates that nodules as big as 250–300mm in length were occasionally exploited, although few blades corresponding to such cores were found. At the other extreme, there is clear evidence for the production of blades as small as 30mm or less in significant numbers. This perceived decline in Long Blade production may suggest that Wawcott XII is a more recent site than Avington VI, transitional towards the Early Mesolithic. This may also be reflected in the knapping methods.

Comparing the Avington VI and Wawcott XII assemblages production of core rejuvenation flakes and crested blades appears to be less frequent at the latter than the former. Such a reduction in frequency might reflect conscious changes in core technology or might simply be a result of the increasing tendency to use smaller nodules of raw material concomitant with the general reduction in the size of the industry. This may also reflect a change in the accessibility of raw materials with large nodules becoming harder to find as climate improved and vegetation masked more of the landscape.

One other small but possibly significant difference between the two assemblages is the absence of any evidence of burning on the artefacts from Avington VI, whereas burnt pieces were observed in the Wawcott XII assemblage but in no great number.

When considering the differences between Wawcott XII and Avington VI such as size of the blades and core technology, it is tempting to suggest that although the two sites are clearly closely related Wawcott XII is somewhat later in date. The location of Wawcott XII, out on the flood plain proper, may be relevant in this context. At the time Avington VI was occupied the flood plain may have been a rather bare and inhospitable environment, in contrast to this the base of the valley slope may have offered more shelter. A century or two later there could well have been a reversal with soil development on the flood plain encouraging plant growth and producing an altogether more hospitable environment.

Chapter 7

Crown Acres

Location

The site of Crown Acres no longer exists. It was destroyed by commercial gravel digging that transformed the Thatcham area of the Kennet Valley over the period from 1950–2000. **Figure 7.1** shows the location of the site as it was in about 1960, situated in a group of small fields bordering the present flood plain of the River Kennet. Records in Newbury Museum identify the grid reference as SU 509666 although Campbell (1977, vol. 2, 141) gives it as SU 511667 an inaccuracy repeated for the entry of the site in the *Gazetteer of Upper Palaeolithic Sites* (Bonsall in Bonsall & Wymer, 1977) also attributed to Campbell.

History and fieldwork

Crown Acres was discovered by Peter Tosdevine and other members of the Newbury Museum Archaeological Group in 1961. At this time a surface collection was made; further field walking and collecting by individuals from the group seems to have continued after this initial exploration. Despite at least one reference to the contrary (Bonsall, 1977) the present writer was not involved with any work at the site during its existence. An aerial photograph of the area, dated April 1971, shows that although gravel digging was taking place in the general area, the group of fields containing the Crown Acres site was untouched. Another dated April, 1976, indicates that the small fields had been consumed by the gravel digging and the Crown Acres site had probably been destroyed by this time. This suggests that there was a 10– 15 year period during which material could have been collected from the site. Subsequently, most of the worked out gravel pits became fisheries belonging to Newbury and Thatcham Angling Associations.

Over the 40 or so years since its discovery, no detailed account of the Crown Acres industry has been published. A brief note referring to the initial finds appeared in the County Journal (Anon, 1964, 98) and this records that the artefacts had been placed in Newbury Museum; this is consistent with the accession records for 1964 at the museum. This initial collection is presumably the material studied by John Campbell whilst engaged in post-graduate studies at the University of Oxford during the late 1960s and subsequently published (Campbell, 1977, vol. 1, 177–180; vol. 2, 141). Some years later, in the early 1980s, Nick

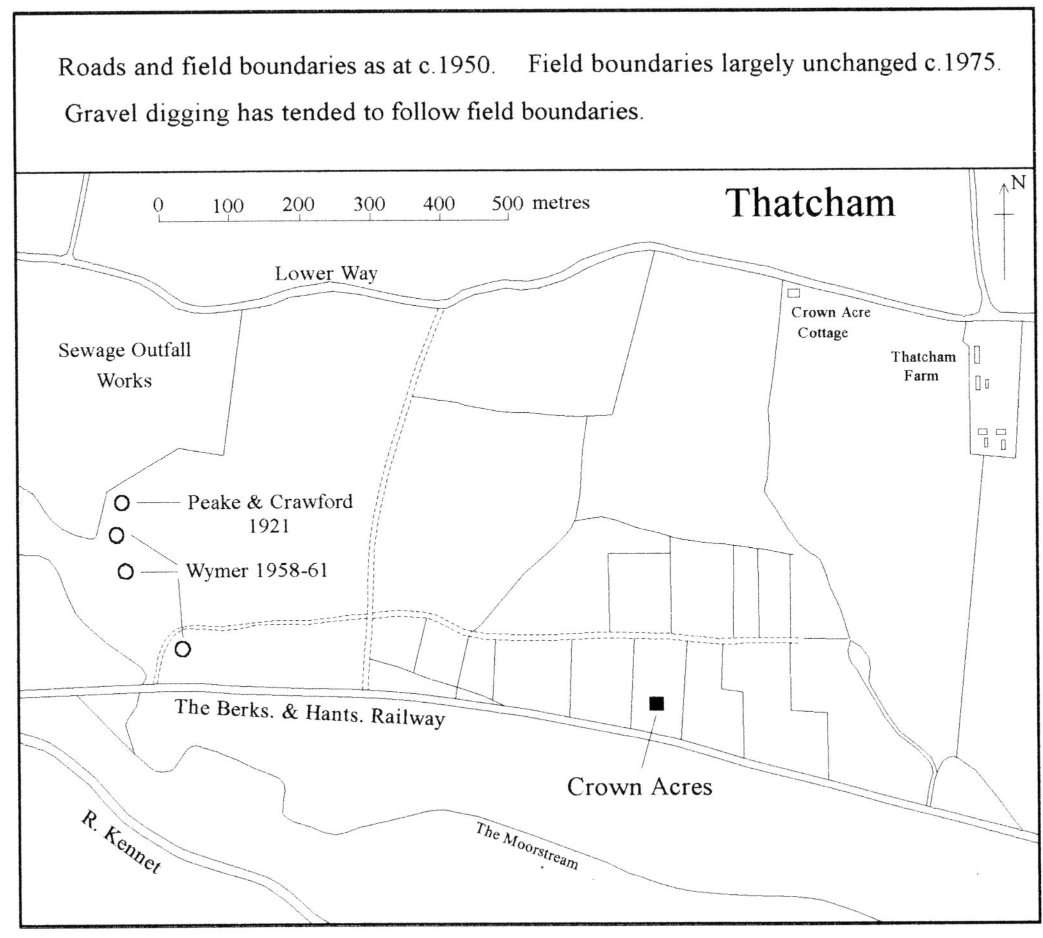

Figure 7.1 Crown Acres: location

Barton also studied the Crown Acres material in Newbury Museum as part of his post-graduate research and deposited a copy of the relevant part of his thesis (Barton, 1986a) in Newbury Museum archive. Comparison of the accounts given by Campbell and Barton suggests that during the period 1964–1984 the Crown Acres assemblage in Newbury Museum changed significantly; some material including blades disappeared at some time during that 20 year period whilst new material, including tools, was added. The Newbury Museum material studied by the writer in 2002 appears to be substantially the same as that studied by Barton indicating that the collection had stabilised. However, in addition to the assemblage stored in Newbury Museum, the writer had the advantage of studying a much larger collection. In 1994 the writer was introduced to John Turner, a former member of the Newbury Museum Archaeological Group, who, in conversation, indicated that he had retained material from Crown Acres in his private collection. Sadly, Mr. Turner died before the writer could visit and view the material but his widow, Jean Turner, generously allowed the writer unrestricted access to the Crown Acres material for research purposes. It is possible that other material from the site exists or once existed in other private collections.

Stratigraphy

The Crown Acres site was trial trenched by members of the Newbury Museum Archaeological Group on at least one occasion but nothing of consequence was found; the site appeared to have been destroyed by ploughing. In a conversation with the writer early in the 1970s Ray Sheridan, a leading member of the group, described the deposits as a black peaty topsoil over gravel in the surface of which were patches of a pale sandy material. At the time, the writer was struck by the similarity of this description to that of the writer's Long Blade site Wawcott XII. The 'pale' deposit at Crown Acres was almost certainly marl, similar if not identical to the deposits which occur widely on the uneven surface of the basal gravels in the Marsh Benham – Wawcott area. This observation was confirmed in 1977 when extensive gravel digging out on the flood plain within 1km and to the south of the Crown Acres site, enabled the writer to record and photograph the exposed stratigraphy over the course of a number of visits to the workings; numerous and extensive marl deposits were recorded. Although the trial excavation at Crown Acres failed to locate undisturbed strata, such evidence as there was suggested that the artefacts had been originally located on or just above the gravel/marl deposits and below the peaty layer, as at Wawcott XII.

The lithic assemblage

Table 7.1 summarises the composition of the Crown Acres assemblage. The artefacts presented here come from two samples: one stored in Newbury Museum and the other which formed part of the private collection of the late John Turner. Those artefacts stored in Newbury Museum may be sub-divided into three groups: some are marked 'Crown Acres, Thatcham, 1961' and include small nondescript pieces of little significance; others are marked 'C.A./J.T' which the writer assumes may be translated as Crown Acres/John Turner; in addition there are a large number of items, including tools, which are not marked in any way but which are curated with the marked pieces. The most likely explanation for these variations, taking into account the discrepancies in the descriptions given by John Campbell and Nick Barton, is that the Newbury Museum collection accumulated from various sources and was built up, and possibly depleted, over a period of years.

John Turner's collection showed that considerable effort had been made with respect to its organisation and storage, although no written records seemed to be associated with it. The collection is predominantly of Neolithic/Bronze age artefacts and the bulk of it originates from only a few sites. It is most unlikely that Mr. Turner collected Long Blade material from anywhere other than Crown Acres and thus the sample studied by the writer may safely be assumed to have come from that site although only a few pieces are actually marked as such. In this context it is worth noting that the writer was able to secure fits between artefacts in the Newbury Museum collection and items in the John Turner collection. When viewed collectively the two collections have a uniformity which suggests that they may be safely evaluated as a single entity. However, this does not mean that the sample is without bias. To judge from his wider collection, under most circumstances at least, John Turner did not retain debitage in any great quantity and this may have been true, at least to some extent, of other members of the Newbury Museum Archaeological Group. Consequently, the proportional frequencies of the various artefact types are likely to be suspect. The background scatter of a few typical Mesolithic artefacts is another cause of uncertainty. There are many Mesolithic sites in the Kennet Valley, as for example those concentrated in the Thatcham and Marsh Benham–Wawcott area, and agricultural and peat digging disturbance has probably caused some mixing. Typologically Mesolithic artefacts are present in both the Newbury Museum and Turner collections from Crown Acres but have notv been included in the analyses on the grounds that they probably result from the mixing described.

Table 7.1: Composition of the Crown Acres assemblage

Artefact type	Newbury Museum	Turner Collection
Backed bladelets	3	
Endscrapers	5	3
Burin	1	
Truncated blades	3	
Cores	7	6
Core rejuvenation flakes	5	16
Crested blades	3	2
Blade fragments	140	324
Complete blades	14	80
Flakes	20	65
Bruised edge pieces	1	2
Totals	202	498

Condition

The Newbury Museum sample contains 245 artefacts although Campbell listed 314 (1977, vol. 2, 141). The Turner collection contains 691 artefacts. All of the artefacts are made of flint. Together the two samples total somewhat just less than 1,000 pieces which is similar to that available from Wawcott XII. The majority of these artefacts divide into those which are patinated blue-white and those which have an ochreous yellow-brown staining. Some artefacts are partially stained and patinated and these differences in surface colouration may occur on opposite sides of the piece. Such differential patination-staining could well relate to the original position of the artefact, according to whether it was at the gravel-peat interface where it would accrue an ochreous staining or, at the marl-peat junction where the blue-white patination would pertain. However, a small number of artefacts exhibit a slightly different appearance, the patination being more distinctly white, sometimes with a brown mottling. One large blade-like flake in the Newbury Museum collection which has been chipped in recent times reveals that the patination has proceeded to a much greater depth than in most of the Crown Acres material. It is possible that this may indicate an earlier occupation at the site. As is to be expected with surface collection from fields which were at least occasionally cultivated, many of the artefacts are slightly abraded and exhibit edge damage; in some cases quite large spalls of 10mm or more in size have been detached. However, the fresher scar surfaces left by such damage are not patinated and can easily be distinguished from deliberate retouch or edge modification caused by ancient use.

Tools

All of the tools referred to in this account are in the Newbury Museum collection unless otherwise specified.

There are two artefacts both with ancient breaks that can be classified as Class B microliths (Clark, 1933; Clark & Rankine 1939) or backed bladelets. One of these (**Fig. 7.2: 1**) was among the original finds of 1961 and this piece is one of the few to have the rare white-mottled white patina; the existing portion shows that it was produced on a neatly made blade originally some 70–80mm in length, struck from a two platform core. Originally it appears to have been retouched along the whole of one side and for part of this length the marginal abrupt retouch has been applied both from the edge and down from a dorsal arête. The break is complex and may indicate an impact force acting along the major axis of the artefact; the other end is also missing. It is difficult to identify the proximal end of the original blade because of the uniformity of the ventral surface. The other microlith (**Fig. 7.2: 3**) exhibits similar characteristics. It is also made on a blade originally 70–80mm long, has the rare white patina and ancient breaks at both ends, one of which may be an impact fracture. The entire length of what survives of the left edge has been retouched.

Another artefact with the white-mottled patina is made on a broader blade and defied typological classification (**Fig. 7.2: 2**). It retains part of the bulb of percussion and a trace of the butt. The upper part of the left edge as drawn is a break surface which may be a spontaneous fracture which occurred as the blade was struck from the core or a fracture associated with the retouch applied to the left edge. The distal end is broken and the fracture is complex. The right edge has suffered some damage in recent times. At the proximal end the central arête exhibits some fine abrasion and if this is ancient rather than post-depositional in origin, it may indicate that this artefact was fitted into some form of haft which its outline would facilitate.

Endscrapers

Endscrapers represent the largest group of tools (**Fig. 7.3: 1–8**) although there are only eight and two of these are doubtful: the

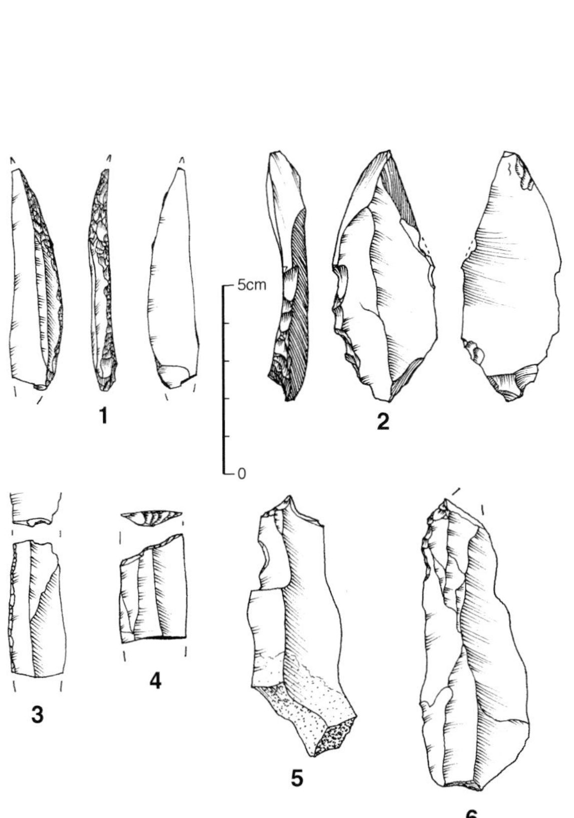

Figure 7.2 Crown Acres: tools. 1-3: backed blades; 4-6: truncated blades. 2-6 are drawn with the proximal end at the top

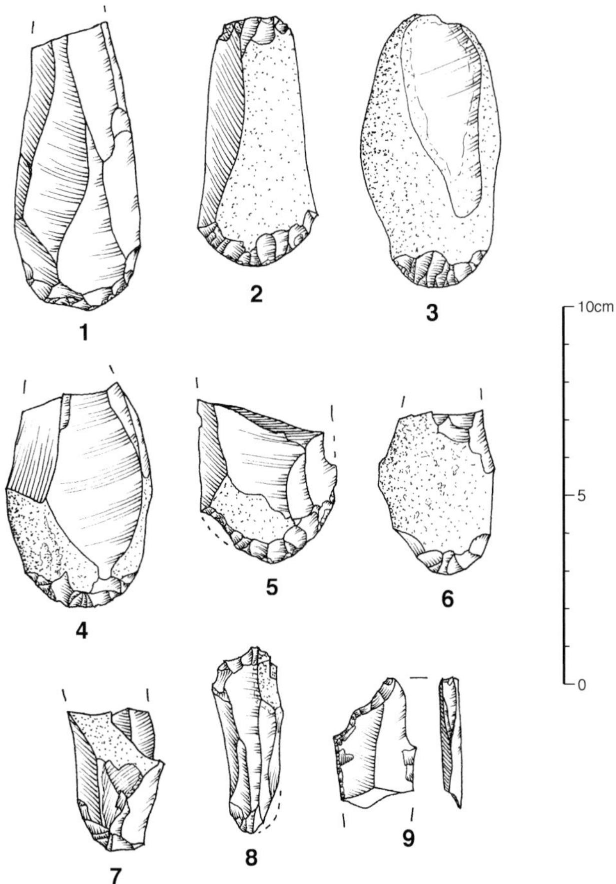

Figure 7.3 Crown Acres: tools. 1-8: endscrapers; 9: burin on a retouched truncation. All are drawn with the proximal end at the top

patination and general character of one (**Fig. 7.3: 6**) is such that it could well be an intrusive Mesolithic specimen and the other (**Fig. 7.3: 8**) could equally well be classified with the utilised pieces. Five of the endscrapers form a reasonably coherent group (**Fig. 7.3: 1–5**), three of these (**Fig. 7.3: 1–3**) are from the John Turner collection. As can be seen from the drawings, all five have curved ends with scraper retouch and in all but one example the end curves to be all but continuous with the sides of the original blade or flake. The patination of all five of these endscrapers is the blue-white observed in so much of the assemblage. Three of the five are broken and the proximal ends are missing, two at least (**Fig. 7.3: 1, 4**) were broken in antiquity; the fractures are simple. One, possibly two, were made on large blades (**Fig. 7.3: 1, 5**), the others on flakes. As a result of breakage the lengths are difficult to ascertain accurately but must originally have varied from less than about 65mm to as much as 85–100mm; in width they range from 34mm–40mm. It is likely that the length:width ratio of these endscrapers was at least 2:1; their thickness varies from 8 to12mm. The scraper edges appear to have been carefully prepared, ranging in width from 26mm to possibly as much as 38mm and in height from 4.5–7.5mm. The included angle varies from a minimum of 35° (**Fig. 7.3: 3**) to a maximum of 75° (**Fig. 7.3: 2**). One of the unbroken scrapers (**Fig. 7.3: 2**) has several tiny scars on the ventral surface where spalls between one and 5mm across have been detached. These appear to be spontaneous removals and suggest that the butt had been subjected to stress applied to the ventral edge after the flake had been detached from the parent core; this might have been caused by hafting which could also account for the breakage and loss of the proximal end of some of the other endscrapers.

There is one double endscraper (**Fig. 7.3: 8**) the broader scraping edge of which occurs on the proximal end. This broader scraper edge is irregular, probably as the result of use; the smaller scraper edge, made on the distal end, is largely missing, most having been lost when a large spall was detached in modern times.

With the exception of the probable Mesolithic endscraper (**Fig. 7.3: 6**) all of the endscrapers have the same patination as the Long Blade assemblage and are in all probability, part of that assemblage although some Early Mesolithic material in the area is patinated in a similar manner.

Burins

There is a single burin in the assemblage (**Fig. 7.3: 9**), it is marked as being one of the original finds and has the less common mottled white patina. The burin is made on a blade the distal end of which has an ancient break; there is also some modern damage along the right edge beyond the burin spall. In addition to the oblique retouch which terminates with the burin edge, there is further retouch contiguous with it along the remaining part of the left edge. The burin edge is 4mm in width.

Truncated blades

There are three examples of retouched truncations at Crown Acres (**Fig. 7.2: 4–6**) one of which is typical truncated blade (**Fig. 7.2: 4**). The oblique truncation on this piece has been formed by deliberate retouch across the proximal end of the blade; the distal end is missing due to a modern break. Another example occurs on a less elegant blade (**Fig. 7.2: 5**); this piece may have been almost identical to the first example: the blade is truncated obliquely by a line of retouch but the form of the tool has been much modified by a spall detached from the ventral surface. Unfortunately, the absence of any patination on this piece makes it difficult to be certain whether this damage is ancient or modern whereas there is no doubt that the third example (**Fig. 7.2: 6**), has been damaged by modern machinery and this has modified a large part of the truncated end. It is likely that it was originally a simple obliquely truncated blade a description that fits all three of these artefacts and in each case the proximal end carries the retouch.

Cores

The sample of cores is small. Thirteen Long Blade cores have been identified in the two collections; seven of these are in the Newbury Museum collection. There are also at least three other pieces of worked flint which are either remnants or fragments of similar cores. A further seven items, cores or shatter pieces, in the Newbury Museum collection appear most-likely to be Mesolithic in origin and there is one such piece in the John Turner collection.

Superficial examination of the cores suggests that flint nodules from a gravel source were rarely used; most of the cores have thin cortex, much less than 1mm, which often exhibits detail in low relief; a few cores have thicker cortex, 2–3mm in thickness. Broadly, the same balance of cortex types is reflected in the flakes and blades. In this respect Crown Acres does not differ significantly from Avington VI and Wawcott XII. The staining and/or patination of the cores are the same as that in the rest of the assemblage. As far as can be ascertained from visual examination, the flint types used at Crown Acres do not differ significantly from those used at Wawcott XII. Generally, the flint appears to have been at least of adequate knapping quality, several cores exhibit unblemished working faces (**Figs 7.4, 7.5**), others however indicate varying numbers of blades which terminated in hinge fractures (**Figs 7.4: 1, 7.5: 1, 2**). In several cases it has proved possible to refit blade fragments to the cores (for example **Fig. 7.5: 1, 3**), but it is impossible to tell whether the breaks occurred spontaneously during knapping or broke after separation although the former does seem more likely in many cases and this would imply raw material failure.

Of the 13 cores, only one is a single platform core, this is a large core 152mm long, 70mm thick and 42mm wide; it was apparently abandoned early in the reduction sequence since only two removals from the face can be identified with any certainty, irregularity in the larger of these two removals suggests that the flint was probably judged substandard by the knapper. Had work continued, a second platform would almost certainly have been added; the existing platform had been made principally by means of a single removal.

The remaining 12 cores assigned to the Long Blade assemblage have two platforms; most of these have directly opposed platforms (**Fig. 7.4; 7.6: 3**) but there are examples in which the platforms are rotated, with respect to each other, about the major axis sometimes by as much as 90° (**Fig. 7.4: 1, 2**). In the case of one small core (**Fig. 7.6: 2**) the platforms appear to be at 180° to each other but the subsequent refitting of two plunging removals revealed that it had been a typical two

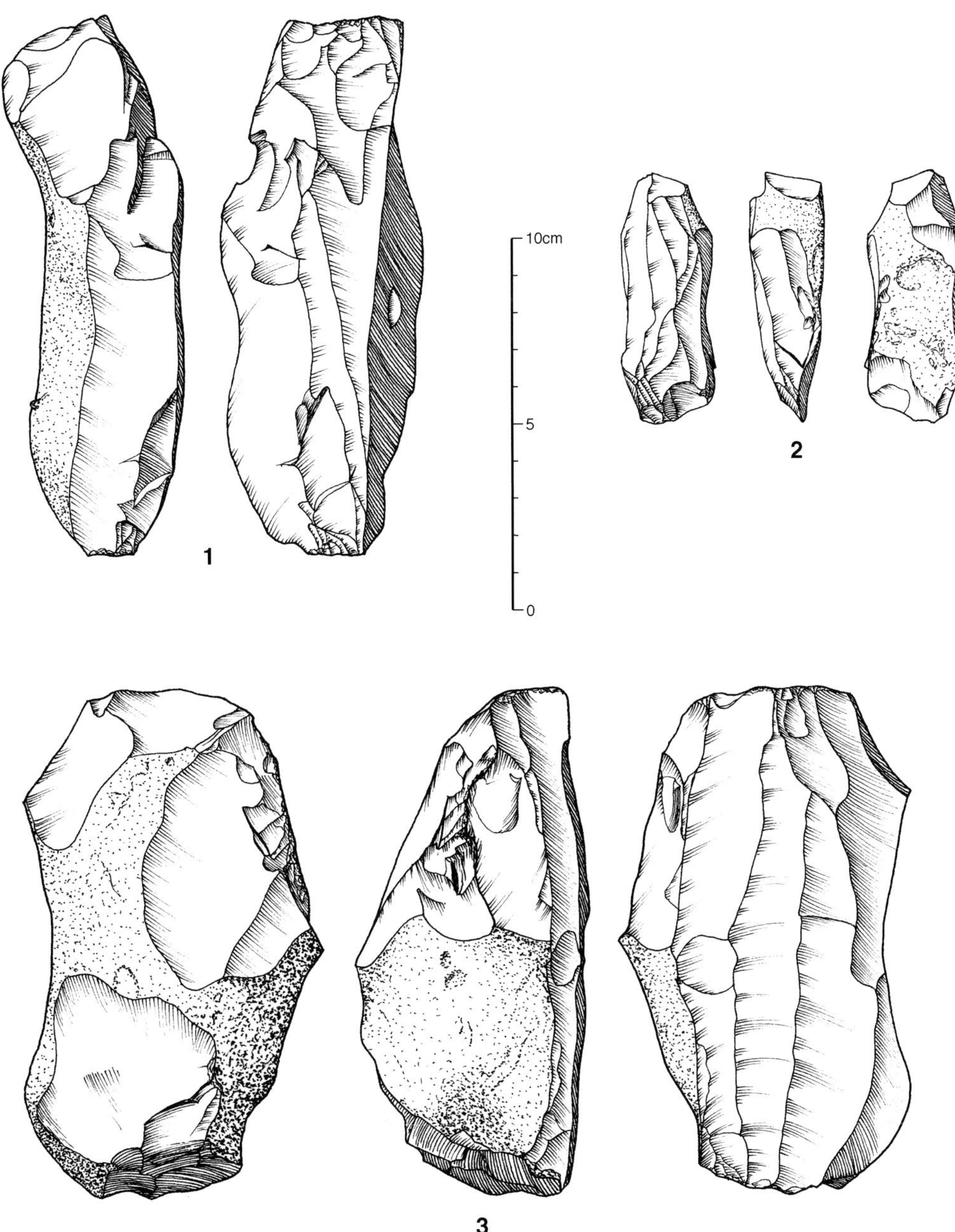

Figure 7.4 Crown Acres: bi-polar cores

platform core with opposed platforms earlier in its reduction sequence. In some of the two platform cores the platforms are of approximately equal size, in others they are notably different; however, as refitting demonstrates, in some cases at least, the smaller platform was once much larger (**Fig. 7.5: 1**). Platforms constructed from a single removal occur but so too do platforms resulting from several removals, sometimes on the same core; examination of the rejuvenation flakes indicates the inter-conversion of these two types. Some of the platforms are retouched, most commonly down the face but there are examples of retouch across the platform. The cores range in length from 152mm–52mm, the majority are less than 100mm; in width they vary from 75mm–25mm. As the refitting programme at Avington VI demonstrates, the size of a core as found may bear little relationship to its initial dimensions. At Crown Acres a few cores show large removals and are probably the residue of much larger cores, for example, in one core the existing platforms interrupt the scars of previous large blades in an arbitrary manner (**Fig. 7.5: 5**). In another example one of the core fragments may have originated from a much larger core than any currently in the assemblage; unusually, this core fragment exhibits what appears to be traces of cresting (**Fig. 7.7: 1**, in addition to the pair of refitted rejuvenation flakes shown, two further removals were subsequently refitted to the face). There is also the possibility that large partially worked nodules were not retained by the collectors. As with the other two Long Blade sites described in this volume, the two platform cores indicate that in some cases a flint nodule of approximately the correct size and shape was selected and little or no extra work other than the construction of the platforms and working face was necessary (**Fig. 7.6: 1**); in some cases additional work may be observed (**Fig. 7.4**) but this is perhaps less frequently the case than at the other two sites. In this context it is worth noting that evidence of cross or lateral flaking is scarcely observed in the blade element.

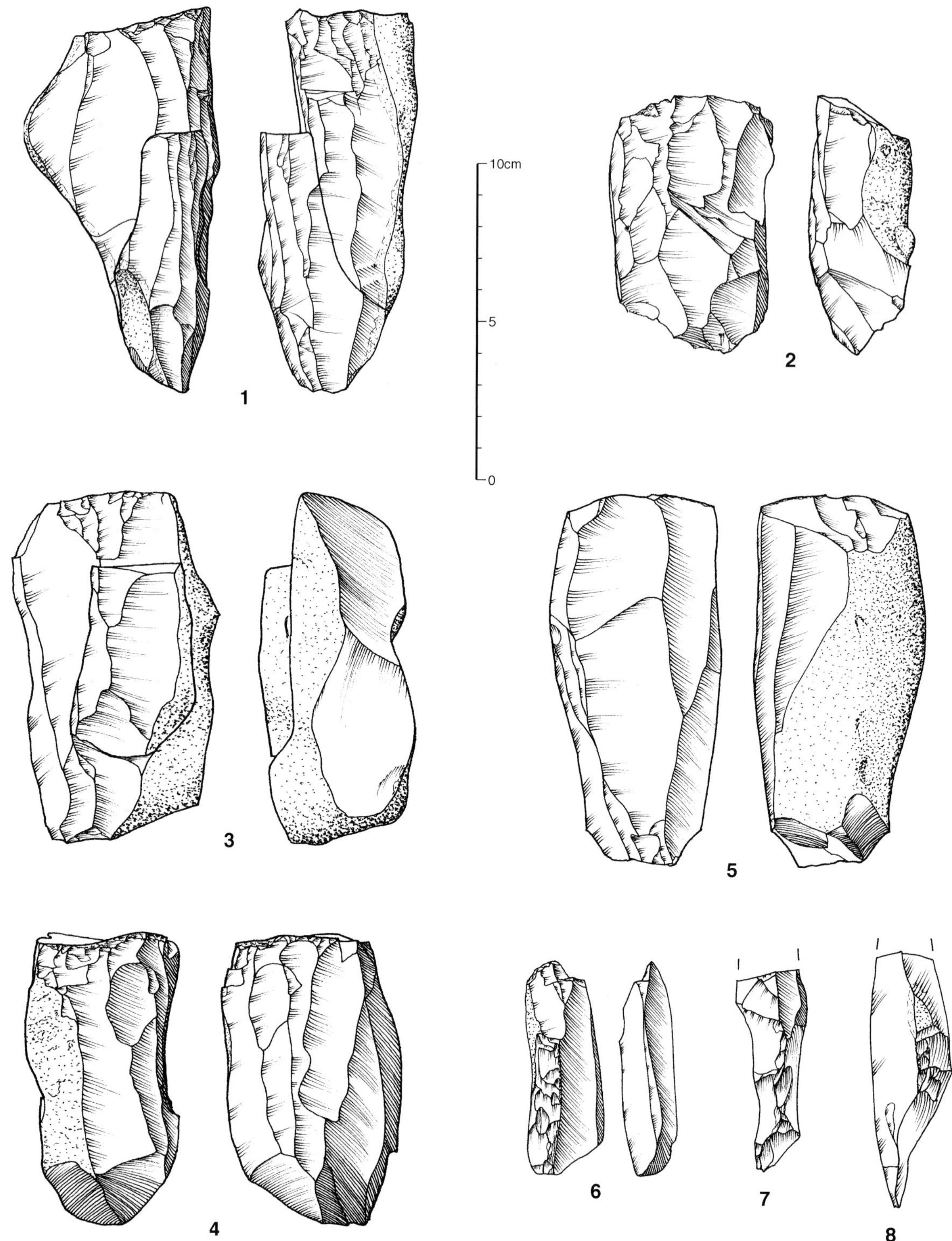

Figure 7.5 Crown Acres: 1-5: bipolar cores; 6-8: crested blades drawn with the proximal ends at the top

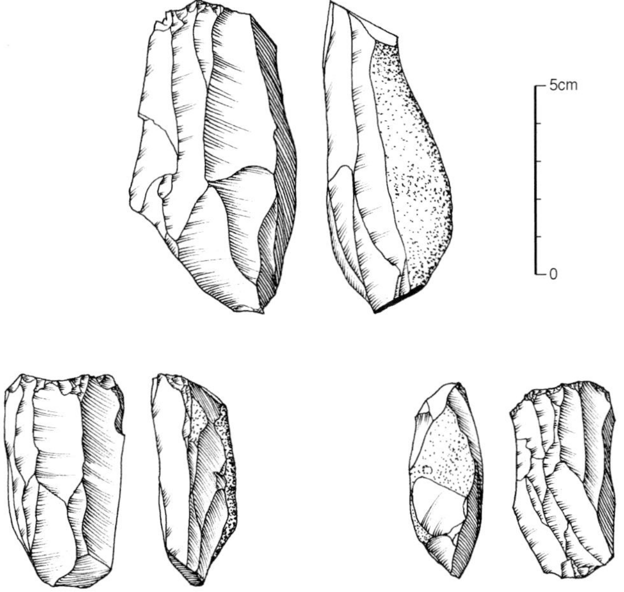

Figure 7.6 Crown Acres: 1-3 bipolar cores

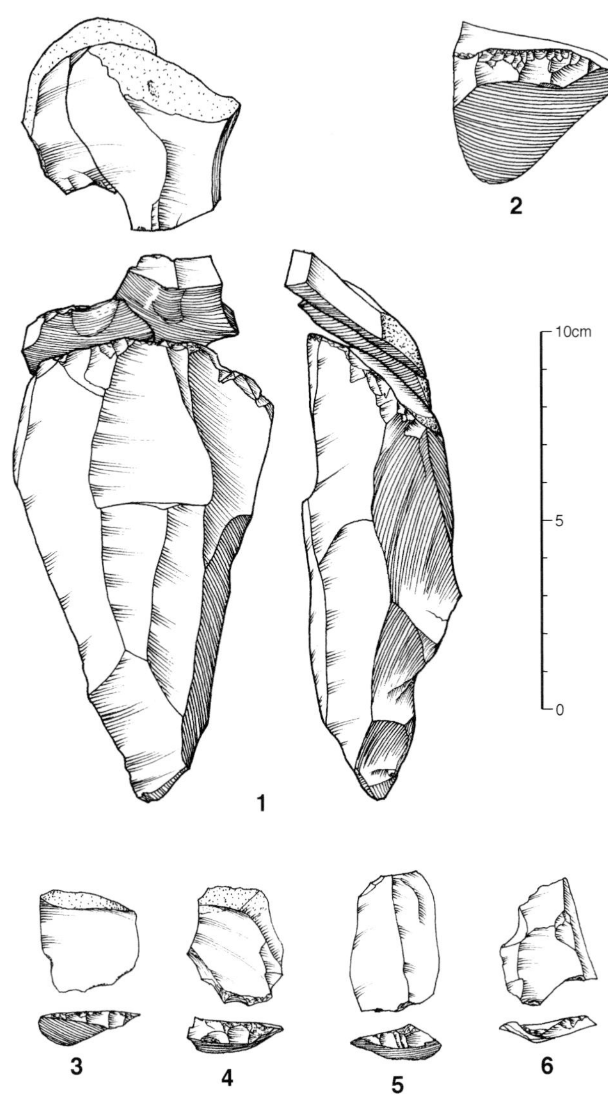

Figure 7.7 Crown Acres: 1: bipolar core with two refitted rejuvenation flakes; 2-6: core rejuvenation flakes

Core rejuvenation flakes

As with the other two sites, the larger core tablets and rejuvenation flakes may be separated with some confidence but the smaller examples are identifiable with less certainty, a situation aggravated when a surface collection is being evaluated. In total, some 20 examples were recognised; 75% of these were from the Turner collection. The largest rejuvenation flakes measured 50–75mm in length and 40–50mm in width (seven examples), a number have been drawn (**Fig. 7.7: 2–6**). Attempts to refit the core rejuvenation flakes to each other and to the cores met with no success other than that shown in **Figure 7.7: 1**.

Crested blades

Campbell (1977, vol. 2, 141) records nine 'ridged flakes' which may refer to crested blades; subsequently, Barton (1986), in his deposition in the archives of Newbury Museum, makes no reference to crested blades but notes the absence of evidence for cresting on the cores. In the much larger assemblage available to the writer, not a single complete example of a fully developed crested blade was identified. This is in marked contrast to the other two sites described in this volume. Of the five examples identified in the Crown Acres collections, only one fragment of a crested blade struck both sides of the central spine was identified (**Fig. 7.5: 7**); the other four exhibit lateral removals from one side only and were thus struck during the reduction process rather than at its initiation (**Fig. 7.5: 6, 8**); in the latter case the missing proximal fragment was located and added, increasing its length from 80mm–106mm. Inspection of the blades revealed scarcely any which showed the existence of a crested blade earlier in the reduction sequence. Thus this aspect of blade core technology is largely absent from the Crown Acres assemblage.

Blades

In the Newbury Museum collection blades are largely represented by fragments. Campbell (1977) records significantly more than Barton (1986a) whose figure corresponds with the same number as currently available. The John Turner collection contains a much larger sample of blades; the proportion of blade fragments is lower than in the Newbury Museum collection but it is still high.

It is difficult to assess the degree of breakage accurately; it seems likely that some blades are missing from the Newbury Museum collection and both collections are surface derived; however, in the Turner collection some 80% of the blade element is in the form of fragments, based on the complete blades and the proximal blade fragments this represents 60% of all blade removals having been broken during or after separation from the core. Examination of the blade fragments reveals that the vast majority have fractures at or near to a right angle to the length axis; obvious oblique fractures are extremely rare. Although there are definite examples of fractures which have occurred in modern times, it is equally clear that a large proportion of the breakage took place in ancient times. These ancient fractures have many forms; some are simple breaks at right-angles to the blade, others are more complex and have projecting lips, some have the characteristically rounded outline of a hinge fracture.

Most of the blade fragments have been assigned to one of three categories: proximal fragments in which the bulb of percussion is retained (37%), middle fragments in which both the proximal and distal sections are missing (28%) and the distal fragments which represent the tip ends of blades (34%). These figures are consistent with a majority of the broken blades having been separated into three sections rather than two.

Generally, the fragments appear to represent between 25%–75% of the original blade but more extreme examples were observed. Refitting resulted in five complete blades being rebuilt, each had been broken into two pieces; a further five blades which had been broken into three or more fragments were partially reconstructed; in each case two sections were reunited. One proximal fragment terminating in a hinge fracture has been refitted to a core exhibiting several similar fractures. The patination of the blade fragments does not differ in any way from that seen in the rest of the assemblage.

Approximately 12 complete blades currently exist in the Newbury Museum collection (March, 2002) and there are nearly 80 in the Turner collection. Statistically, this is probably enough for analysis but an element of doubt remains because the blades were recovered during surface collecting and, as a result, small blades, as well as perhaps less regular pieces may be under represented although the range and size of the blade fragments suggest that the collectors were thorough and collecting bias is not a great concern.

Set out and viewed collectively, most of the complete blades have a blue-white patination, relatively few are yellow-brown ochre in appearance, some blades exhibit both types of coloration, occasionally depending on whether it is the dorsal or ventral side that is viewed; a small number of blades have the denser more definitely white patination. Although virtually all of the blades are sharp, two are slightly abraded and could conceivably relate to an earlier occupation. As might be expected, damage resulting from modern agricultural operations is frequently observable.

Commonly, the blades are regular in outline, most are more or less parallel sided and often have a blunt outline at the distal end although pointed forms are present; a few blades have convex sides and, in extreme examples, are elliptical in outline. Blades with a triangular outline are extremely rare. As previously noted, scarcely any blades have evidence of earlier lateral flaking; consequently, the complete blades have been sub-divided into three groups: cortical blades (>10 % cortex), total 19 blades; non-cortical regular, total 58 blades and non-cortical irregular, total 14 blades. The relative scarcity of non-cortical irregular blades could be a function of the collecting process. **Figure 9.2** summarizes the metrical size data for Crown Acres in a comparison with the other Kennet Valley sites. Platform retouch was universal in the complete blades and proximal blade fragments, in the great majority of cases it was down the working face but occasionally it was across the striking platform.

Metrical analysis shows that the longest blades are respectively 137–135mm whereas 81% are 100mm or less, and there are 12 blades between 21–40mm in length. The distribution of length within the sample reveals a broad maximum in the region 41–80mm with a minor maximum at 101–110mm; this secondary maximum may be the result of either collecting bias or small sample error or both. When the lengths and widths are plotted, the resulting dispersion indicates a median line with a gradient of 1:3 for width:length; this correlates well with the other two sites (**Fig. 9.2**). When the relative proportions of length, width and thickness are analysed using triangular co-ordinates (**Table 7.2**), there did not appear to be any significant difference between the blades at Crown Acres and those at Wawcott XII, given the size of the samples.

Table 7.2: Triangular coordinates for the blades

Blades with >10% cortex (19 blades)	Regular blades with <10% cortex (58 blades)
0.708	0.726
0.227	0.215

Analysis of the Striking Platform Quotient again correlates well with the same analysis for Wawcott XII, at both sites more than half of the blades produce values <0.2 and the great majority of blades produced values <0.4; however, at Wawcott XII a few blades produced values >1.0 but <1.5, no such blades were observed in the Crown Acres assemblage. Blades with bruised edges, a significant feature in the Avington VI Long Blade assemblage, are almost entirely absent in the Crown Acres assemblage as they are in the Wawcott XII assemblage.

Flakes

There are some 80 or so flakes, mostly unbroken; three refitting pairs have been found among which one conjoin involve flakes from both the Newbury Museum and Turner sets. The largest flakes were 60–95mm in length and generally 50–75mm in width with one measuring 101mm; such flakes presumably resulted from the working of large nodules, perhaps of the order of 200mm or more in size. As might be expected, the amount of cortex varied from 0%–100% and helps to suggest a variety of sources for the original flint nodules including occasionally gravel flint. The patination is in keeping with the rest of the assemblage. Examination of the general character of the flakes suggests that they derive from the full range of reduction processes. Many of the flakes, the larger ones in particular, exhibited prominent bulbs of percussion suggestive of direct percussion, probably with a hard hammer, in many cases the blow landed on an area of cortex but in other cases it struck the scar of a previous removal.

Bruised edge pieces

Ancient bruised edges could only be recognised with certainty on three artefacts. One large blade in the Newbury Museum collection exhibits ancient bruising; it is much more strongly patinated (white) than is typical for the assemblage as a whole. A proximal fragment, 115 x 31 x 15mm, from a large blade in the Turner collection also exhibits true bruising resulting from ancient use. The third example is an exceptionally thick blade-like flake, 107 x 37 x 27mm, also in the Turner collection, which has areas heavy bruising on both edges.

Refitting

At various times during the examination of the two collections, attempts were made to secure refits. Two refits had been established previously in the Newbury Museum collection, a plunging blade had been added to a core (**Fig. 7.5: 1**) and, separately, a further two plunging blade fragments had been reunited to each other; another blade was then added to this latter pair from the same collection. The number of refits is currently just over 30, in nearly all cases they are binary refits and include the partial or complete rebuilding of broken blades and removals refitted to cores. Seven of the refits, less than 25% of all the refitted pieces, link items from the Newbury Museum collection to items from the Turner collection. The most extensive series involves what appears to be a fragment of a large two platform core refitted to a pair of rejuvenation flakes with a further two removals refitted to the working face of the core (**Fig. 7.7: 1**).

Conclusions

Crown Acres, as is the case with the other two sites described in this volume, did not yield any directly dateable material nor did it produce any organic remains. Further, as has been noted, there are some difficulties with the assemblage which is a surface collection brought together over about 20 years by different collectors. Some but not all pieces are marked and it can only be assumed that the curation of the unmarked tools and debitage has been careful enough to avoid any mixing. Consequently, it would seem unwise to draw detailed conclusions on the data presented but some points of interest are worth putting forward.

It is difficult to ignore the parallels between Crown Acres and Wawcott XII. Both sites were situated on gravel which incorporated marl deposits in its uneven surface; peat subsequently developed over these sediments. Although Wawcott XII has been presented as a flood plain site, the flood plain in the Wawcott–Marsh Benham area may be differentiated into a central zone which is slightly lower than the northern and southern zones which flank it; the central zone has no known evidence of occupation whereas the other two zones can be rich in such evidence, for example, the northern zone embraces sites such as Wawcott IV and Wawcott XXX and the southern zone encompasses Wawcott XV and the Marsh Benham site. All four of these sites are Early Mesolithic. Wawcott XII is situated at the edge of the southern zone close to the central zone of the flood plain.

The late Ray Sheridan an independent archaeologist who worked at the site of Crown Acres described it to the writer as being on the edge of the bluff overlooking the reed beds of the flood plain. Taking into account the fact that Crown Acres is 10km downstream from Wawcott XII, it is reasonable to suppose that the comparatively small difference in elevation between the central and flanking zones of the flood plain in the Wawcott–Marsh Benham area has increased to a point where in the area of Crown Acres it has become an easily recognisable bluff, as identified in the excavations at the Thatcham Mesolithic sites (Wymer, 1962). This bluff may have formed as a result of deposition caused by the confluence of the River Lambourn and the Kennet, only 1 or 2km upstream. The writer is firmly of the opinion that in this part of the Kennet Valley considerable amounts of peat were dug in the 18th and 19th centuries and the present topography is misleading. Part of the evidence for this is to be found in the account of peat digging written by Harold Peake (1935). Further evidence of the considerable changes brought about by peat digging is offered by the study of the water levels in the general area, especially with respect to the main river, which was a navigable waterway before both major peat digging and the construction of the Kennet and Avon Canal in the late 18th century, further evidence may be found in the Ordnance Survey maps of the period 1920–1950 which detail the pattern of drainage channels in the Newbury–Thatcham area.

All this evidence suggests strongly that in the post-glacial period alluvial deposits which included peat developed on the flood plain and extended laterally until they covered both Crown Acres and the Early Mesolithic sites. The peat and marl which in part covered the latter sites were not swept up onto the sites by flooding (an intrinsically unlikely event) in a chalk stream environment but were simply the later deposits in a long development subsequently reshaped by human exploitation in the 18th and 19th centuries when the greater part of them was removed. The removal of the greater part of these deposits and the concomitant change in the drainage pattern allowed much of the remainder to dry out, shrink and decay, leaving the topography that may be seen today or the little that gravel digging has left. As previously noted, extensive gravel digging in 1977 on the flood plain, south of the railway, enabled the writer to observe and record sections cut into the flood plain deposits, at least one section was entirely consistent with the activities of peat diggers; other sections suggested normal river channels rather than lake deposits. In all probability, the Crown Acres site and that at Wawcott XII were identically situated whereas the Avington VI Long Blade site, like the Three Ways Wharf and Church Lammas sites in the Colne Valley were situated in tributary valleys away from the flood plain where there would have been more shelter, perhaps at an earlier date.

Superficially, there are many similarities between the Crown Acres and Wawcott XII assemblage and some differences. The assemblage at Crown Acres has a Long Blade element and thus the site is linked additionally to the Avington VI Long Blade site. Tools are moderately well represented at Crown Acres, unlike the situation at Wawcott XII where, in particular, the absence of endscrapers is puzzling and prevents any comparison in this respect. However, it is possible that endscrapers were collected off the site by an unknown collector during an earlier ploughing in the 1950s. The endscrapers from Crown Acres exhibit similarities to those from Avington VI. Although essentially a common and long-lived type, the burin from Crown Acres is similar to the two smaller burins from the Avington VI assemblage. There is evidence to suggest that cores larger than any which currently exist in the Crown Acres collections once existed at the site and in many ways the cores at Crown Acres are comparable both to those found at Wawcott XII, as well as those at Avington VI. The most striking difference is the degree to which the technique of cresting prior to blade production varies at the three sites; this is common at Avington VI, much reduced at Wawcott XII and rare at Crown Acres. This virtual absence could be explained by suggesting that cores were already prepared before they were brought to Crown Acres; however, the presence of blades with varying large amounts of cortex and the wide range of simple waste flakes tends to contravene this hypothesis and leads us to suppose some changes in the chaîne opératoire, possibly reflecting either differences in the age of the assemblage, environmental change and/or altered accessibility to raw materials.

Comparison of blades is difficult in view of the inherent problems with the collection but it is perhaps relevant to note that the ratio of cores:blades is similar at Crown Acres where it is 1:6.9 and at Wawcott XII where it is 1:5.7. In the circumstances, the much higher degree of blade fragmentation at Crown Acres may well be significant; at Crown Acres the 90 complete blades are outnumbered by the 155 proximal fragments in a ratio of 0.58:1; even if allowance is made for possible missing blades the ratio would still be less than 1:1; if the analysis is based solely on the John Turner collection then the ratio is 0.69:1. This situation is reversed at Wawcott XII where 128 blades outnumber 67 proximal fragments in the ratio 2:1. However, these results need to be treated with some caution.

The incidence of bruised edge blades and flakes appears to be much the same at Crown Acres as it is at Wawcott XII and at both sites it is much reduced compared to Avington VI. A further similarity between Crown Acres and Wawcott XII is the low but definite incidence of burnt artefacts as none were observed at Avington VI.

Taking all the evidence into consideration there are clear similarities linking the Crown Acres site with that at Wawcott XII and, to some extent, with the Avington VI Long Blade site the nature of which will be reviewed in chapter 9.

Chapter 8

Isolated Long Blade Finds in the Kennet Valley

In addition to the excavated sites described in the preceding chapters, there are a few isolated Long Blade finds from the Hungerford – Thatcham part of the Kennet Valley which deserve further mention (**Fig. 8.1**). These finds vary from small clusters of indisputable Long Blade artefacts which may imply the existence of a site yet to be discovered, to odd pieces which may be nothing more than isolated losses, far removed from their original point of manufacture, dropped by individuals on or between sites. Low numbers of finds may be either a reflection of the thickness of overburden covering an as yet undiscovered site or simply a true indication that there is no site to be discovered. Furthermore, although the Long Blade assemblages described in this volume are clearly distinct from the local Early Mesolithic individual artefacts may be less diagnostic and cannot always be ascribed to Long Blade or Early Mesolithic with certainty or may indeed be transitional between the two periods. However, despite this cautionary note, further Long Blade sites have been identified in the immediate area of the junction of the Dun and Kennet Valleys (SU335692) and in close proximity to the Mesolithic site of Wawcott III (**Fig. 8.1**). The site at the valley junction, known as Undy's Farm or the Charnham Lane Development, would appear to be the most certain of these.

Charnham Lane

Undy's Farm was situated on the northern outskirts of Hungerford until its buildings were demolished and some of the land taken over for the Charnham Lane Development in the late 1980s. Initial archaeological exploration in advance of the commercial development was carried out during 1987; further more extensive exploration followed in 1988 – 89 (Ford 2002). The finds and associated archive have been deposited in Newbury Museum. The exploration encompassed both the edge of the valley side and that part of the flood plain intended for development. Finds included worked flints of Long Blade character, as well as both Early and Later/Late Mesolithic types and artefacts of Neolithic and Early Bronze Age date. Less than 12 of the flint artefacts are indisputably of Long Blade origin although it is reasonable to suppose that some less diagnostic material may have merged with non-specific debitage of more recent periods. Although the field investigations did not locate any concentrations within the planning area, the few Long Blade artefacts were found relatively close together within an area approximately 50m in diameter.

The condition of the artefacts is variable; some are sharp and have no patina, others are slightly abraded and occasionally have a blue-white patination. **Table 8.1** summarises the content of the collection.

Table 8.1: Long Blade artefacts from Charnham Lane

Endscrapers	2
Truncated blades	2
Cores	4
Crested blades	2
Blades & blade fragments	6

All of the cores are large and have two platforms (**Fig. 8.2**); the largest is 190mm long and made on a piece of tabular flint as were some cores at Avington VI. This core has two working faces both of which were developed on the edges of the nodule (**Fig. 8.2**); remnants of four sets of lateral removals indicate that a bi-directional crested blade was produced for each face. The other three cores are remarkably similar in size and are more or less well-made (**Fig. 8.2: 3, 4**). All of the cores have good parallels in the Avington VI Long Blade assemblage and they imply the existence of blades of similar length to those at that site. It is also notable that two bi-directional crested blades have been found at Charnham Lane (**Fig. 8.2: 2**) and there is also a semi-cortical blade which was evidently detached after the removal of a crested blade. Three large blade fragments and an endscraper (**Fig. 8.3: 1**) provide further signs of cresting making a total of 8 artefacts out of a total of 16 which show evidence of this technique. The statistics of small samples are justly viewed with suspicion but, given the significant use of cresting in the Avington VI assemblage, this is at least a suggestive observation.

Two complete blades and four fragments were found at Charnham Lane and are regarded as Long Blades. Two of the fragments further suggest the existence of large well-controlled blades probably with lengths in excess of 150mm. There are two endscrapers in this little assemblage (**Fig. 8.3: 1, 4**); both are unusual in that the scraper edge was made on the proximal end of the blade. One is exceptionally large and was made on a crested blade and has some additional retouch along one side contiguous with the scraper edge. The other endscraper is much smaller and made on a plain blade; this tool appears to have broken when in use, the fracture is complex and resulted in the detachment of a small spontaneous spall.

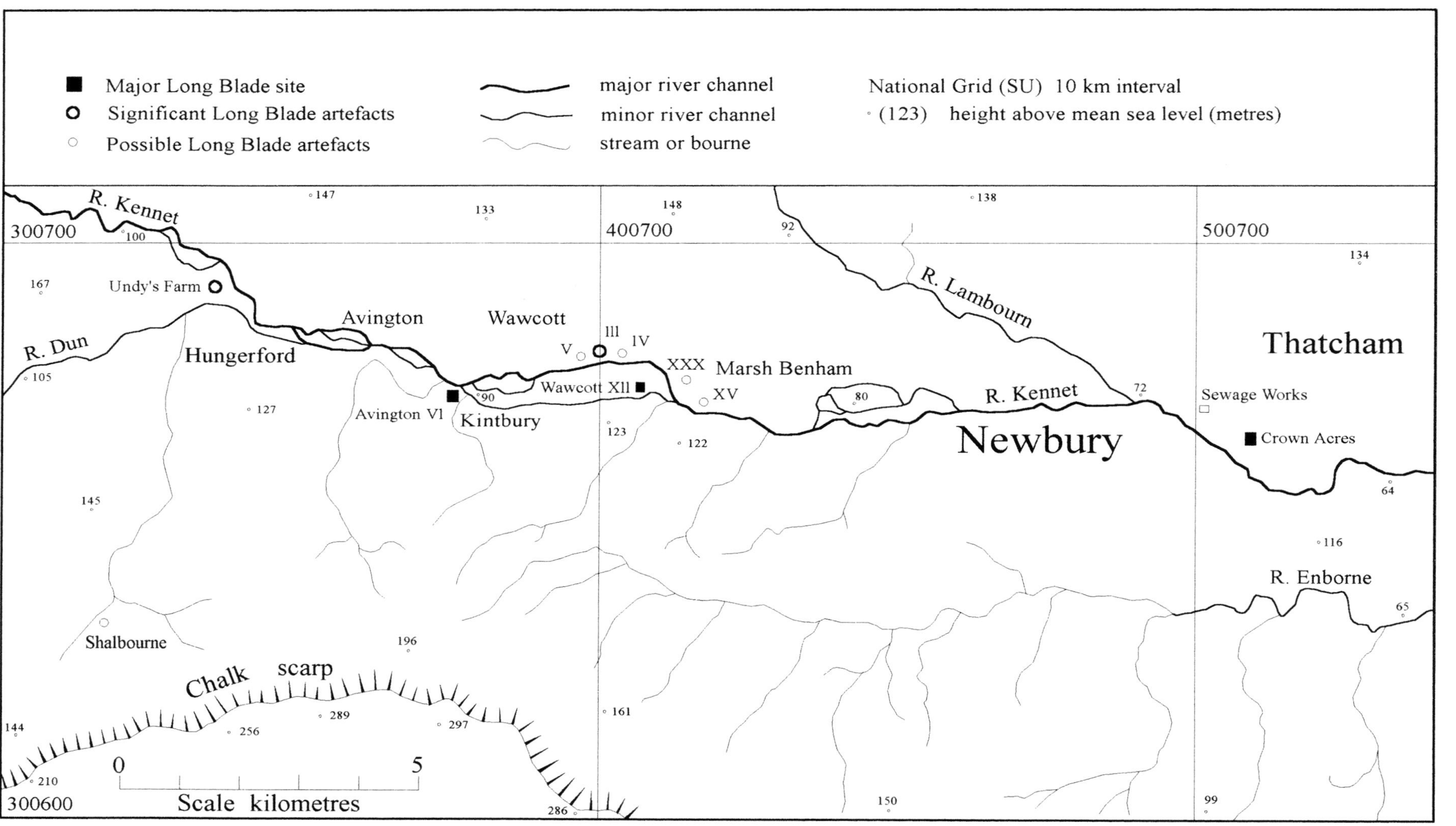

Figure 8.1 The Kennet Valley between Hungerford and Thatcham

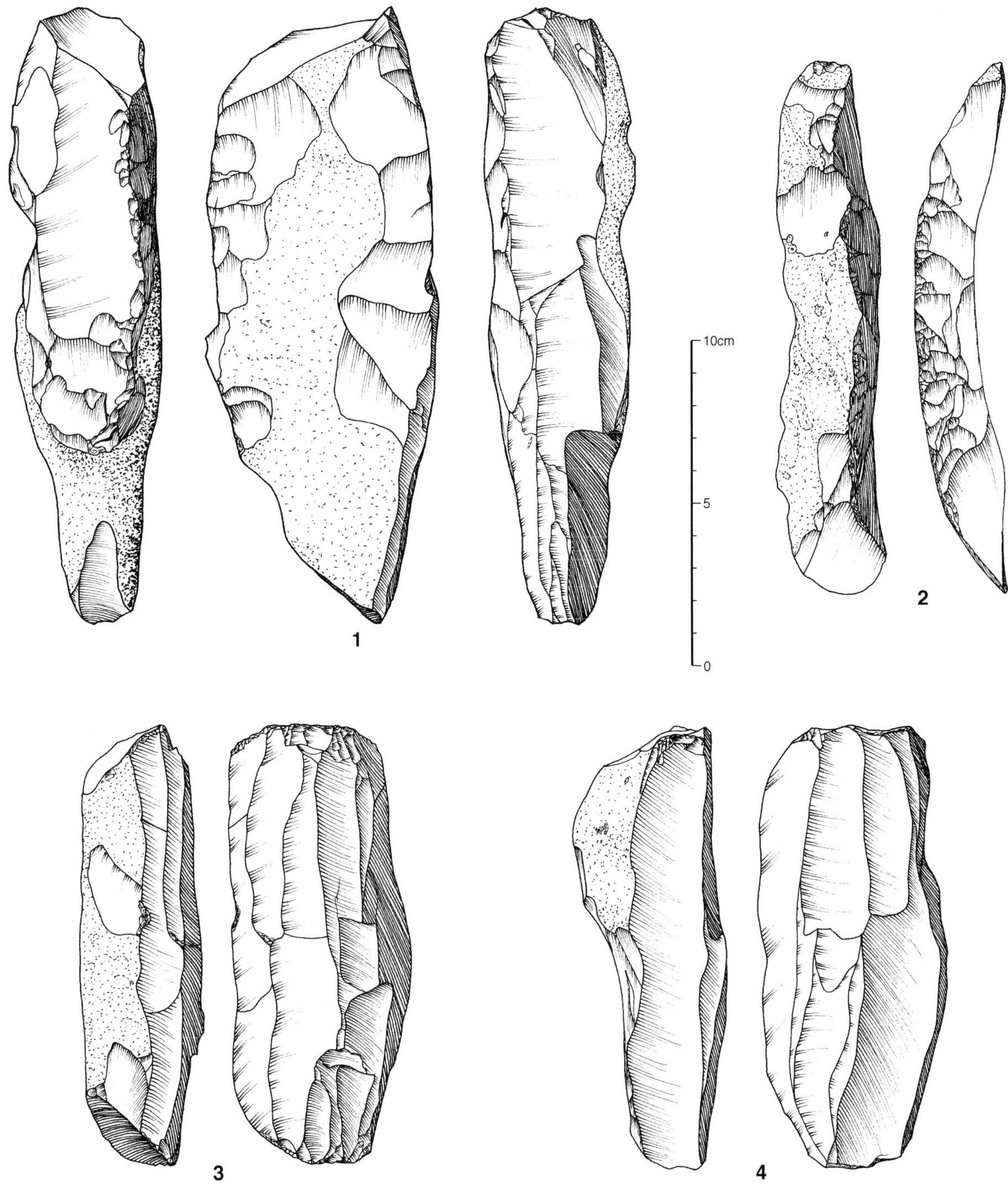

Figure 8.2 Charnham Lane: 1, 3, and 4: bipolar cores; 2: crested blade

There are two blades which have been truncated at the distal end (**Fig. 8.3: 2, 3**). One is a particularly elegant and well-made tool; the other example was originally much the same but has suffered considerable modern damage at the proximal end, part of which has been broken off. Together, the endscrapers and truncated blades represent a large proportion of this small assemblage. However, comparing **Table 8.1** with **Table 3.2**, suggests that, excluding small retouched pieces which may easily have been missed in the machined trenches at Charnham Lane, tools are almost as numerous here as they are in the much larger assemblage at Avington VI. Whether these few artefacts are all that is left of a site that was perhaps destroyed by agriculture stretching back continuously from the immediate past to Bronze Age times, or is the background scatter associated with an as yet undiscovered site situated outside of the area explored in advance of the commercial development, is an unanswered question.

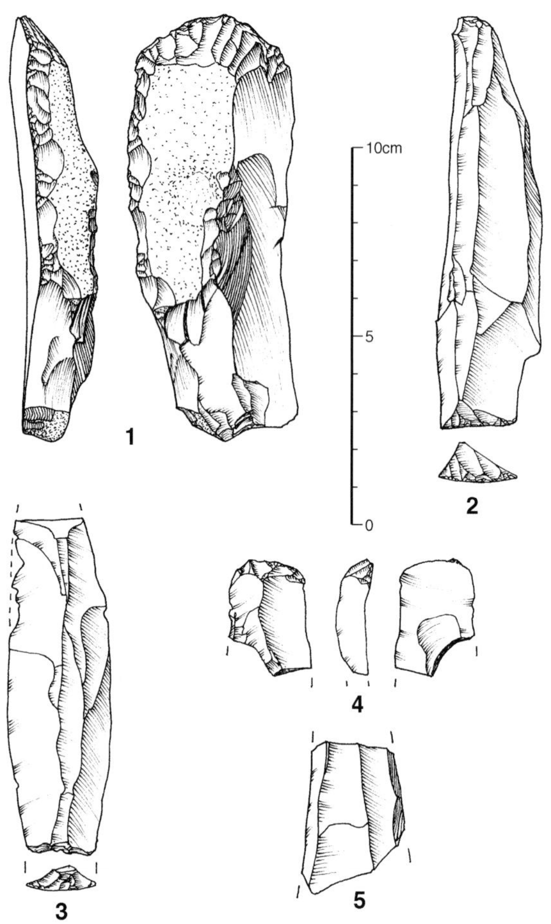

Figure 8.3 Charnham Lane: 1 and 4: endscrapers; 2-3: blades with retouched distal truncations; 5: fragment of a Long Blade. Drawn with proximal ends at the top

Wawcott IV and Wawcott XXVI

The material recovered from Wawcott sites IV and XXVI is more problematic although the slightly shouldered point fragment and the curved backed blade from the former have Late Glacial affinities (**Fig. 8.4: 1, 2**). A small excavation was carried out at Wawcott IV in 1962 (Froom 1963) and the field enclosing the two sites was subjected to a wide-ranging series of small trial trenches in 1969; in this exercise significant amounts of archaeological material were located in several areas. Given that a large proportion of the artefacts recovered from the two sites appears to be Early Mesolithic, and that much of it is patinated, there exists the possibility that an even earlier occupation may be present, certainly some pieces of debitage are more in keeping with some of the material described in this volume than with the local Early Mesolithic. This raises the possibility of an occupation in which the industry is transitional between the Long Blade and Early Mesolithic. Although ideally any earlier occupation might be expected to be stratified below succeeding occupations, in reality this may not be the case; deposition in this type of situation during the Late Glacial–Early Post-glacial is likely to have been slow for a variety of reasons and the general dampness would have encouraged plant growth, this in turn would have attracted a variety of animals. Elk and wild cattle are known to be attracted to such locations. These are large heavy animals and will sink deeply into soft ground; their bones have been identified amongst the organic finds from these sites as well as those of wild pig; the latter love to root around vigorously and deeply in such areas. The activities of beaver should also be taken into account; they too can be active diggers. Thus it is possible that any fine detail in the stratification, if it ever existed, could have been destroyed. Much the same situation appears to have existed at Thatcham site III (Reynier, 2000; Wymer 1962). With both horizontal and vertical overlap, disentangling a series of occupations may well prove exceptionally difficult. As previously noted, the few stray finds, in some cases single items, may represent nothing more than casual losses away from any site; equally, they could originate from a site too deeply buried to be disturbed by ploughing.

Finally, it must remain a matter for speculation as to how the occupants of the sites described in this volume exploited the area, whether they restricted their activities to the river and its immediate environs or ranged much more widely. Similarly, little useful can be written with regard to the frequency and duration of occupation although the lack of disturbance which is evident at Avington VI and hinted at elsewhere suggests brief periods of occupation. So far, the sites recognised are closely associated with the River Kennet but this may only reflect modern archaeological effort; however, field walking is unlikely to detect deeply stratified sites; if there are sites of the character described in this volume away from the narrowly defined Kennet Valley, their discovery may be a matter of chance, as was that of Avington VI. The ability of early people to navigate across country without modern devices such as map and compass or the latest GPS system should not be underestimated; nonetheless, rivers and streams constitute exceptional landmarks and the river- estuarine distribution of the Kennet, Colne and Thames Valley Long Blades sites could well have connected through to the Somme and Seine where similar sites occur. For the purpose of prospecting for new sites it is also worth noting that several south coast rivers, for example the Test and the Hampshire Avon, have their headwaters close to the Hungerford area.

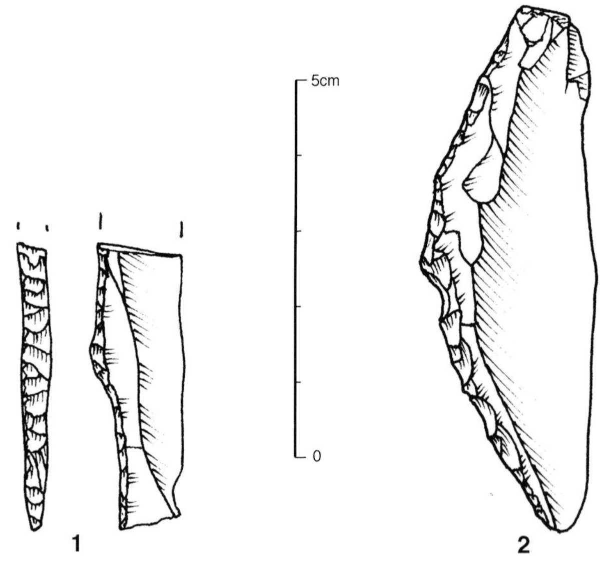

Figure 8.4 Wawcott IV: 1: fragment of shouldered point; 2: curved backed blade, drawn with the proximal end at the top

Chapter 9

Synthesis and Overview

As defined in chapter 1, the term 'Long Blade' has been used for over 30 years in association with Kennet Valley sites to differentiate artefacts which are significantly longer than those found on the Mesolithic sites, certainly greater than 100mm. This definition and the distinction it made has proved useful and the term is now more broadly applied to denote a particular type of assemblage containing few tools, Long Blades and bruised edge pieces. Such assemblages not only occur elsewhere in southern Britain but also in Holland, Belgium, France and Germany. As in the Kennet Valley, these sites include retouched items also found in Final Magdalenian, Ahrensburgian, Laborien and Azilian assemblages and this begs the question of whether Long Blades may be defined culturally or whether they represent a particular activity or technological facies of a cultural phenomenon expressed diagnostically at other sites. As is the case with virtually all of the known Long Blade sites, those in the Kennet Valley lack secure means of both relative and absolute dating. However, the Kennet Valley sites, Avington VI in particular, do allow a number of points to be made with some confidence.

Tools

There are few retouched artefacts in the Kennet Valley Long Blade assemblages described in this volume but this is consistent with other sites of this kind and may be a reflection of their function. For example, at Sproughton, Suffolk, only seven endscrapers, five burins and four microliths were found among the 3,783 artefacts recovered from the controlled excavation (Wymer, 1976, 5). Similarly, the Long Blade scatter A at Three Ways Wharf, Uxbridge, contained only six obliquely blunted points which constituted about 1% of the total of 700 artefacts in this concentration (Lewis, 1991, 252) and at La Fuillotte in the Paris Basin the excavated assemblage at locus 4 contained less than 2% or only 15 retouched pieces out of 925 artefacts and this decreases to less than 1% in the surface collection of 1,115 pieces (Bodu *et al.*, 1995). Even at Belloy sur Somme where the retouched constituent is higher there are still only 63 recognisable tools in an assemblage of 'several hundred' artefacts (Fagnart, 1991, 222).

Among the tools, the small retouched pieces also referred to as microliths are the most indicative. At Avington VI there are obliquely blunted or Ahrensburgian points, as well as one or, possibly, two Blanchéres or Malaurie points and a tanged point. The Wawcott XII assemblage also contains an obliquely blunted point and there is an abruptly backed bladelet with a slight shoulder from Wawcott IV (**Fig. 8.4: 1**) similar to one found at Bad Breisig a late Allerød/Younger Dryas site in the Neuwied Basin on the Middle Rhine (Waldmann *et al.*, 2001). Obliquely blunted and Malaurie points were also found at Bad Breisig (ibid.) and the late Allerød/Younger Dryas site of Le Closeau in the Paris Basin (Bodu & Valentin, 1997). These artefacts suggest that Long Blade assemblages may represent a late western expression of the Ahrensburgian (Coudret & Fagnart, 1997; Thévenin, 1997, 405, fig. 8D) with wider connections south of the Paris Basin (Bodu *et al.*, 1995). All of these small retouched pieces may be armatures for darts or arrows and could, as Rozoy (1998) suggests, indicate a shift in hunting techniques in favour of the bow and arrow at the end of the Last Glacial when changing climate and habitats was starting to displace reindeer and horse in favour of red deer and bovids.

Endscrapers and burins have been found both at Avington VI and Crown Acres and the latter site also has examples of truncated blades. These tools are known in similarly small numbers at other Long Blade sites such as Sproughton, Suffolk (Wymer, 1976), Three Ways Wharf, Uxbridge, Middlesex (Lewis, 1991) and Belloy sur Somme (Fagnart, 1989; 1991) as well as sites in the Paris Basin (Bodu *et al.*, 1995). Their affinities lie with Upper Palaeolithic forms also made on larger blades and flakes rather than the smaller Mesolithic types. As at the Late Upper Palaeolithic site of Hengistbury Head, Dorset, the endscrapers from the Kennet Valley Long Blade sites divide between flake and blade types in an approximate ratio of 5:2 and the blade endscrapers tend to a length:width ratio exceeding 2:1 (Barton, 1992). Burins and truncated blades although rare in the Kennet Valley sites are also similar to those at Hengistbury Head where burins are in particular more numerous. However, the paucity of these types of tools suggests that the tasks for which they were required were not significant in contexts with Long Blades. Indeed, it is the Long Blade technology which is the most significant feature of Avington VI, Wawcott XII, Crown Acres and Charnham Lane.

Intentions, products and raw material

Evaluation of the cores and refitted groups from the Kennet Valley Long Blade sites shows that the intention was to produce blades. Flakes were only produced spontaneously or in the preparatory stages of the intended blade production. However, the blades are not homogeneous in character. There are many relatively thick irregular blades and these seem to have been less susceptible to breakage than the thinner more regular Long Blades which may have been the knappers' ideal. Indeed, as at Sproughton (Wymer, 1976, 8) and La Fuillotte locus 4 (Bodu *et al.*, 1995) blades longer than 100mm are less frequent at the Kennet Valley sites than shorter blades. As might be expected the lengths of the cores correlate with the lengths of the blades (**Fig. 9.1, 9.2**) and although the size of a discarded core may bear no relation to its initial size, it is nonetheless useful to compare the 'as found' sizes of the cores. The largest occur at Avington VI whilst those at Wawcott XII and Crown Acres are similar (**Fig. 9.1**). This probably reflects the use of flint from the same sources. Visual examination of the cores suggests that, in the main, the flint raw material at all of the sites came from local exposures of weathered chalk and clay-with-flint and also possibly from exposures where the base of the Tertiary strata yielded particularly large flint nodules; flint from the flood plain gravel was rarely used. The only possible exception to this pattern is the dark flint used for several of the small cores at Wawcott XII which has not been found at the other sites.

Debitage

Many of the cores from the Kennet Valley Long Blade sites have or once had two platforms and it is possible that most or all of the single platform cores are simply undeveloped two-platform cores. Two-platform cores are a feature of the Long Blade assemblages as at Sproughton (ibid.), Three Ways Wharf scatter A (Lewis, 1991), Belloy sur Somme (Fagnart, 1991) and La Fuillotte (Bodu *et al.*, 1995). At the last named site refitting has enabled the description of the alternating use of the platforms as rapid and rhythmic (ibid., 216); the knappers were turning the core to suppress the influence of any spontaneous detachments that might reduce the regularity of the blade removals and cause faults such as abrupt and hinge terminations. In other words, the use of two platforms helped to maintain the regularity of the working face and allowed use of its full length in the production of good regular blades with thin sections. This technique can also be seen at Avington VI in refitted groups 264, 154 and 118 but in others such as 150 the method varies; instead of the two platforms being worked alternately to achieve removals from the same working face they are used independently to remove short sequences of blades from separate faces.

As at La Fuillotte, the preparation of the nodules on the Kennet Valley sites was often quite elaborate. Using a soft stone hammer the nodules were generally opened up by the removal if necessary of any protrusions followed by the cresting of an edge and the removal of one or more crested blades. This approach seems similar to that in the Kennet Valley assemblages although the incidence of cresting appears to be higher at Avington VI suggestion some variation in technique. The relative frequency of cresting in the Kennet Valley sites has been assessed by comparing the number of crested blades to the number of cores and to the number of plain blades. In these analyses, only those blades with cresting flake scars present on both sides of a central arête were counted as crested in order to avoid inflating the number. By including blades removed after the primary crested piece which nonetheless retain cresting scars on one side although including both would not have altered the results since at Avington VI and Wawcott XII the two forms have a constant ratio to each other (1.8:1) whereas at Crown Acres the data shows radical differences either way.

The differences shown in **Table 9.1** between the large and small area samples at Avington VI simply illustrates the tendency for the crested blades to be abandoned in the major concentrations of worked flint C19–20 and D21–22; they are approximately twice as common in these concentrations as compared to across the site in general. The data for the main concentrations have been used for comparisons with the other Kennet Valley sites.

Table 9.1: Relative frequencies in the occurrence of crested blades

Sample	Crested blades per core	Blades per crested blade
Avington VI A - E 18 - 20	0.37	93
Avington VI C19 - 20	0.78	78
Avington VI A - E 21 - 23	1.3	28
Avington VI D21 - 22	2.4	25
Wawcott XII	0.46	18
Crown Acres	0.08	250

At Avington VI crested blades appear to be approximately three times more common in concentration 2 (D21–22) than in concentration 1 (C19–20). When a comparison of crested blades:cores are made between the sites, Wawcott XII appears to correlate with Avington VI A–E 18–20, particularly if it is accepted that cores may be over-represented in a surface collection compared to crested blades. At Crown Acres, no matter what speculative allowances are made for it being a surface collection, crested blades are rare. Analysis of the ratio of plain or simple blades:crested blades results in a more complex picture but the relative scarcity of crested blades at Crown Acres is again emphasised and the value for Wawcott XII is likely to be anomalous because surface collecting may only have produced a fraction of the smaller blades originally present (**Fig. 9.2**).

The variation within the data for Avington VI poses the question as to whether such variability is the result of intrinsic statistical instability or a fundamental trait in the flint knapping technique. Refitting of the Avington VI cores has demonstrated that some nodules were successfully developed into blade cores without the production of a crested blade; others had one crest which could result in a single crested blade or two if struck from each platform whilst in yet other cases more than one crest was developed on a core. Thus the number of true crested blades per core could vary from zero–three or more.

Once one or two platforms had been set up and the crested blade removed from one or both ends the detachment of blades ensued. The blade butts show that both plain and faceted platforms occur at the three main Kennet Valley Long Blade sites. There is plenty of evidence for adjustment of the platform by retouch prior to striking of the blades and this has usually been applied down the working face. Similarly the platforms were frequently rejuvenated to keep the core going.

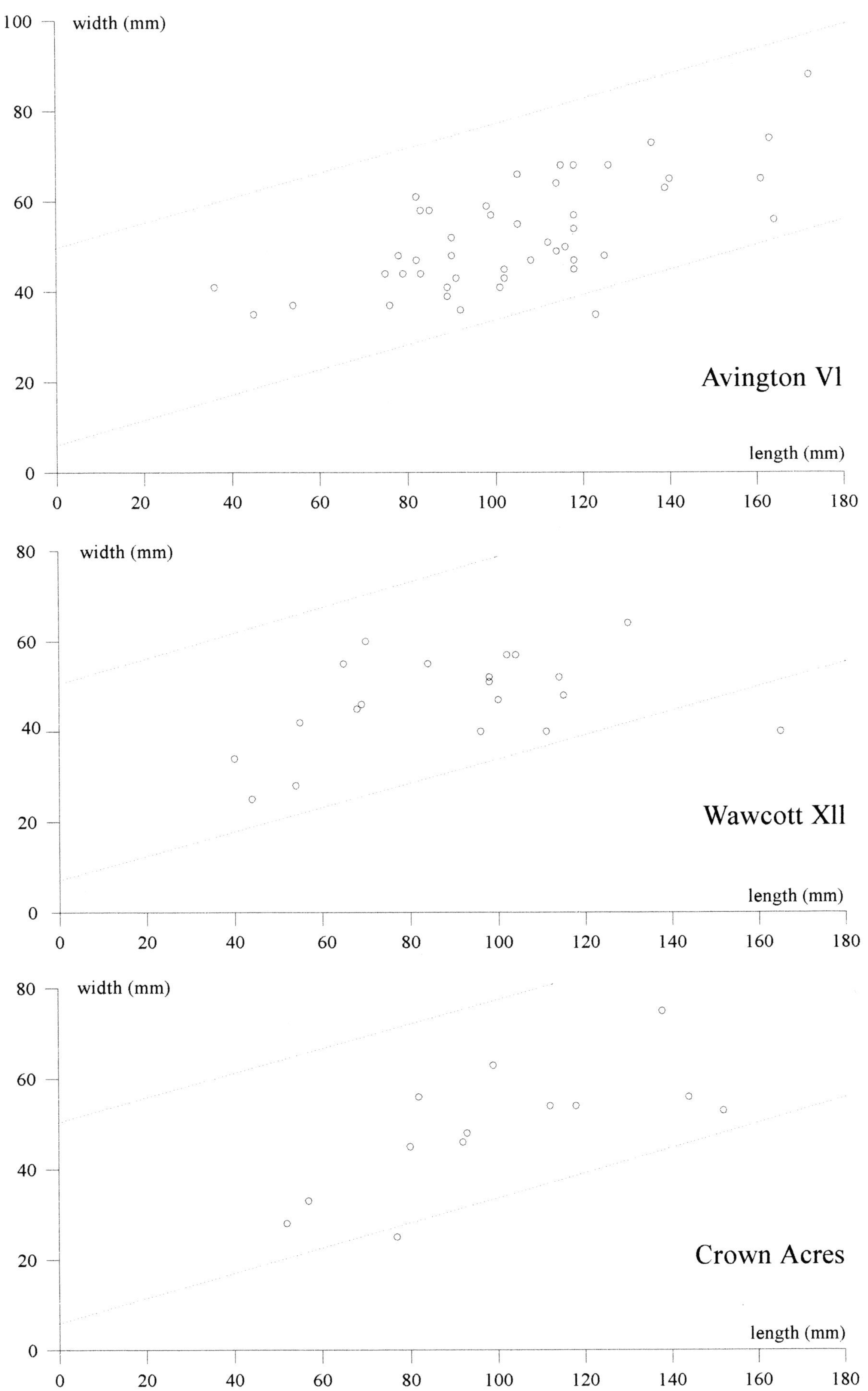

Figure 9.1 Length: width dispersion diagrams for bipolar cores from Kennet Valley Long Blade sites

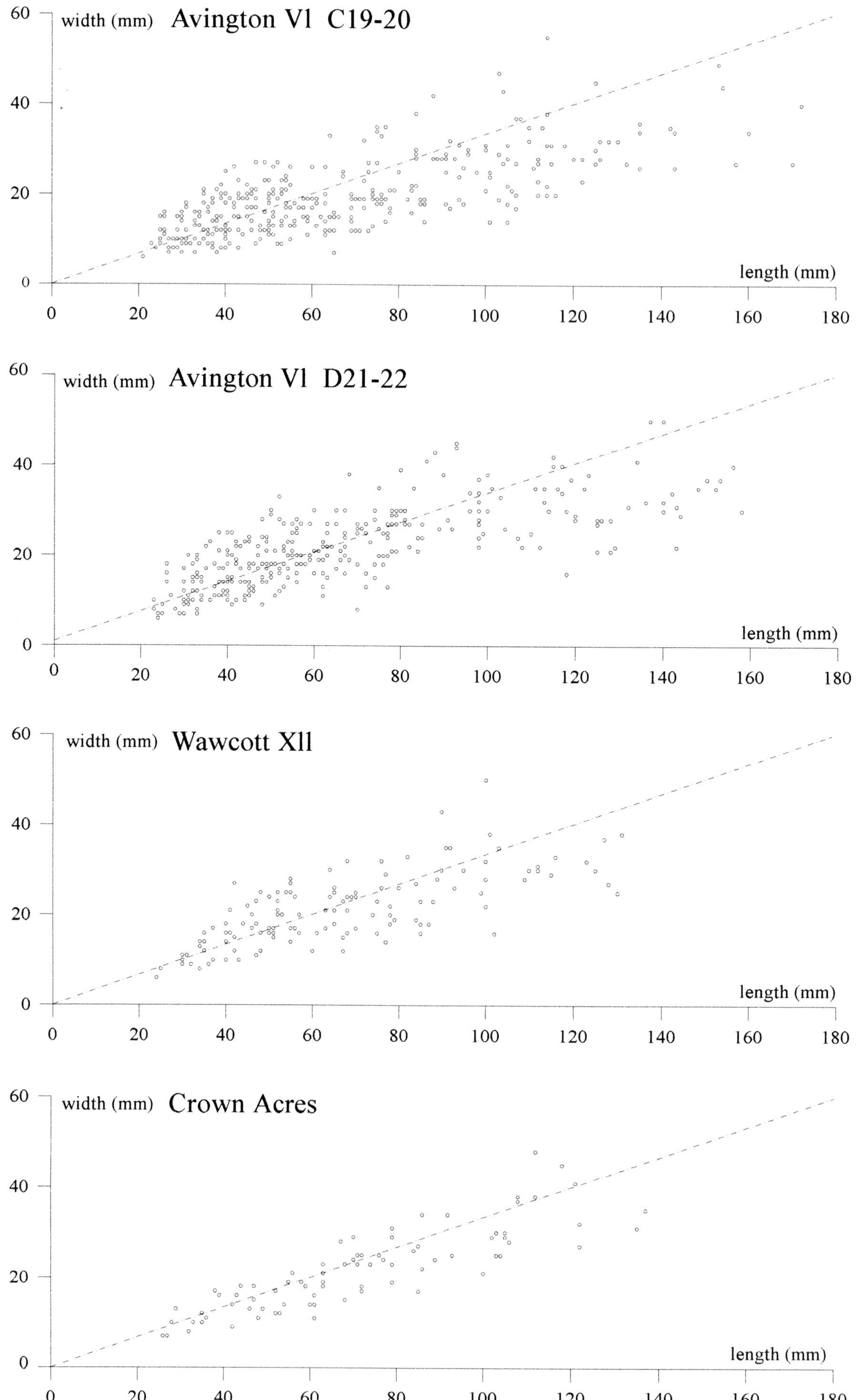

Figure 9.2 Length: width dispersion diagrams for blades from Kennet Valley Long Blade sites

Blades

Careful excavation ensured that all the artefacts were recovered at Avington VI and an estimate of the average blade production per core can be calculated. For the purpose of this estimate, a minimum number of blades was counted as the number of complete blades added to the number of proximal fragments per core In the larger areas the values for blades per core are similar with values of 34 and 36 for transects A–E 18–20 and A–E 21–23 respectively. In both of the main concentrations C19–20 and D21–22 the value was 60. These numerical values are broadly in agreement with the results from refitting and do not differentiate between the two concentrations at Avington VI. The higher values for the concentrations simply reflect the fact that the greater density and lesser dispersal of artefacts within them by comparison with the surrounding area. When the other Kennet Valley sites are brought into this analysis, the values are 8 for Wawcott XII and 19 for Crown Acres; this could result from factors inherent in surface collecting but probably also reflects the smaller nodules in use at these sites. As the size of the raw material selected or available for core production decreased it is logical that the number of blades per core would also decrease although a parallel decrease in the size of the blades would tend to offset such a decrease.

Breakage is a major feature of the blade component at the three main Kennet Valley sites. A reasonable estimate of the degree of fragmentation has been obtained by dividing the number of proximal ends by the minimum number of blades. The results are shown in **Table 9.2.**

Table 9.2: Degree of blade fragmentation at the Kennet Valley sites

Site	Avington VI A - E 18 - 20	Avington VI A - E 21 - 23	Wawcott XII	Crown Acres
Degree of fragmentation	0.315	0.375	0.344	0.592

Given that Wawcott XII is a surface collection, it is unwise to separate its value from that for Avington VI; however, the value for Crown Acres which is based only on the John Turner collection, differs significantly, whereas the values for Avington VI and Wawcott XII show that approximately one in three of the blades are broken, at Crown Acres over half are broken. From the evidence of the refitting at Avington VI it seems probable that a high proportion of blades broke during knapping rather than later as result of deliberate segmentation or trampling for which there is no evidence. Spontaneous breakage during knapping could have been due to faults in the flint or because long regular removals were too thin. Such breakage has also been recorded at La Fuillotte in the Paris Basin where 80% of the regular blades in locus 4 broke during detachment (Bodu *et al.*, 1995) and it is probably the cause of fragmentation at Wawcott XII and Crown Acres although there may be some distortion in the figures for these sites due to modern breakage caused by farming machinery. However, as the agricultural histories of these two sites are similar the higher degree of fragmentation at Crown Acres can be regarded as a real archaeological phenomenon.

Variation in blade size is also observable across the main Kennet Valley sites. At Avington VI the size of the complete blades does not vary much across the site although the blades from concentration 2 (D21–22) do tend to be slightly larger than those concentration 1 (C19–20). By comparison, the blades in the assemblages from Wawcott XII and Crown Acres are smaller (**Fig. 9.2**). In a similar manner, when the relative values of length, width and thickness are expressed as triangular co-ordinates, the differences observed within the Avington VI assemblage are probably insignificant but the blades from Wawcott XII and Crown Acres, although similar to each other, appear to be slightly broader and thicker when compared to those from Avington VI. The somewhat tighter dispersal of the blades from Crown Acres evident in figure 137 could well be the result of differential collecting; it was noted when examining the blades in the John Turner collection that 'irregular' blades were few in number.

Bruised edge blades

The incidence of bruised edge artefacts is often a particular characteristic of Long Blades sites (Fagnart & Plisson, 1995, 96, fig. 1). As elsewhere, the bruised edge blades found in the Kennet Valley Long Blade assemblages show the characteristically heavy edge damage on crested blades and the large flakes and blades detached during the early stages of a reduction sequence. The frequency of these expedient tools is much higher at Avington VI than at Wawcott XII and Crown Acres. The cause of this variation is uncertain but has also been noted in the Paris Basin where the site of La Fouillotte has numerous bruised edge artefacts whereas the otherwise comparable assemblages from Bas du Port du Nord and Les Clos Mailloux at Muides-sur-Loire between Blois and Orléans have none (Bodu *et al.*, 1995).

Where the artefacts were found *in situ* in the Avington VI Long Blade horizon they were more frequent within the main concentrations of knapping debris and such association has also been recorded at such sites Belloy sur Somme near Amiens (Fagnart, 1989;1991) and La Fouillotte in the Paris Basin (Bodu *et al.*, 1995). By observation and determination of the centre of percussion (p. 36) it is concluded that the Avington VI bruised edge pieces were used as hammerstones in the production of Long Blades. A similar conclusion has been drawn by Fagnart and Plisson by use wear investigation of 26 of these artefacts from Belloy sur Somme and Bodu *et al.* (1995) endorse this use with the evidence from La Fouillotte where 3.6% of the artefacts from the knapping concentration in locus 4 were bruised edge blades. As in the Kennet Valley, the area around La Fouillotte lacked other non-flint stones suitable for use as hammerstones and the use of the bruised edge blades is identified as a specialised knapping technique which gives the soft hammer characteristics noted in some of the debitage. Given this technical function, the variation in frequency of bruised edge blades at different sites may represent differing lithic resources, knapping techniques or activities rather than being a culturally diagnostic trait.

Overview

The sites of Avington VI, Wawcott XII, Crown Acres, Charnham Lane and possibly Wawcott IV have all produced assemblages characterised by Long Blade technology. Although they share this technology they vary slightly in the number and type of small retouched tools that they contain and more considerably in the frequency of bruised edge artefacts, crested blades and the amount of breakage among the blades which was probably produced during debitage. These variations have also been observed between other sites with Long Blade technology in south-eastern England northern France and the Somme Valley. They may be a product of differing activities or reflect slight differences in knapping techniques used to adapt the Long Blade method to local variations in flint and other lithic resources. However, there is also the possibility that the variation seen in the Kennet Valley assemblages may reflect change through time (Dumont, 1995). This is currently a difficult argument to sustain given the lack of secure dating evidence for the sites but if the Avington VI Long Blade assemblage is the oldest of these known sites then the presence of Type A microliths, the reduction in core/blade size, as well as the decline of crested blades and bruised edge artefacts may be indicative of a transition towards the Early Mesolithic, as is perhaps also suggested by the variation between scatters A and C at Three Ways Wharf, Uxbridge (Lewis, 1991). This may also be reflected in the location of Avington VI in an appropriately sheltered tributary valley whereas the other sites are on the flood plain. However, there is only meagre pollen evidence and an OSL age estimate to suggest a Late Allerød-early Younger Dryas age for Avington VI, and little or no dating evidence for the other Long Blade or Early Mesolithic sites in the Kennet Valley. Clearly this is a priority for future work and detailed study of the Mesolithic assemblages may also clarify whether there was a technological and typological transition or unconformity between 10,000 and 9,300 years ago (Froom in preparation).

The Kennet Valley sites also share other traits with other Long Blade sites in England and France. They are situated on the alluvial plain close to abundant sources of flint. As the faults in some of the nodules at Avington VI show, this flint was not always of perfect knapping quality but this may have been less crucial where raw material was so plentiful. At Avington VI where there was no disturbance, the occupation surface lacked any evidence of domestic activities. The site was used for knapping and apparently little else. The composition of the other assemblages suggests that although subsequently disturbed they were probably the same. Bone is not preserved at any of the sites, there are no indications of hearths or burning and the tools required for everyday tasks are rare. The D-shaped and circular holes associated with concentration 1 at Avington VI may have held posts perhaps supporting a wind break but the spatial distribution of the artefacts suggests that at most this might have given the knappers some protection as no clear living space is delineated around them.

Although it may be said that there are many gaps in our current knowledge of Long Blade sites in the Kennet Valley the detailed study of a small part of the Late Glacial landscape has shown the potential for further research and the discovery of further sites both along the Kennet and its tributaries. However, above all, the assemblage at Avington VI shows the intentions, method and detailed knapping techniques of just a few individuals working to survive in a relatively inhospitable environment.

References

Anon. 1964. Archaeological notes from Reading Museum. *Berkshire Archaeological Journal* 61: 96–109.

Anon. 1995. An Upper Palaeolithic site at Church Lammas, Staines, Surrey. *English Heritage Archaeological Review 1994/95*: www.eng-h.gov.uk/ArchRev/rev94_95/chlammas.htm

Barton, R.N.E. 1986a. *A Study of Selected British and European Flint Assemblages of Late Devensian and Early Flandrian Age*. D.Phil thesis, University of Oxford.

Barton, R.N.E. 1986b. Experiments with long blades from Sproughton near Ipswich, Suffolk. In: D.A. Roe (ed.) *Studies in the Upper Palaeolithic of Northwest Europe*, 129–141. Oxford: BAR.

Barton, R.N.E. 1991. Technological innovation and continuity at the end of the Pleistocene in Britain. In: N. Barton, A.J. Roberts & D.A. Roe (eds.) *The Late Glacial in north–west Europe: human adaptation and environmental change at the end of the Pleistocene*, 234–245. CBA Research Report No. 77. London: Council for British Archaeology.

Barton, R.N.E. 1992. *Hengistbury Head Dorset. Volume 2: The Late Upper Palaeolithic and Early Mesolithic Sites.* Oxford University Committee for Archaeology Monograph No. 34. Oxford: Oxford University Committee for Archaeology.

Barton, R.N.E., Antoine, P., Dumont, S., Munaut, A.V. 1998. New Optically Stimulated Luminescence (OSL) dates from a Late Glacial site in the Kennet Valley at Avington VI, Berkshire, UK. *Quaternary Newsletter* 85: 21–31.

Bodu, P. & Valentin, B. 1997. Groupes à Federmesser ou Aziliens dans le sud et l'ouest du bassin parisien. Propositions pour un nouveau modèle d'évolution. *Bulletin de la Société Préhistorique Française*: 94: 341–347.

Bodu, P., Hantaï, A. & Valentin, B. 1995. La Long Blade Technology au sud du Bassin parisien: découvertes récentes. In: J–P. Fagnart & A. Thévenin (eds.) *Le Tardiglacaire en Europe du Nord–Ouest,* 211–222. Paris: Éditions du CTHS.

Bonsall, C. & Wymer, J (eds.) 1977. *Gazetteers of Upper Palaeolithic and Mesolithic sites in England and Wales.* CBA Research Report No.20. London: Geo Abstracts & Council for British Archaeology.

Campbell, J.B. 1977. *The Upper Palaeolithic of Britain: a study of Man and Nature in the late Ice Age.* 2 volumes. Oxford: Clarendon Press.

Clark, J.G.D. 1932. *The Mesolithic Age in Britain*. Cambridge: Cambridge University Press.

Clark, J.G.D. 1933. The classification of microlithic culture: the Tardenosian of Horsham. *Archaeological Journal* 90: 52–77.

Clark, J.G.D. 1938. Reindeer hunting tribes of northern Europe. *Antiquity* 12: 154–171.

Clark, J.G.D. & Rankine, W.F. 1939. Excavations at Farnham, Surrey, 1937–38: the Horsham culture and the question of Mesolithic dwellings. *Proceedings of the Prehistoric Society* 5: 61–118.

Collins, P.E.F., Fenwick, I.M., Keith–Lucas, D.M. & Worsley, P. 1996. Late Devensian river and floodplain dynamics and related environmental change in northwest Europe, with particular reference to the site at Woolhampton, Berkshire, England. *Journal of Quaternary Science* 11: 357–375.

Coudret, P. & Fagnart J–P. 1997. Les industries à Federmesser dans le basin de la Somme: chronologie et identité des groupes culturels. *Bulletin de la Société Préhistorique Française*: 94: 349–359.

Dumont, S. 1995. Nouvelles recherches sur la transition tardiglacaire–préboréal dans le sud et l'est de l'Angleterre. In: J–P. Fagnart & A. Thévenin (eds.) *Le Tardiglacaire en Europe du Nord–Ouest,* 517–527. Paris: Éditions du CTHS.

Fagnart, J–P. 1989. Le Paléolithique final dans le nord de la France. In: J–P. Mohen (ed.) *Le Temps de la Préhistoire*, 304–306. Paris: Société Préhistorique Française Edition Archéologia.

Fagnart, J–P. 1991. New observations on the Late Upper Palaeolithic site of Belloy-sur-Somme (Somme, France). In: N. Barton, A.J. Roberts & D.A. Roe (eds.) *The Late Glacial in north-west Europe: human adaptation and environmental change at the end of the Pleistocene*, 213–226. CBA Research Report No. 77. London: Council for British Archaeology.

Fagnart, J–P. & Plisson, H. 1997. Fonction des pièces mâchurées du paléolithique final du Bassin de la Somme: caractères tracéologiques et données contextuelles. In: J–P. Fagnart & A. Thévenin (eds.) *Le Tardiglacaire en Europe du Nord–Ouest,* 95–106. Paris: Éditions du CTHS.

Ford, S. 2002. *Charnham Lane, Hungerford, Berkshire*. Thames Valley Archaeological Services Monograph Series 1.

Froom, F.R. 1963. The Mesolithic around Hungerford, parts I–III. *Transactions of the Newbury District Field Club* 11 (2): 62–87.

Froom, F.R. 1965. The Mesolithic around Hungerford, parts IV–V. *Transactions of the Newbury District Field Club* 11 (3): 45–51.

Froom, F.R. 1970. The Mesolithic around Hungerford, part VI. *Transactions of the Newbury District Field Club* 12 (1): 58–67.

Froom, F.R. 1972a. Some Mesolithic sites in southwest Berkshire. *Berkshire Archaeological Journal* 66: 11–22.

Froom, F.R. 1972b. A Mesolithic site at Wawcott, Kintbury. *Berkshire Archaeological Journal* 66: 23–44.

Froom, F.R. 1976. *Wawcott III: a stratified Mesolithic succession*. British Archaeological Report 27. Oxford: British Archaeological Reports.

Froom, F.R., Cook, J., Debenham, N., & Ambers, J. 1994. Wawcott XXX: an interin report on a Mesolithic site in Berkshire. In: N. Ashton & A. David (eds.) *Stories in Stone*, 206–212. Lithic Studies Society Occasional Paper No.4. Oxford: Lithic Studies Society.

Hinout, J. 1997. Quelques aspects de l'Épipaléolithique dans le nord du basin parisien. *Bulletin de la Société Préhistorique Française*: 94: 337–340.

Holyoak, D.T. 1980. *Late Pleistocene Sediments and Biostratigraphy of the Kennet Valley, England*. Unpublished Ph.D thesis, The University of reading.

Lewis, J. 1991. A Late Glacial and early Postglacial site at Three Ways Wharf, Uxbridge, England: interim report. In: N. Barton, A.J. Roberts & D.A. Roe (eds.) *The Late Glacial in north–west Europe: human adaptation and environmental change at the end of the Pleistocene*, 246–255. CBA Research Report No. 77. London: Council for British Archaeology.

Peake, H.J.E. 1931. *The Archaeology of Berkshire*. London: Methuen.

Peake, H.J.E. 1935. The origin of the Kennet Valley peat. *Transactions of the Newbury District Field Club* 7: 116–126.

Putman, F. 1931. Palaeolithic implements. *Transactions of the Newbury District Field Club* 6(2): 69.

Rankine, W.F. 1956. *The Mesolithic of southern England.* Research Papers of the Surrey Archaeological Society No. 4.

Reynier, M. 2000. Thatcham revisited: spatial and stratigraphic analyses of two sub-assemblages from Site III and its implications for Early Mesolithic typo-chronology in Britain. In: R. Young (ed.) *Mesolithic Lifeways: current research from Britain and Ireland*, 33–46. Leicester Archaeology Monographs No.7. Leicester: University of Leicester, School of Archaeological Studies.

Rozoy, J-G. 1998. The re-population of northern France between 13,000 and 8000 BP. *Quaternary International* 49/50: 69–86.

Schild, R. 1996. The North European Plain and eastern Sub-Balticum between 12,700 and 8,000 BP. In: L.G. Strauss, B.V. Erikson, J.M. Elandson and D.R. Yesner (eds.) *Humans at the end of the Ice Age: the archaeology of the Pleistocene–Holocene transition*, 129–157. New York: Plenum Press.

Taute, W. 1968. *Die Steilspitzen-Gruppen im nördlichen Mitteleuropa. Ein Beitrag zur Kenntnis der späten Altsteinzeit*. Fundamenta Reihe A, 5. Köln: Böhlau.

Thévenin, A. 1994. L'Azilien' et les cultures à pointe à dos courbé: esquisse géographique et chronologique. *Bulletin de la Société Préhistorique Française*: 94: 393–411.

Waldmann, G., Jöris, O. & Baales, M. 2001. Nach der Flut. Ein spätallerødzeitlicher Rückenspitzen-Fundplatz bei Bad Breisig. *Archäologisches Korrespondenzblatt* 31: 173–184.

Worsley, P. & Collins, P.E.F. 1995. The Geomorphological context of the Brimpton Late Pleistocene succession (south central England). *Proceedings of the Geologists' Association* 106: 39–45.

Wymer, J. 1962. Excavations at the Maglemosian site of Thatcham, Berkshire, England. *Proceedings of the Prehistoric Society* 28: 329–361.

Wymer, J. 1976. The Long Blade industry from Sproughton. *East Anglian Archaeology* 3: 1–10.

Plate 1 Avington VI: Looking south across the Long Blade surface as exposed in 1978 showing the D-shaped hole excavated out on the right of concentration 1 and the edge of concentration 2 to the left

Plate 2 Avington VI: Looking west across the Long Blade surface as exposed in 1978. The square trench behind the D-shaped hole is the base of the 1972 trial pit. The feature at the base of the baulk is the Mesolithic pit.

Plate 3 Avington VI: Concentration 1, transect C19-20, as excavated in 1978. At the centre of the concentration the artefacts have dropped into the top of the circular hole about 15 cm across

Plate 4 Avington VI: Close up on concentration 1 as excavated in 1978